MAKING
PLACE

Making Place is Volume 8 in the series
21ST CENTURY STUDIES
Center for 21st Century Studies
University of Wisconsin–Milwaukee
Richard Grusin, General Editor

MAKING PLACE

Space and Embodiment in the City

EDITED BY

Arijit Sen and Lisa Silverman

INDIANA UNIVERSITY PRESS

BLOOMINGTON AND INDIANAPOLIS

This book is a publication of

Indiana University Press
Office of Scholarly Publishing
Herman B Wells Library 350
1320 East 10th Street
Bloomington, Indiana 47405 USA

iupress.indiana.edu

Telephone 800-842-6796
Fax   812-855-7931

♾ The paper used in this publication meets the minimum requirements of
the American National Standard for Information Sciences—Permanence of
Paper for Printed Library Materials, ANSI Z39.48–1992.

Manufactured in the United States of America

Library of Congress Cataloging-in-Publication Data

Making place : space and embodiment in the city / edited by Arijit Sen and
Lisa Silverman.
     pages cm. — (21st century studies)
  Includes bibliographical references and index.
  ISBN 978-0-253-01142-8 (cl : alk. paper) — ISBN 978-0-253-01143-5
(pb : alk. paper) — ISBN 978-0-253-01149-7 (eb) 1. Cities and towns—
Psychological aspects. 2. Cities and towns—Social aspects. 3. Spatial
behavior—Social aspects. 4. Place attachment—Social aspects. 5.
Environmental psychology. I. Sen, Arijit, [date]- II. Silverman, Lisa.
  HT153.M32 2014
  307.76—dc23

                         2013024342

1 2 3 4 5 19 18 17 16 15 14

CONTENTS

ACKNOWLEDGMENTS

Many of the essays in this volume featured in two interdisciplinary symposia held at the at the Center for 21st Century Studies at the University of Wisconsin–Milwaukee in fall 2010 and spring 2011 titled "Embodied Placemaking in Urban Public Spaces." We are grateful to the staff of the Center, especially director Richard Grusin, associate director John Blum, former interim director Merry Wiesner-Hanks, and former deputy director Kate Kramer for their support in the organization of the symposia and the publication of this volume. Many thanks are also due to the College of Letters and Science for the co-sponsorship of the symposia, as well as to the Graduate School, the School of Architecture and Urban Planning, the Center for Jewish Studies, the Buildings-Landscapes-Cultures collaborative project, the Cultures and Communities Program, the Urban Studies Program, the Peck School of the Arts, and the Departments of Anthropology and Geography for their support.

At Indiana University Press, we thank Rebecca Tolen and Sarah Jacobi for their help and advice, and we thank two external reviewers for insightful comments that greatly improved the manuscript.

We also wish to thank the following colleagues, friends, and family for their assistance and encouragement: Cheryl Ajirotutu, Anna Andrzejewski, Caitlin Boyle, Simone Ferro, Robert Greenstreet, Marta Gutman, Ryan Holifield, Gregory Jay, Louis Nelson, Harry van Oudenallen, and Vaishali Wagh.

Both the symposia and the essays in this volume underscore the emerging scholarship on the built environment carried out under the aegis of Buildings-Landscapes-Cultures, a new collaborative area of research and doctoral studies at the University of Wisconsin–Milwaukee and –Madison that focuses on the study of everyday cultural landscapes. This program focuses on the study of the built environment within a historical framework, seeking to understand the relationship between built form and culture as well as the complex relationship between cultural practices, material culture and human agency. Buildings-Landscapes-Cultures affiliates include students and faculty with diverse research and teaching interests, including art and architectural history, cultural landscapes, public history, urban history, and cultural geography.

Arijit Sen and Lisa Silverman

MAKING
PLACE

Introduction

Embodied Placemaking: An Important Category of Critical Analysis

ARIJIT SEN AND LISA SILVERMAN

Space, Place, and the Body

In 1943 British Parliamentarians engaged in heated debate about how to rebuild the House of Commons chamber, which had been destroyed in 1941. Some argued that its rebuilding should have been used as an opportunity for expansion to improve its formerly cramped conditions, reshaping it from a rectangle into a semicircle. Prime Minister Winston Churchill, however, sided with opponents by insisting that the new building should conform to the size and shape of the old. He knew that the chamber would be crowded and filled to capacity during critical votes and debates, and it was important that these activities proceed with members spilling out into the aisles, lending on great occasions "a sense of crowd and urgency." On slow days the chamber was barely filled, but on others it became a throbbing center of civic debate. It continued to be both a symbolic center of state power as well as a vibrant democratic institution, but in its newly rebuilt form it would also trigger resurgent memories of a place bombed during the war and proudly reconstructed as a symbol of a nation's resilience. Churchill's understanding of the situation is best summed up in his now-famous declaration: "We shape our buildings, and afterwards our buildings shape us."[1]

Churchill's astute observations suggest his deeper understanding of the complex relationship between place and how our bodies engage it. His "sense of place" of the House of Commons extended beyond the building's architectural form and its functional use to include its spatial ambience and the meaning produced when individuals and groups used the building.

This understanding underscores the fact that changing physical modifica-
tions allows individuals to personalize and transform a location when they
occupy it. Churchill's recognition of the building as more than a mere institutional setting for governance suggests its function as a stage that derived its
meaning from the event, the audience, the performers, as well as the physical qualities of the setting. What he perceived—and what this volume seeks
to address—is that the meaning of buildings, neighborhoods, and cities is
not static, but variable in its personal, cultural, historical, social, economic,
and political contexts. Churchill's stress on the importance of a crowded,
and therefore urgent, ambience indicates his awareness of the role of the
body in turning a government institution into a place of vibrant civic discourse. In other words, he understood the role of embodiment in the making of the built environment.

Recently the epistemological boundaries according to which we understand culture and history have shifted because of a so-called "spatial turn"
in the humanities and social sciences.[2] This spatial turn, which puts space
and place at the center of analysis of culture and history, is undoubtedly a
result of fluctuations in social thought emerging from broader economic,
social, political, and cultural transformations, including increasing globalization and its impact on media, migration, identity, and subjectivities, as
Barney Warf and Santa Arias explain.[3] For other scholars the spatial turn
refers to seeing the transformation of economies, emerging digital cultures,
and ecological movements as global processes that prompt us to rethink the
role of locality, space, and spatiality in understanding culture and history.[4]
But despite these new considerations, the concept of placemaking—as well
as how it can be used as a practical tool of analysis by scholars who do not
traditionally study the built environment—remains difficult to comprehend
and apply. In this volume we argue that using "embodied placemaking" as a
category of analysis—that is, foregrounding not only place but also the body's
role within it as mutually constituent elements of the built environment—
can open up deeper and innovative ways of understanding the human experience across a variety of disciplines.

Place is a slippery concept. In the past when describing physical landscapes, scholars of the built environment carefully distinguished between
their use of the terms "space" and "place." Space has traditionally been considered more abstract; one common view defined space as a boundless,
empty, three-dimensional abstraction within which existed a set of interrelated events or objects. Others stressed the socially constructed nature
of space, thus drawing attention to the material qualities that delimit its

bounds.[5] Place, on the other hand, always refers to a physical location, but its existence can be either real or imagined and its meaning constantly reinterpreted and reclassified. Scholars, however, who challenge this simple dichotomy obviate the need for a distinction between space and place, arguing that, although space may exist in the abstract, as a social construction it, too, necessarily entails very real and often contested divisions, borders, and boundaries. Indeed, Henri Lefebvre, an early seminal thinker, had already suggested that social orders are so crucial to the construction of spaces that, according to his definition, the material, political, and ideological conditions of those who produce space are its most important constitutive elements.[6]

Place, then, denotes a material world that can be limited not only by physical borders but also by much less explicit temporal and socially constructed boundaries. The roots of the term "placemaking" can be traced to Martin Heidegger's foregrounding of the constitutive relationship between people and their physical environment in his notion of *Dasein* (being-in-the-world), which implies not only that we cannot exist independently of the world around us but also that the world around us cannot exist independent of the people who inhabit it.[7] In other words, it is only through our consciousness, actions, and interactions that the physical landscape is brought into existence.[8] By focusing on embodiment—that is, on the mutually constitutive relationship between place and the body—we underscore the notion that a physical environment cannot exist without the human inhabitants who experience it in their everyday lives, and its meaning is dependent upon the larger political and economic contexts within which these individuals operate in any specific location.

Architectural historian Dell Upton expands upon this notion when he asks us to consider place as more than a functional container where humans live, interact, and participate in daily activities. He suggests that a place or landscape, which he terms "the scene," "undeniably offers itself to us as a transparent totality, coherent and final. Compared to the ephemeral nature of human consciousness and social action, the continuity of the material world and its apparent unchangeability seem to promise constant or certain meaning. Yet the stability of physical form falsely certifies stability of meaning; there may be no meaning at all."[9] As his research underscores, the ability of a place to accommodate human activity is inextricably interconnected to how a person acts and behaves within its bounds. Yet, Upton also stresses that the symbolic underpinnings of a "scene" remain difficult to decipher. He argues that in order to understand fully the meaning of a place, we must make visible some of those "unseen" political processes of spatial production that typically remain hidden. In order to do so, we need to be aware how larger psychological, political, experiential, and ideological contexts affect individual behavior.

Like place, embodiment is also a concept that is difficult to define. On one hand, to embody something is to express, personify, and give concrete and perceptible form to a concept that may exist only as an abstraction. This act of making an abstract idea corporeal and incarnate occurs when we read place as a material product of human imagination and experience. Place, however, is not a neutral site into which human beings enter; our current experiences as well as memories of past events frame how we understand and reproduce it.[10] Emphasizing embodiment allows us to identify and underscore the important element of human agency in both the physical construction as well as the social production of place. It also helps us comprehend what Michel de Certeau helpfully terms "tactics," those everyday forms of engagement that empower individuals to resist, counter, circumvent, and transform the world around them.[11] This ability to understand and engage the physical world in terms of the embodied experiences of individuals alerts us to place's emancipatory possibilities. Embodied placemaking can thus become, to use James C. Scott's term, a "weapon of the weak" and can offer possibilities of radical citizenship and urbanism as suggested by Henri Lefebvre.[12]

On the other hand, "to embody" also suggests the act of becoming part of a body. Viewed as an act of incorporation, embodiment allows us to see the powerful ideological role played by place in the formation of human subjects. In other words, the experience of place can constitute—that is, be a substantial part of—our senses of individual and communal self-identification and can situate us within larger social contexts. Embodied placemaking, we suggest, is the primary mode by which individuals, societies, and social systems reproduce themselves. As historian Paul Connerton shows, everyday forms of engagement with place may be "products of habits and bodily practices that produce a combination of cognitive and habit-memory."[13] In fact, our repeated and mundane place-based behavior tends to become so habitual and taken for granted that its powerful influence is often not explicitly evident. Nevertheless, scholars such as Iain Borden have demonstrated how such place-based behavior shapes us and elicits culturally sanctioned responses.[14] Borden argues, "Any experience of materiality must be understand [sic] as a continual production and reproduction of that condition. And this condition involves four things: an acting subject, a mode of engagement, a condition of materiality, and a resultant meaning and critique."[15]

Thus, the term *embodied placemaking* underscores the human element upon which making place hinges, and in using it we posit that a study of place that omits consideration of the bodies that engage its terms remains incomplete. Our focus on this process as it occurs in the city reflects the fact that the dynamism of placemaking has been and remains most evident in urban public spaces, where the greatest numbers of people are exposed to spatial change. As this volume makes clear, placemaking in the city is always a process fraught with ideological, economic, and symbolic conflicts—but only because of the people who are engaged in it. By foregrounding the political possibilities of placemaking, we hope to illuminate both its emancipatory and its oppressive possibilities. By drawing attention to the role of the human body and its performative and affective engagement with the material world, we aim to show how these are essential elements to the incessant processes of social construction and production. In doing so we posit that scholars of history, literature, anthropology, art history, and a host of other fields can use embodied placemaking as a powerful framework in which to understand authorship and ownership of the built environment and, therefore, the human experiences that take place within it.

Embodied Placemaking: An Interdisciplinary Genealogy

Our approach to the concept of embodied placemaking in the city draws upon a rich tradition of performance artists, practitioners, and designers who explore visceral engagements with the environment and make place by performing, building, and acting. Site-specific installations by contemporary artists such as Zander Olsen, Peter Westerink, Andy Goldsworthy, Janet Zweig, and Ernest Zacharevic are examples of such crafts. Performance artists such as Improv Everywhere and choreographers such as William Forsythe and Anna Halprin do so by experimenting with the human body and its kinesthetic awareness in order to create and recreate place. Works of landscape architects and architects such as Zaha Hadid, Steven Holl, Lawrence Halprin, Diller Scofidio + Renfro, and James Corner explore the relationship between place and the human body.[16] Recent work exploring materials, digital fabrication, and performative architecture also examines the affective and experiential qualities of the material world.[17] Our approach to embodied placemaking also borrows from historical archaeology and material culture scholars such as Henry Glassie, James Deetz, and Bernard L. Herman.[18] These scholars argue that the material world, like speech, works according to specific rules of composition. Whether scholars or practitioners, performance artists or designers, all of them consider embodied placemaking by bringing to center stage the physical aspects of the material world.

Scholarship about embodied placemaking in cities borrows from particular "ways of thinking about the city" that may be classified loosely as studies dealing with the production of urbanity. They include work by a variety of academics, theorists, artists, designers, and novelists who examine how urbanity is incessantly reproduced due to human actions and imaginations.[19] Unlike the proponents of popular political, economic, and ecological models that explain the culture of cities as a product of larger political and economic forces, the former scholars argue that the urban built environment influences how humans interact with these larger forces.[20] They acknowledge that larger socioeconomic and political structures may indeed frame the culture of cities, but they also stress that individuals, too, have both the power and the agency to negotiate these larger frameworks in creative ways. Bourdieu's concept of *habitus* and Giddens's theory of structuration are two theoretical models that help explain the dialectical thinking of agency and structure proposed in this volume.[21]

A scholarly focus on the role of the body in the interactions between people and places began with the emergence of negative characterizations of the industrial city as a place lacking the possibilities for intimate recognition and face-to-face interactions experienced in traditional towns. Confronted with the seeming powerlessness of individuals to influence city life, late-nineteenth and early twentieth-century scholars and novelists often portrayed the city as a dystopic, crowded hub where strangers confront each other as they traverse the urban landscape.[22] These texts outline the tactics—that is, the elaborate behavioral strategies, including nonverbal communication, maintenance of personal space, and marking of territories—that inhabitants used as they tried to retain a sense of control and privacy in the metropolis.[23] They also suggest that strangers acknowledge and engage each other by reproducing psychological and physical boundaries as they physically negotiate their surroundings; it is as if individuals produce personal bubbles to shield them from the impersonality and strangeness of urban culture.

One prominent example can be found in the work of Walter Benjamin, whose examination of strolling as a novel practice in nineteenth-century European streets forms the basis of a trend for the study of haptic—that is, tactile, sensorial, affective, and corporeal—engagement with the city.[24] This writing and research is, in turn, connected to more positive characterizations of urban culture in the late twentieth century. Writers such as

Lewis Mumford, William Whyte, and Jane Jacobs view the city as a stage for urban drama.[25] Contemporary authors such as Sharon Zukin, AbdouMaliq Simone, Quentin Stevens, Iain Borden, Joachim Schlör, Deborah Parsons, and Susan Ossman continue such traditions, albeit within a more global framework.[26] These scholars examine how experiences in the city are embodied and gendered through acts of walking, mapping, seeing, touching, and smelling. According to them, the performative potential of the city is what allows individuals to influence and transform its culture.

The field of psychogeography, dedicated to the examination of humans' emotional, psychological, and physiological engagement with the material world in cities, developed in the 1950s. As part of this trend, scholars such as Ivan Chtcheglov and Guy Debord used maps to document the embodied experience of time and space in cities.[27] Later, Henri Lefebvre's *Rhythmanalysis* provided us with a method to gauge and study the experiential and temporal rhythms of urban places.[28] Lefebvre's work engages with a rich genre of movies called "city symphonies" in the 1920s that attempted to capture the embodied, poetic, and experiential moods of urban life.[29]

More contemporary scholarship of embodied placemaking has been concerned with challenging two long-held assumptions behind the production of place. First, the belief that individuals can performatively reproduce place challenges a "mistaken isomorphism" between place and culture in traditional scholarship. In the past we tended to see cultures as "discrete, object-like phenomena occupying discrete space," where Indian culture was limited to India, Egyptian culture to Egypt, and so on.[30] This correlation among firmly bounded concepts of place, nation, and culture rendered the cultural production of place an essentially local and national practice and limited its study to the application of only a few methodologies. Many scholars now recognize the fluidity with which people, goods, and ideas are formed, rendering the consideration of discrete and disjointed place-based cultures less relevant. Indeed, their explorations of how people react physically and emotionally to the places they inhabit provide powerful evidence of how cultural ideas travel and how human beings mediate between multiple cultures. Their research shows how contemporary migrants creatively deploy their bodies in space in order to reproduce their worlds, thereby incessantly reconfiguring memories and histories in new locations.[31]

Second, new scholarship has challenged the primacy of vision in how we understand place by positing that place is also touched, remembered, smelled, heard, and experienced kinesthetically.[32] Many public historians turned toward this methodology at the end of the twentieth century, leading them to ask new questions about authorship such as: Whose values are acknowledged in our histories? Whose version of cultural authorship do we value in our scholarship? Applications of such ideas can be seen in Dolores Hayden's Power of Place project, Donna Graves and Jill Shirk's California Japantowns project, and Marci Reaven's New York City Place Matters project.[33] These projects have reframed the practice of heritage preservation by suggesting practical ways to capture the voices and histories of underrepresented minorities.[34] Folklorists Michael Ann Williams and M. Jane Young forcefully argued this point in 1995 with their "ethnography-of-speaking" approach, which emphasized not only form but also "social use" and "process" as categories of analysis.[35] They urged material culture scholars to go beyond a reliance on linguistic and sociolinguistic models to examine the process of the production of space through "personal narratives that reveal how people feel about and talk about houses as well as the associational values these buildings have for them."[36] Oral narratives, they claimed, point us toward intangible meanings, encourage sensory awareness, and show us the importance of personal preferences within larger cultural patterns. For us, these seminal projects and new avenues of thinking serve as points of departure for studying and documenting the politics of placemaking as an embodied phenomenon.

Spatial Ethnography: A Comprehensive Methodological Approach

Despite the rich literature that forms the basis of these innovative approaches to studying the built environment, it remains difficult to observe, research, and write about embodied placemaking. We simply lack a comprehensive methodology that encompasses the language, methods, and ability to describe, capture, and record its processes adequately. This volume attempts to redefine and reshape previous concepts and nomenclatures by introducing a comprehensive methodology of "spatial ethnography" that allows us to incorporate both material and abstract approaches to the study of people and place and encourages us to consider the various levels—from the personal to the planetary—according to which spatial change occurs. Taken together, the case studies in each of these chapters can serve as a methodological guide for using embodied placemaking as a category of critical analysis to add rigor and depth to more traditional historical, anthropological, geographical, and other analyses by focusing on how the meanings of places are constantly produced and reproduced.

To be sure, geographers interested in interpreting human actions within larger regional and geopolitical contexts already use the term "spatial ethnography." Writing about spatial ethnographies of labor, for example, Sharad Chari and Vinay Gidwani explain that "the grounds for ethnographic knowledge of work must be seen in their diverse cultural and cosmological forms, but these forms must also be anchored in lived experience as it is forged in the interplay of active socio-cultural relations and spatial processes."[37] Our use of the term, however, differs in that we emphasize spatial ethnography as a method necessary to understand place as material culture. Our sense of spatial ethnography also posits that, as Winston Churchill alluded, once place is produced, it also influences human actions and practices. Place itself—like the people who make it—contains possibilities for agency.

Such a dialectical, ontological position, however, produces a curious epistemological dilemma. At its most intimate scale—the level of the human body—the concept of *place* produces the following challenge: A person moves and, as a result, his or her body occupies a different physical location. Each transient moment thus produces a new place, new context, new act, and new meaning. To conduct spatial ethnography at such a granular scale is difficult, since it requires accounting for the rapidity with which people reproduce place. On the other hand, one must also take into consideration that change also occurs according to the slower pace of geological time, or according to the gentle sweep of big history. Considerations of place in the context of these broader scales necessarily elicit more stable cultural patterns.[38] Consequently, as a comprehensive methodology, spatial ethnography must account for this important scalar variation.

The concept of spatial ethnography presented in this volume thus focuses on devising ways to understand embodied placemaking as a process inflected by a variety of scales. For instance, we can study placemaking from the point of view of an individual, family, kin, or community. We can then apply any number of geographical scales of analysis to this point of view, such as architectural, urban, regional, or global. Finally, we can then choose to consider placemaking within a broad span of geological time, through the intergenerational memory of a particular culture, or through the most intimate and transient scale of a person's lifetime. In other words, this methodology requires us to position our point of view and ourselves within the same matrix of scales that shapes the world we live in. The choice of scale affects the nature of the evidence we collect and the means we adopt for collecting the data.

When it comes to the process of gathering data, spatial ethnography foregrounds an ethnographic storytelling approach that compares multiple temporal, cultural, and geographical case studies, a strategy that George Marcus calls "multi-sited ethnographies" or that Durham Peters calls "bifocality."[39] The latter approach oscillates between fine-toothed micro-histories, on the one hand, and big sweeps of history, on the other.

Spatial ethnography points toward noncognitive and affective forms in which people acquire spatial information. It also draws upon work by Maurice Merleau-Ponty, showing that affect and cognition are never fully separable.[40] Kevin Lynch's work on mental maps of cities in 1960 does, to some extent, clarify a number of these positions. But even his references to the cognitively constructed cartographies by which humans read, remember, and organize spatial information do not take into consideration the complexity of scale.[41] Spatial ethnography recognizes this aspect by incorporating detailed interpretations of material culture with studies concerned with the breadth of public history, or even those that take into account the extremely long temporality of environmental history. As a methodology, it provides room for a compendium of incremental, multi-scalar case studies.

Each chapter in this volume presents a case study that examines the phenomenon of embodied placemaking from various historical, geographical, and social contexts, using different kinds of evidence and interpretive techniques. Each offers a mix of archival analysis with demographic information and relies on detailed documentation of places and fine-tuned observations of the human activities that occur within them. Some of the examples in this volume carefully study human performance and the body, analyzing movement, procession, vision, tactility, and a sense of order. Some focus on the multisensory qualities of place and how human beings experience them, and take seriously the concept of positionality—that is, the examples assume that different people experience the same place in different ways due to varying contexts, and also acknowledge that this multiplicity of experiences influences what we study and how we study it.

The contributions to this volume begin with Setha Low's "Placemaking and Embodied Space," which focuses on the politics of embodied placemaking in the literal realm of political engagement from the point of view of an anthropologist who considers how material space, objects, and human bodies interact with social and political institutions. Her chapter offers an introduction and genealogy of the development of embodied placemaking, outlining the historical tools and concepts that scholars from a range of disciplines have used in past decades to define, describe, consider, and analyze the spaces of everyday life. She then demonstrates the application of these theories using her fieldwork at the Plaza de la Cultura in San José, Costa Rica, as an example. By tracing how space is considered in its most abstract form—in scholarship—and through maps and quantification, Low's essay offers an approach to the qualitative experiences of everyday spaces through the lens of embodied placemaking that helps contextualize the chapters that follow.

Swati Chattopadhyay and Emanuela Guano cast the keen eyes of the architectural historian and ethnographer, respectively, on contemporary issues of urban protest and resistance to power, showing how institutional, state, community, and even individually advocated inscriptions onto the material landscape function to produce spaces of engagement, public discourse, and even conflict in the city. In her essay on political wall writing in India, Chattopadhyay's analysis of urban walls in Calcutta as sites of political engagement suggests that these material spaces are no mere blank surfaces on which individuals and groups inscribe their messages. These walls, as she notes, serve to create new "conditions of legibility," rendering the very act of reading them a political undertaking that forges new identities and spatial imaginations for urban citizens. In a similar vein, Emanuela Guano examines in detail the inscription of what she terms a "political imaginary" onto the city of Genoa at the time of the 2001 Group of Eight summit. In that case the Italian state created a militarized security zone within the city to serve as a protected space for the summit. This act, Guano argues, produced a cognitive urban boundary inside of which normality and everyday urban life were suspended, in effect setting the stage for the actualization of the very same disturbances and disruptions the government had presumably sought to avoid. Affective engagements with the material environment emerge as the focus of the next two essays, by Jennifer Cousineau and Arijit Sen, which draw particular attention to the lived, embodied qualities of the built environment and the important role these play in structuring and transforming self-identification and collective identities of observant Jews in London and South Asian Muslim immigrants in Chicago. Their accounts focus on the performance, enactment, and experience of the everyday as transient and temporal phenomena that replicate culture. Cousineau's analysis shows how the experiences of London's Jewish community are inflected not only by religious proscription and gender but also by the cognitive boundaries according to which these categories are proscribed. Her study of London's most heavily populated Jewish area reveals it as a volatile and transient field of physical and conceptual relationships that is constantly reproduced through experience. Sen's study, in contrast, frames the experiences and enactment of identity of the ethnically diverse patrons of a Muslim-owned South Asian restaurant in Chicago. His analysis shows that individuals can cognitively decipher spatial order at the same time their bodies experience it affectively.

Emphasizing the role of memory and lived experience in the production of place forms the basis of the final two essays, by Karen Till and Lisa Silverman. They reveal how the history of displacement and violence relates to memories of place and how these are used in performance and memory work of those seeking to come to terms with the past. Till examines collaborations between the Mapa Teatro Laboratory of Artists in Colombia and the displaced inhabitants of the El Cartucho neighborhood in Bogotá, Colombia, between 2001 and 2005. She argues that the artists' installations, exhibitions, and performances addressing place-memory function as unique methods of disruption of the dominant narratives of modernity as they challenge its residents' displacement from acts of urban planners and city government. Similar disruptions emerge from the oral histories of Austrian Jewish émigrés that form the focus of Silverman's essay. Her examination of their descriptions of Vienna before their expulsion from the city in 1938 reveals how their personal engagements with the city's built environment—how they moved through the city, where they lived, and where they did not go—were integral to their Jewish self-understandings. What emerges from these readings is a collective, cognitive map of Vienna constructed through memory that reveals just how deep-seated the boundaries of "Jewish space" were in the city before 1938.

Whether it is the politics, the strategies of inscription and domain differentiation, or the affective use of memory in construing place, the following chapters all underscore the need for scholars to reexamine places as performative, interactive, and emergent processes rather than mere inert cultural artifacts. In cities, new places often replace older ones, industrial buildings can be converted to loft apartments, and new residents might move into established neighborhoods at a rapid pace. Entire streets can be converted temporarily to markets while protesters occupy centrally located parks and other public spaces to express their views. Handbills, wall writings, and temporary occupations create new sites of civic discourse and political protest. Alternate uses and changing lifestyles constantly redefine traditional places and attribute new meanings to them.

In applying spatial ethnography as a methodology, all of the chapters recognize that the question "Who makes place?" is political, since various social agents participate in the process of making it. They take as a given that the question "Whose place?" becomes a contested one when the voices and stories of vulnerable and less powerful inhabitants of places emerge.

Moreover, they understand that the question "Which place?" is one that depends upon a recognition of the complex matrix of physical, social, and temporal relationships of which it is comprised, as well as a consideration of how historical time and memory influence how these are interpreted. By keeping such questions in mind as they consider the body and place mutually constituent elements, these chapters all show how any understanding of human experiences in the city must necessarily consider both place and the body as crucial in shaping the possibilities for agency.

NOTES

1. Winston S. Churchill, "Speech on Rebuilding the House of Commons," October 28, 1943, in *Winston S. Churchill: His Complete Speeches, 1897–1963,* ed. Robert Rhodes James (New York: Chelsea House, 1974), 7:6869–71.

2. The work of Michel Foucault has been a key aspect of the spatial turn for many in the humanities and social sciences. Geographers such as Doreen Massey, Edward Soja, and Tim Cresswell, and architectural historians such as Dell Upton, who have traditionally foregrounded space as the focus of their analyses, ideas, and debates associated with the spatial turn have produced new histories of places and suggested new methods to understand and study the built environment. Historians, environmental historians, and anthropologists such as Peter Sahlins, Stephen Greenblatt, David Lowenthal, Pierre Nora, Edward Casey, William Cronon, and Michael Herzfeld have also written about placemaking and cultural contact during the age of discovery, European colonial expansions, world wars, and in oceanic cultures. They have examined the role of place and placemaking during migrations, diasporas, travel, and trade during premodern contact among oceanic cultures. See, for instance, Tim Cresswell, *Place: A Short Introduction* (Malden, Mass.: Blackwell, 2004); Doreen Massey and Pat Jess, eds., *A Place in the World? Places, Cultures, and Globalization* (Oxford: Open University Press, 1995); Karen Halttunen, "Groundwork: American Studies in Place—Presidential Address to the American Studies Association," *American Quarterly* 58 (March 2006): 1–15.

3. Barney Warf and Santa Arias, *The Spatial Turn: Interdisciplinary Perspectives* (New York: Routledge, 2008).

4. The speed and intensity of contemporary globalization has produced what David Harvey calls "time-space compression" and Anthony Giddens terms "time-space distanciation." Technology and economic systems have annihilated the importance of space by rendering the physical and experiential impact of distance insignificant. Increased immigration and transnational migration are additional factors. Scholars such as Mike Featherstone, Ulf Hannerz, David Harvey, Arjun Appadurai, Manuel Castells, and Edward Soja have also written on migration, cosmopolitanism, identity, and politics in the current era of globalization. See Anthony Giddens, *The Consequences of Modernity* (Stanford, Calif.: Stanford University Press, 1990); Carol Breckenridge, Sheldon Pollock, and Homi Bhabha, eds., *Cosmopolitanism* (Durham, N.C.: Duke University Press, 2002); Mike Featherstone, *Global Culture:*

Nationalism, Globalization, and Modernity: A Theory Culture and Society Special Issue (Thousand Oaks, Calif.: Sage Publications, 1990); David Harvey, *The Condition of Postmodernity: An Enquiry into the Origins of Cultural Change* (New York: Wiley-Blackwell, 1991). For an account of trends within the ecological movements, see Carolyn Merchant, *American Environmental History: An Introduction* (New York: Columbia University Press, 2007), 193–205.

5. Of course, debates about the definition of space by early thinkers such as Newton, Kant, and Leibniz, who grappled with important foundational questions, including whether it existed as an external absolute or a property of cognition, have shaped the basis of how more contemporary scholars use the concept of space. On the early debates, see Wolfgang Lefèvre, *Between Leibniz, Newton, and Kant: Philosophy and Science in the Eighteenth Century* (Dordrecht: Kluver Academic Publishers, 2001).

6. Lefebvre's and Foucault's seminal works have been critical for scholars in how they understand the organization of space. The scholarship of recent cultural geographers emphasizes the political aspects of placemaking. Some examples include Don Mitchell, *The Right to the City: Social Justice and the Fight for Public Space* (New York: Guilford Press, 2003); Richard Schein, *Landscape and Race in the United States* (New York: Routledge, 2006); James Duncan and Nancy Duncan, *Landscapes of Privilege: The Politics of the Aesthetic in an American Suburb* (New York: Routledge, 2004); Gillian Rose, *Feminism and Geography: The Limits of Geographical Knowledge* (Minneapolis: University of Minnesota Press, 1993); Doreen Massey, *Space, Place, and Gender* (Minneapolis: University of Minnesota Press, 1994); Gill Valentine, *Social Geographies: Space and Society* (New York: Prentice Hall, 2001).

7. Martin Heidegger, *Being and Time*, trans. John Macquarrie and Edward Robinson (London: SCM Press, 1962). According to Heidegger, the general philosophical tradition that humans exist independently of the world around them (i.e., the "subject-object" model) does not adequately describe the human experience, nor does it allow us to properly and accurately describe the embodied experiences (as opposed to the abstract philosophical concerns) that constitute our everyday lives. See William Blattner, *Heidegger's Being and Time: A Reader's Guide* (London: Continuum, 2006), 48.

8. Miles Richardson's work on Costa Rican plazas, for example, represents a good application of such principles. Richardson shows how a sense of being in place and being out of place produces cultural meanings of places. Miles Richardson, "Being-in-the-Market versus Being-in-the-Plaza: Material Culture and the Construction of Social Reality in Spanish America," in *The Anthropology of Space and Place: Locating Culture*, ed. Denise Lawrence-Zúñiga and Setha M. Low (Malden, Mass.: Blackwell, 1982), 74–91.

9. Dell Upton, "Seen, Unseen, and Scene," in *Understanding Ordinary Landscapes*, ed. Paul Groth and Todd W. Bressi (New Haven, Conn.: Yale University Press, 1977), 174–79.

10. This point is a given for those who focus on the built environment. For a discussion in the context of Freudian psychoanalysis, object relations theory, and the Other, see David Sibley, *Geographies of Exclusion: Society and Difference in the West* (London: Routledge, 1995).

11. Michel de Certeau, *The Practice of Everyday Life*, trans. Steven Rendall (Berkeley: University of California Press, 1984). Sibley, *Geographies of Exclusion*, especially addresses the power of place in the production of identity and a sense of exclusion.

12. James C. Scott, *Weapons of the Weak: Everyday Forms of Peasant Resistance* (New Haven, Conn.: Yale University Press, 1985); and Henri Lefebvre, "The Right to the City," in *Writings on Cities*, trans. Eleonore Kofman and Elizabeth Lebas (Oxford: Blackwell, 1996), first published in French as a separate book, *Le droit à la ville* (Paris: Anthropos, 1968). Lefebvre's theory is also discussed by cultural geographers such as Don Mitchell, David Harvey, and Edward Soja. See Don Mitchell, *The Right to the City: Social Justice and the Fight for Public Space* (New York: Guilford Press, 2003); David Harvey, "The Right to the City," in *New Left Review* 53 (September-October 2008): 23–40, http://www.newleftreview.org/?view=2740; Edward Soja, *Seeking Spatial Justice* (Minneapolis: University of Minnesota Press, 2010), 6.

13. Paul Connerton, "Bodily Practices," in *How Societies Remember* (New York: Cambridge University Press, 1989), 88. Although Connerton doesn't state it explicitly, his work is related to theoretical concepts discussed by Deleuze and Guattari, Spinoza, Bergson, and Bourdieu. See, for example, Herman Roodenburg, "Pierre Bourdieu: Issues of Embodiment and Authenticity," *Etnofoor* 17, nos. 1/2 (2004): 215–26. According to Patricia Ticineto Clough, scholars in this line of thinking "treat affectivity as a substrate of potential bodily responses, often automatic responses, in excess of consciousness. For these scholars, affect refers generally to bodily capacities to affect and be affected or the augmentation or diminution of a body's capacity to act, to engage, and to connect, such that autoaffection is linked to the self-feeling of being alive." Patricia Ticineto Clough, introduction to *The Affective Turn: Theorizing the Social*, ed. Patricia T. Clough and Jean Halley (Durham, N.C.: Duke University Press, 2007), 1–2.

14. Iain Borden, "Thick Edge: Architectural Boundaries in the Postmodern Metropolis," in *InterSections: Architectural Histories and Critical Theories*, ed. Iain Borden and Jane Rendell (New York: Routledge, 2000), 221–46.

15. Iain Borden, "Machines of Possibility," inaugural professorial lecture, Bartlett School of Architecture, University College of London, October 21, 2004.

16. There is a rich history of design practitioners exploring the haptic engagement between humans and their environment. See Charles W. Moore, Kent C. Bloomer, and Robert J. Yudell, *Body, Memory, and Architecture* (New Haven, Conn.: Yale University Press, 1977); and Christian Norberg Schulz, *Genius Loci: Towards a Phenomenology of Architecture* (New York: Rizzoli, 1991).

17. Branko Kolarevic and Ali Malkawi, *Performative Architecture: Beyond Instrumentality* (New York: Spon Press, 2005).

18. Henry Glassie, *Folk Housing in Middle Virginia* (Knoxville: University of Tennessee Press, 1975); James Deetz, *In Small Things Forgotten: An Archaeology of Early American Life* (New York: Anchor Books, 1996); Bernard L. Herman, "Time and Performance: Folk Houses in Delaware," in *American Material Culture and Folklife: A Prologue and Dialogue*, ed. S. Bronner (Ann Arbor, Mich.: UMI Research Press, 1985), 155–75. See also Dell Upton, *Another City: Urban Life and Urban Spaces in the New American Republic* (New Haven, Conn.: Yale University

Press, 2008); Jennifer Nardone, "Roomful of Blues: Jukejoints and the Cultural Landscape of the Mississippi Delta," in *Perspectives in Vernacular Architecture*, vol. 9, *Constructing Image, Identity, and Place* ed. Alison K. Hoagland and Kenneth A. Breisch (Knoxville: University of Tennessee Press, 2003), 166–75; Gerald L. Pocius, *A Place to Belong: Community Order and Everyday Space in Calvert, Newfoundland* (Athens: University of Georgia Press, 1991); and Richardson, "Being-in-the Market."

19. For a discussion of such scholarship, see Quentin Stevens, *The Ludic City: Exploring the Potential of Public Spaces* (New York: Routledge, 2007), 5–66; and Ash Amin and Nigel Thrift, "The Legibility of the Everyday City," in *Cities: Reimagining the Urban* (Malden, Mass.: Polity Press, 2002), 7–30.

20. Work on urban culture that focuses on political economic factors includes Robert E. Park, "The City: Suggestions for the Investigations of Human Behavior in the Urban Environment," in *The City*, ed. Robert E. Park and Ernest W. Burgess (Chicago: University of Chicago Press, 1925), 1–46; Louis Wirth, "Urbanism as a Way of Life," in *American Journal of Sociology* 44 (July 1938): 1–24; Sharon Zukin, *Landscapes of Power: From Detroit to Disney World* (Berkeley: University of California Press, 1991); David Harvey, *The Urban Experience* (Baltimore, Md.: Johns Hopkins University Press, 1989); and David Harvey, *The Condition of Postmodernity* (Malden, Mass.: Blackwell, 1990).

21. Pierre Bourdieu, *Outline of a Theory of Practice*, (Cambridge: Cambridge University Press, 1977); Anthony Giddens, *The Constitution of Society: Outline of the Theory of Structuration* (Berkeley: University of California Press, 1984). The notion of habitus is, in fact, inseparable from a consideration of space. See Pierre Bourdieu, "Structures and the Habitus," in *Material Culture: Critical Concepts in the Social Sciences*, vol. 1, part 1, ed. Victor Buchli (London: Routledge, 2004), 116–77.

22. Georg Simmel, "The Metropolis and Mental Life," in *The Sociology of Georg Simmel*, trans. Kurt Wolff (New York: Free Press, 1950), 409–24; Edgar Allan Poe, *The Man of the Crowd* (first published in 1840), Electronic Text Center, University of Virginia Library, 1994, http://etext.virginia.edu/toc/modeng/public/PoeCrow.html; Charles Baudelaire, *The Painter of Modern Life*, (New York: Da Capo Press, 1964), orig. published in *Le Figaro* in 1863.

23. Edward T. Hall, *The Hidden Dimension* (New York: Anchor Books, 1966).

24. Walter Benjamin, *One Way Street* (London: Verso, 1997), 171; see also Benjamin's Arcades project and, more recently, Tim Edensor, *The City* (London: Ashgate, 2010); and Tim Ingold and Jo Lee Vergunst, *Ways of Walking: Ethnography and Practice on Foot* (London: Ashgate, 2008).

25. Lewis Mumford, *The Culture of Cities* (1938; New York: Harcourt Brace, 1996); Lewis Mumford, *The City in History: Its Origins, Its Transformations, and Its Prospects* (1961; New York: Harcourt, 1989); Jane Jacobs, *The Death and Life of Great American Cities* (New York: Random House, 1961); William H. Whyte, *City: Rediscovering the Center* (New York: Doubleday, 1988); William H. Whyte, *The Social Life of Small Urban Spaces* (Washington, D.C.: Conservation Foundation, 1980).

26. Sharon Zukin, *The Cultures of Cities* (Malden, Mass.: Blackwell, 1995); AbdouMaliq Simone, "Movement: The Zawiyyah as the City," in *For the City Yet to Come: Changing African Life in Four Cities* (Durham, N.C.: Duke University

Press, 2004); Stevens, *Ludic City*, 5–66; Borden, "Thick Edge," 221–46; Joachim Schlör, *Nights in the Big City* (London: Reaktion Books, 1998); Deborah Parsons, *Streetwalking the Metropolis* (Oxford: Oxford University Press, 2000); Susan Ossman, *Picturing Casablanca: Portraits of Power in a Modern City* (Berkeley: University of California Press, 1994).

27. Situationist International, the twentieth-century avant-garde movement in France, experimented with embodied experiences in the city and helped produce the field of psychogeography. The Situationists, however, were not only interested in describing and experiencing the city; they also sought to capture and document such experiences. For a discussion of the urban analysis of scholars associated with the Situationist International movement, see Simon Sadler, "Formulary for a New Urbanism, Rethinking the City," *The Situationist City* (Cambridge: MIT Press, 1998), 62–104.

28. Henri Lefebvre, *Rhythmanalysis: Space, Time, and Everyday Life* (London: Continuum, 2004).

29. Two of these "city-symphony" movies are *Man with a Movie Camera* (Russian, *Chelovek s kinopparatom*, 1929), directed by Dziga Vertov; and *Berlin: Symphony of a Metropolis* (German, *Die Sinfonie der Großstadt*, 1927), directed by Walter Ruttmann, cowritten by Carl Mayer and Karl Freund.

30. Akhil Gupta and James Ferguson, "Beyond Culture: Space, Identity, and the Politics of Difference," in *Cultural Anthropology* 7, no. 1 (1992): 7. This seminal article argues that correlating place with culture produces epistemological problems and blind spots. Appadurai discusses such practices, arguing that the tendency to equate cultural authenticity with place falsely situates people of color and colonized cultures, since an individual is marked constantly and tied to a mistaken notion of autochthony. See Arjun Appadurai, "Putting Hierarchy in Its Place," *Cultural Anthropology* 3 (February 1988): 38–39.

31. For instance, geographer Nigel Thrift's work on nonrepresentational theory draws from complex associations with theoretical genealogies such as interactionism, actor-network theory, Deleuze, Dewey, and performance theory. We draw attention to Thrift's emphasis on practice, action, and performance as a way to rethink everyday routines and corporeal practices that establish meaning in the built world. Nigel Thrift, *Non-Representational Theory: Space, Politics, Affect* (New York: Routledge, 2007); Melissa Gregg and Gregory J. Seigworth, eds., *The Affect Theory Reader* (Durham, N.C.: Duke University Press, 2010); Gilles Deleuze and Félix Guattari, *A Thousand Plateaus*, trans. Brian Massumi (Minneapolis: University of Minnesota Press, 1987); Bruno Latour, *Reassembling the Social: An Introduction to Actor-Network Theory* (New York: Oxford University Press, 2007).

32. See Yi Fu Tuan, *Space and Place: The Perspective of Experience* (Minneapolis: University of Minnesota Press, 1977); David Seamon and Robert Mugerauer, *Dwelling, Place & Environment: Towards a Phenomenology of Person and World* (Malabar, Fla.: Krieger Publishing, 2000); Tony Hiss, *The Experience of Place: A New Way of Looking at and Dealing with Our Radically Changing Cities and Countryside* (New York: Vintage Books, 1990).

33. Dolores Hayden, *The Power of Place: Urban Landscapes as Public History* (Cambridge: MIT Press, 1996). For more on the California Japantowns project or

the Place Matters project, see http://www.californiajapantowns.org and http://www.placematters.net.

34. According to architectural history, architects, patrons, and builders are all seen as authors of the built environment. Vernacular architecture and cultural landscape scholars posit the folk builder or the community as producers of the built world. They tend to downplay the experience of individuals as they study larger aggregates, viz. cultural practices. A good critique of the canon is Dell Upton, "Architectural History or Landscape History?" in *Journal of Architectural Education* 44 (August 1991): 195–99.

35. Michael Ann Williams and M. Jane Young, "Grammar, Codes, and Performance: Linguistic and Sociolinguistic Models in the Study of Vernacular Architecture," in *Perspectives in Vernacular Architecture* vol. 5, *Gender, Glass, and Shelter*, ed. Elizabeth Collins Cromley and Carter L. Hudgins (Knoxville: University of Tennessee Press, 1995), 40–51. For a definition of the ethnography-of-speaking approach, see 42–43. Williams and Young's argument is not unique. Gerald L. Pocius, in his work on Calvert, Newfoundland, argues that "Calvert's past today comes from talk in the context of sociability and thus depends ultimately on ongoing social relationships. The past cannot be preserved by saving things because the past does not consist of fossilized static items that are conserved and stored away." Pocius, *Place to Belong*, 54.

36. Williams and Young, "Grammar, Codes, and Performance," 46.

37. Sharad Chari and Vinay Gidwani, "Introduction: Grounds for a Spatial Ethnography of Labor," *Ethnography* 6, no. 3 (2005): 267–81; and Katharyne Mitchell, *Crossing the Neoliberal Line: Pacific Rim Migration and the Metropolis* (Philadelphia: Temple University Press, 2004).

38. For considerations of place in the context of broader scales, see the Big History Project, http://www.bighistoryproject.com; David Christian, *Maps of Time: An Introduction to Big History* (Berkeley: University of California Press, 2005); and William Cronon, "A Place for Stories: Nature, History, and Narrative," *Journal of American History* 78, no. 4 (1992): 1347–76.

39. George E. Marcus, "Ethnography in/of the World System: The Emergence of Multi-sited Ethnography," *Annual Review of Anthropology* 24 (1995): 95–117; John Durham Peters, "Seeing Bifocally: Media, Place, and Culture," in *Culture, Place, and Power: Essays in Critical Anthropology*, ed. Akhil Gupta and James Ferguson (Durham, N.C.: Duke University Press, 1997), 75–92.

40. Much of that work comes out of Merleau-Ponty's writings on the body and its role in perception. Merleau-Ponty's work has been the inspiration for recent work on affect and embodied practices. See David Abram, *The Spell of the Sensuous: Perception and Language in a More-Than-Human World* (New York: Pantheon Books, 1996); James R. Mensch, *Embodiments: From the Body to the Body Politic* (Chicago: Northwestern University Press, 2009). Other theorists whose work has influenced recent scholars include Bergson and Spinoza. Henri Bergson, *Matter and Memory*, trans. N. M. Paul and W. S. Palmer (New York: Zone, 1991); Baruch Spinoza, "Ethics," in *Collected Works*, ed. Edwin Curley (Princeton, N.J.: Princeton University Press, 1985). For more contemporary foundational work on affect theory, see Brian Massumi, *Parables for the Virtual: Movement, Affect, Sensation* (Durham, N.C.: Duke University Press, 2002).

41. Kevin Lynch, *The Image of the City* (Cambridge: MIT Press, 1960).

1.

Placemaking and Embodied Space

SETHA LOW

Within the field of space and culture there has been increasing interest in theories that include the body and walking as bodily movement as
integral parts of spatial analysis. These concerns have been addressed partially through the historical analysis of the docile body to social structure
and power in work of Michel Foucault, and sociologically in the notions
of *habitus* by Pierre Bourdieu and "structuration" by Anthony Giddens, as
well as the works of many others.[1] Nonetheless, many researchers, architects,
and landscape practitioners need theoretical formulations that provide an
everyday material grounding and experiential, cognitive, and/or emotional
understanding of the intersection and interpenetration of body, space, and
culture.[2] I call this material and experiential intersection "embodied space."
These understandings require theories of body and space that are experi-
ence-near and yet allow for linkages to be made to larger social and political processes.

Spatial analyses in fields that deal with the built environment—for
example, cultural landscape studies, architecture and vernacular architecture, material culture, and cultural anthropology and geography—often
neglect the body because of difficulties in resolving the dualism of the subjective and objective body and distinctions between the material and representational aspects of body space. The concept of embodied space, however,
draws these disparate notions together, underscoring the importance of the
body as a physical and biological entity, as lived experience, and as a center of agency, a location for speaking and acting on the world. Embodied
space actually allows these disparate disciplinary and methodological modes

of practice and analysis to come together through a focus on bodies as they create space through mobility and movement.

The term "body" refers to its biological and social characteristics, and "embodiment" as an "indeterminate methodological field defined by perceptual experience and mode of presence and engagement in the world."[3] "Embodied space" is the location where human experience and consciousness take on material and spatial form. In earlier publications I have discussed the theories of the body, proxemics, phenomenology, language and discourse, and spatial orientation that I employ to construct the concept of embodied space.[4] Here, I would like to focus more on the "placemaking" potential of embodied space. To do so, I draw on one component of that conceptualization—spatial orientation—and add a second conceptual element, that of mobility and movement, particularly through walking.[5] I define and briefly review the literature that I am drawing upon and then illustrate the spatial orientation and movement approach with an ethnographic description of everyday paths and routines from my research on the Costa Rican plaza. Based on this discussion, embodied space is posited as a foundational concept for understanding the creation of place through spatial orientation, movement, and action.

Spatial Orientation

Nancy Munn begins her analysis of spatial orientation of the body through the notion of spacetime "as a symbolic nexus of relations produced out of interactions between bodily actors and terrestrial spaces." Drawing in part upon Lefebvre's concepts of "field of action" and "basis of action," and his insistence that space is produced and consumed actively through embodied practices and experiences, Munn constructs the notion of a "mobile spatial field."[6] I have found her notion useful for understanding how the body creates and makes its own space in that her spatiotemporal construct can be understood as a culturally defined, corporeal-sensual field stretching out from the body at a given locale or moving through locales.

Munn illustrates this notion of the body as a mobile spatial field through an ethnographic example derived from the spatial interdiction that occurs when Australian Aborigines treat the land according to ancestral Aboriginal law. She is interested in the specific kind of spatial form being produced: "a space of deletions or of delimitations constraining one's presence at particular locales" that creates a variable range of excluded or restricted regions for each person throughout their life.[7] For instance, in following their moral-religious law, Aborigines make detours that must be far enough away to avoid seeing an ancient place or hearing the ritual singing currently going on there. By detouring, actors carve out a "negative space" that extends beyond their spatial field of vision. "This act projects a signifier of limitation upon the land or place by forming transient but repeatable boundaries out of the moving body."[8] Munn applies this idea to contemporary Aborigines' encounters with powerful topographic centers and "dangerous" ancestral places.

The importance of this analysis is the way Munn demonstrates how the ancestral law's power of spatial limitation becomes "embodied" in an actor-centered, mobile body, separate from any fixed center or place. "Excluded spaces" become spatiotemporal formations produced out of the interaction of actors' moving spatial fields and the terrestrial spaces of body action. Further, these detours, what Munn calls the production of "negative space," are a new kind of spatialization of respect and a model for understanding the relationship of distance, detour, social regard, and status in other cultural groups, including our own. The power of this idea is that she suggests constructing the person (actor) as an embodied space, in which the body, conceived of as a moving spatial field, makes its own place in the world.

Stuart Rockefeller radicalizes this notion of actors' mobile spatial fields into a theory of public places formed by the individual movement, trips, and digressions of migrants crossing national boundaries. Starting with Munn's idea that the person makes space by moving through it, he traces how movement patterns collectively make up locality and reproduce locality. Places, he argues, are not in the landscape, but simultaneously in the land, people's minds, customs, and bodily practices.[9]

Movement and Walking

Other theorists have emphasized the importance of movement in placemaking, conceptualizing space as movement rather than a container.[10] For example, the geographer Allan Pred traces the history of microgeographies of daily life in southern Sweden to determine how everyday movement and behavior generate spatial transformations in land tenure that result in changes in the local social structure. He concludes that place always involves "appropriation and transformation of space and nature that is inseparable from the reproduction and transformation of society in time and space," and he demonstrates how social change occurs through everyday bodily practices.[11] Michel de Certeau's insightful analysis of the spatial tactics of orientation and movement also focuses on how the mundane acts of walking and meandering resist state order and regimes of city planning.[12]

John Gray, in his ethnographic research on sheep herding in the Scottish borderlands, draws inspiration from de Certeau by emphasizing the analogy of walking and language, with walking designated as the equivalent of speaking (la parole), rather than language (la langue) and the appropriation of space. Like de Certeau's urban dwellers, the hirsel, a unified place that includes both a shepherd's sheep and their grazing area, is constituted by the shepherd's walking and biking in the hills to care for his animals. The act of shepherding, or "agoing" around the hill, is a kind of space-making requiring a shepherd's detailed knowledge of not only the terrain but also how the sheep bond to parts of the terrain, and how these parts are linked together by paths to form a hirsel. The emphasis on walking the hills demonstrates how places, which may be separately named and recalled, are connected to one another and form a unified whole.[13]

Rachel Thomas is more concerned with "mobility" than simply walking in the urban context. Mobility and access are complex concepts that involve the perceptible environment, the perception of the pedestrian, and the ability of the body to express itself. In her research on urban accessibility to public space, she emphasizes the role of sensory perception in the choice of route based on fieldwork in Grenoble.[14]

Tim Ingold's seminal research on walking and linear movement connects these approaches through the integration of psychology and anthropology influenced by the work of James Gibson on perceptual systems.[15] Gibson argues that perception is a psychosomatic act that can only be experienced through the body.[16] Similar to Maurice Merleau-Ponty, who claims the body is a vehicle in the world, Gibson asserts that all perception is embodied.[17] Ingold suggests that linear movement connects body movement and visual perception through lines of vision and the lines and paths of walking. He contrasts lines as free-flowing movement in an open landscape with lines that connect predetermined points of arrival and departure, and suggests that places are constituted by these lines of movement. Multiple forms of linear movement integrate the person, memory, experience, and the environment and include everything from the path to the locomotor mode accompanied by gestures, rhythm, and cadence.

Ethnographic research carried out in 2004–2005 in northeast Scotland by Ingold and Jo Lee Vergunst takes the notions of lines and body movement and applies them to walking, an activity that is fundamental to everyday life. They argue that the relationship between walking, embodiment, and sociability is crucial: "That is, we do not assume a priori that walking affords an experience of embodiment, or that social life hovers above the road we tread in our material life. Rather, walking affords an experience of embodiment to the extent that it is grounded in an inherently sociable engagement between self and environment."[18] Based on their study of Aberdeen walkers, Ingold and Vergunst conceptualize the relationship between bodies and environments in three ways: (1) the walker may look or sense the environment; (2) the walker may turn inward to thoughts, memories, or stories while experiencing the sensory perception; and (3) walkers may become aware of or even cross the boundary of the body and environment through their embodied and emotional interactions. The details of steps are integral to how the walk proceeds, while emotions are engendered not only by grand vistas but also by the care taken in maintaining balance or way-finding.

Vergunst's analysis of the lines and rhythms of walking on Union Street weaves the history and contemporary ethnography of Aberdeen, Scotland, with a study of walking and the street.[19] Although Vergunst does not go as far as to argue that walking and the accompanying gestures of arm swinging and turns and twists create embodied space, he does explore the way that embodiment is materially inscribed in the city. Using sound, movement, rhythm, and shape of the walker's body, he uses walking the street as a means for understanding the historical development of the city. By interviewing walkers while they are walking, he is able to trace their way-finding decisions and adjustments in speed, tempo, and diversion. His discussion of "walking the mat," a walk down Union Street in a small, single-sex group and during the walk meeting up with another group of the opposite sex, is reminiscent of narratives about *la retreta* and *el paseo* in Spanish American culture.

Embodied Space Fieldwork Illustration

The theoretical premise that individuals as mobile spatiotemporal fields create space and locale and the importance of walking in the creation of space are illustrated by a field study of walking and bodily movements and activities undertaken as part of a fifteen-year ethnography of two plazas in the center of San José, the capital city of Costa Rica.[20] I collected these data on walking and body movement long before I had theorized the body's role in placemaking. As a modern dancer I felt that a significant part of the spatial experience of the plaza was created by the movement of people, not just by the users who spent their days there. Vicki Reisner, a dance ethnologist at the Library of Congress, and I struggled to find a way to record and communicate this ephemeral but profoundly material aspect of space and place.

Parque Central represents Costa Rica's Spanish colonial history in its spatial form and context. Its relatively long history spans the colonial, republican, and modern periods, and a number of historical photographs and portrayals of earlier periods of plaza design and social life were available in local archives. During the research period of 1985 through 1987, Parque Central was a vibrant center of traditional Costa Rican culture, inhabited by a variety of largely male workers, pensioners, preachers and healers, tourists, shoppers, female sex workers, and people who just wanted to sit and watch the action. When I returned in 1993 and 1994, it was under construction: the cement kiosk was being renovated and the surrounding benches, pathways, and gathering spaces were in the process of being redesigned. By 1997 it had reopened, and its design and use had changed.

The Plaza de la Cultura, a contemporary plaza only one block west and one block north of Parque Central, is a more recently designed urban space heralded as an emblem of the "new Costa Rican culture." Because it was opened in 1982, I was able to interview individuals involved in its design and planning, while at the same time it could be studied as a well-established place. The Plaza de la Cultura proved to be an excellent comparison to Parque Central, providing contrasts in design, spatial configuration, surrounding buildings and institutions, activities, and kinds of inhabitants and visitors.

These two urban spaces were planned, built, designed, and maintained in different historical and sociopolitical contexts, and both were constrained by limits imposed by the available resources as well as by the central government's political objectives. The environments thus produced are observably different: Parque Central is a furnished and enclosed space of trees, paths, and benches, while the Plaza de la Cultura is an open expanse with few places to sit, providing an open vista leading to a view of the National Theater. Using movement maps derived from dance choreography, behavioral maps from environmental psychology, interviews with people who remember the ritualized courtship walks known as paseos, and my field notes, I explored what an embodied spatial analysis tells us about spatial differences produced by the rhythms and bodily movements in Parque Central and Plaza de la Cultura.

The methodology developed traces the peoples and their routes, behaviors, desires, and fears that come into contact and produce space through what Allan Pred defines as the microgeographies of everyday life. Like

Vergunst's description of Union Street and Munn's analysis of excluded spaces, Pred's placemaking is created by the temporal and spatial attributes of users' walking, bodily movements, and social activities.

> Since each of the actions and events consecutively making up the existence of an individual has both temporal and spatial attributes, time-geography allows that the biography of a person may be conceptualized and diagrammed at daily or lengthier scales of observation as an unbroken continuous *path* through time-space subject to times of constraint. In time-geographic terms a *project* consists of the entire sequence of simple or complex tasks necessary to the completion of any intention-inspired or goal-oriented behavior.[21]

The paths and projects of individual plaza users are presented as a series of movement maps and behavioral maps organized by time and day within each plaza. The overlap of the movement and behavior maps combined with ethnographic description identify a series of distinct locales and places defined by class, age, and gender.

Two kinds of data were collected to describe everyday plaza life: movement maps by gender at two-hour intervals on a typical day, and behavioral maps of group activities by time and location. These maps recorded plaza users' movements and activities supplementing photographs, participant observation, and unstructured interviewing. Taken together, these data identify the locales, paths, and projects that mediate the socio-spatial differences of the two plazas and provide insights into how individuals produce distinct spaces by their everyday routines and practices. The majority of the observations were completed in 1987, over twenty years ago, and therefore do not reflect the current space and movement patterns in these locations; nonetheless they serve to illustrate how movement and walking create space, and how bodily movements and activities produce different kinds of spatial experience.[22]

Movement Maps

Pedestrian movement, usually walking but also skipping by children or running by teenagers, is one way that space is inscribed through the rhythms of everyday life. Movement maps were created by recording the pathway of each pedestrian during a fifteen-minute or thirty-minute observation period. Vicki and I arrived at a simplified system of notation based on her research experience recording dance in its cultural context. We worked out a system that recorded pathways used along with gender and estimated ages of the observed pedestrians. The entrances were rotated throughout the observation period, and notes were made of who was sitting in the plaza at the time and other significant behavioral details (e.g., a pedestrian shakes another man's hand as he walks through).

I used maps of the plazas and colored pencils to draw each person's trajectory around or through the area. Some people cut through quickly, walking in a relatively straight line with no detours or stops. Others wandered through, talking to friends and even stopping to sit for a moment before moving on. Groups and individuals, males and females, young, adult, and elderly were recorded initially until I found that the numbers of people flowing through were too great to record. Then I tried every third or every fifth person so that I had the details correctly documented. In Parque Central I usually stood on the kiosk (bandstand) so that I could see in all directions, while in the Plaza de la Cultura I could sit almost anywhere and see the entire site. Either way, it was tiring and time-consuming but a thoroughly rewarding way to capture the ebb and flow of the people making their way through and around the plazas.

Unfortunately, when it came time to translate these intricately colored and detailed maps into a format for publication, I could not find a way to communicate what we had found. Instead, I turned to Stephane Tonnelat, an architect and professor of sociology and environmental psychology at the Centre National de la Recherche Scientifique (CRNS), to find a way to present these complicated spatial representations. He designed the illustrative movement maps to summarize the findings, although it is important to note that the originals had none of their clarity. In the new illustrations, the width of the line indicates the number of people walking and moving in the same direction, while the different textures indicate gender-normative male and female bodies.

Movement maps were collected from 8:00 AM to 6:00 PM in both plazas. The three maps in figure 1.1 (figures 1.1a, 1.1b, 1.1c) record observations in Parque Central on a Thursday in July, a day that started out cloudy and damp but became sunny in the afternoon. At 8:00 AM a few men move from northwest to east, and east to west and southwest, while only two women, a young woman and an elderly woman in a couple, travel in a southern route across the park. By 10:00 AM more people are crossing and circling, moving from the northwestern to eastern pathway that faces the Metropolitan Cathedral. There are still more men than women, and only men are exiting at the southwestern corner (figure 1.1a). By noon the direction of movement shifts significantly as the majority of people exit at the southwestern corner; these seem to be men and a few women catching the buses home that stop

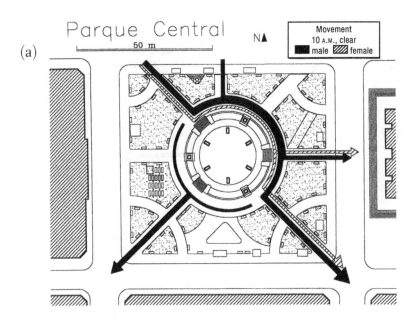

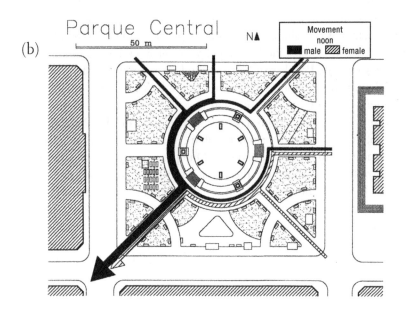

Figure 1.1. Parque Central: Movement Maps: (a) 10:00 AM (b) 12 noon. Created by author.

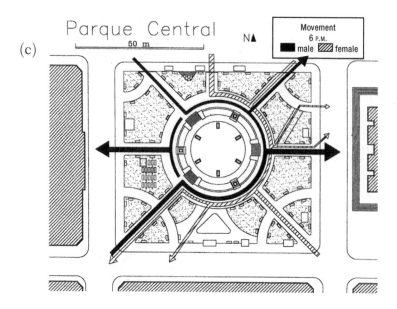

Figure 1.1. Parque Central: Movement Maps: (c) 6:00 PM. Created by author.

along Fourth Avenue (figure 1.1b). The afternoon is the busiest time, with many more women moving through, mostly in an eastern to southwestern direction on their way to shop, meet friends, or pick up children from school. Between 4:00 and 6:00 PM the flow of people reversing their morning journey reaches its peak. People exit both east and west, but the western exit is used predominantly by young men going to the bars located on the west-northwestern edge of the park (figure 1.1c).

The movement maps from a Wednesday in June on the Plaza de la Cultura (figure 1.2) record a similar pattern, with an increase in activity from the morning to the early afternoon. One popular pedestrian pathway, from the southwest corner near the entrance to the Gran Hotel and the National Theater to the northeast corner on Central Avenue, is used as a shortcut by people moving in either direction (figure 1.2a). At 4:00 PM, however, there is a lull when a sudden rainstorm temporarily stops all activity. Only four young men venture out into the rain during the half-hour observation period (figure 1.2b). But by 6:00 PM activity has picked up again. A secondary pathway from northwest to southeast emerges with men walking in either direction, from Pops Ice Cream Parlor on Central Avenue (northwestern corner) to the lower level of the plaza and Second Avenue, where there is a bus stop that services the eastern part of the city (figure 1.2c).

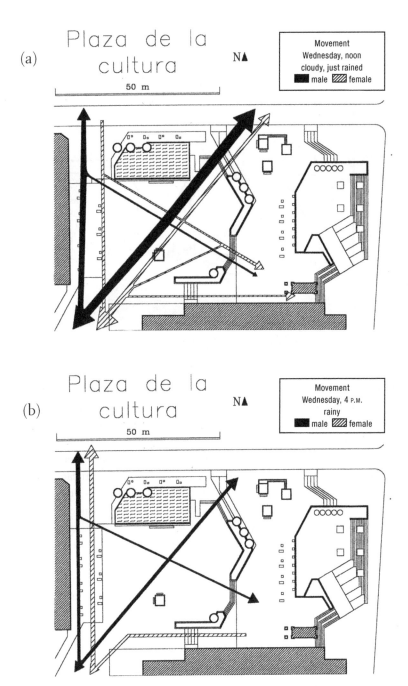

Figure 1.2. Plaza de la Cultura: Movement Maps: (a) 12 noon (b) 4:00 PM. Created by author.

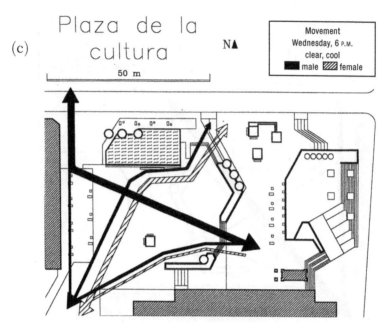

Figure 1.2. Plaza de la Cultura: Movement Maps: (c) 6:00 PM. Created by author.

Comparing the movement maps of Parque Central and Plaza de la Cultura shows that spaces of movement in the two locations are created and experienced differently. The maps reveal "rivers" of intermittently pulsating movement that make up time-geography paths, segregated for the most part into male and female spheres. When integrated with participant observation field notes and photographs of people walking, the movement maps suggest that there are two predominant spatiotemporal fields in each plaza: one made by those who are traveling through, creating path- or river-like spaces, and the other made by those who have taken up residence by sitting on a bench or leaning on a wall. Many people move from one category to another, of course, but overall there seems to be both a residential space and a transient space, with distinct characteristics and activities on both plazas.

What is noteworthy, however, is the manner in which the movement creates spaces that articulate with each other. In Plaza de la Cultura people take up residency in large part to watch the nonresidents who flow through and create paths. There is constant visual contact between the subspaces. In Parque Central, however, the residents are much less interested in the non-residents who move through the space. Parque Central, with its internally focused groups of men, talking and looking at each other while gambling, reading, or working, and not necessarily interacting with passersby, generates a centripetal space, socially and spatially bounded. Plaza de la Cultura, on the other hand, consists of an outwardly focused, centrifugal space of groups of men and women who are constantly looking around and talking to passersby, and who frequently break out of the group to meet someone or to join another group.[23] In fact, one could argue that the entire reason to be in the Plaza de la Cultura is to come in contact with others.

The design of the Plaza de la Cultura reinforces this openness and increases the possibilities of interaction and movement across groups, while the shaded, enclosed corners of the pre-1994 Parque Central provide more privacy and seclusion. But the differences observed in the interaction and movement patterns express more than just the design of the space; here is an example of the landscape architecture and the embodied spaces reinforcing each, and it is difficult to segment out the extent to which each plays a determinant role.

Behavioral Maps

The behavioral maps are also quite dated, having been collected during a variety of field visits in 1985, 1987, 1993, and 1997. The ones included here are only illustrative, drawn from *On the Plaza: Public Space and Culture*.[24] I think, however, that it is important to add these behavioral maps to the movement analyses as a corrective to what I perceive as too much reliance on walking and linear movement in the works of both Vergunst and Gray.[25] As I noted before, there is an interaction between the paths and locales; the so-called activity nodes of environmental psychology are part of the circulation of bodies and often the focus of walking and other intentional movement. Behavioral maps augment the movement maps, provide context, and add another methodological dimension to our understanding of embodied space.

The behavioral observations were made by recording continuous activities and by using timed samples recorded on maps from 8:00 AM until 10:00 PM on a series of sunny weekdays in January, although the majority of activity occurred during the late morning, afternoon, and early evening. Only a few of the behavioral maps are included to illustrate the points made; however, the bulk of the maps were used as the basis for this overview. The maps were drawn on 8½" x 11" plaza plans using black ink and colored pencils to record ongoing behaviors and locations of individuals. Since the colored pencil data could not be reproduced here, circles and written descriptions are used in an attempt to convey the richer data of the originals, again by Stephane Tonnelat.

Parque Central

In Parque Central morning is a time for men to sit and read the newspaper. By 10:00 AM almost every bench is occupied by an adult man reading his paper (figure 1.3a). The shoeshine business in the northeast corner is slow, and neither fruit nor lottery vendors are doing much business. The passersby are mainly on their way to the bus or shopping. The most active person is the municipal employee who sweeps the sidewalks and picks up fallen leaves and trash.

By noon the tempo has picked up (figure 1.3b). The men on their benches are joined by friends with animated voices as the walkways fill with men and women meeting for lunch or catching the bus home. The religious man starts his healing routine in the northwest corner, and the missionaries set up a prayer meeting that begins at noon under the arbor. One group of elderly men leaves Parque Central to go home for lunch and siesta, and they do not return. Others also leave but will return after their lunch. As one seventy-year-old man said: "The plaza is now my place of employment now that I no longer work. I am underfoot at home. The house is my wife's domain, and I feel better being out of the house during the day."

In the afternoon a few older women appear, bringing their children to the library, shopping with friends, or resting from a busy morning in town (figure 1.3c). The shoeshine business is at its peak as middle-class men stop to get their shoes shined on their way back to work from lunch. Sometimes during the mid afternoon, "Vicky" begins his routine with a guitar and a hat for tips, telling sordid jokes on the kiosk platform. Vendors of ice cream, peanuts, and snow cones circulate along the edge of the crowd. The police walk by in pairs, stop and watch for a while, and then continue on their patrol of the street.·

By 4:00 PM most of the older men have left, and young and middle-age couples meet in Parque Central for coffee or to take the bus home. The number of women is the highest at this time, yet they still make up only about 20 to 30 percent of the population, very different from the all-male newspaper readers of the morning. At 6:00 PM the light begins to fade and the air is cooler (figure 1.3d). A new group of pushcart vendors with hot corn, caramelized peanuts, or skewered beef appear on the edge of the sidewalk. As couples circumambulate around the kiosk, they stop to buy food and talk to the vendors, drawn by the smell of the sizzling grilled beef or roasting peanuts.

At 7:00 PM Parque Central becomes quiet. The shoeshine men have left for the day, and only a few couples, some single young men, and the

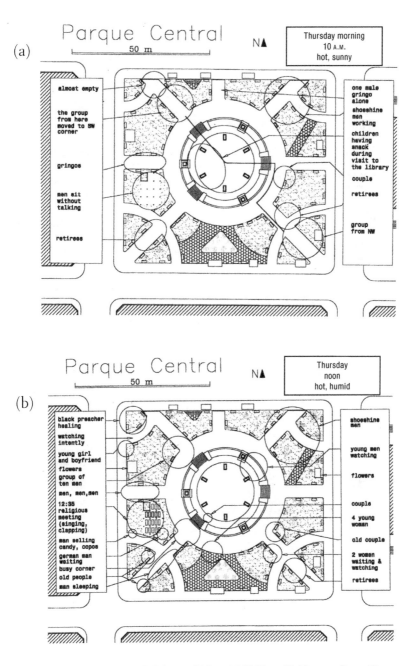

Figure 1.3. Parque Central: Behavioral Maps: (a) 10:00 AM (b) 12 noon. Created by author.

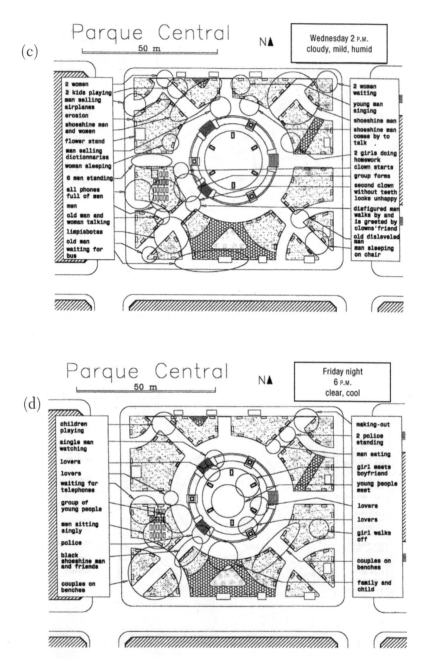

Figure 1.3. Parque Central: Behavioral Maps: (c) 2:00 PM (d) 6:00 PM. Created by author.

vendors remain. If it is a nice evening, more people will wander by on their way to the cinema or to have drink. A small group of street kids run by trying to beg money from a passing gringo (American), and young female sex workers sit under the arbor waiting for business. By now the lines for the buses are not as long, and tired workers wait in groups talking about the day or buying lottery tickets from the corner vendors. Later in the evening, between 9:00 and 10:00 PM, Parque Central is almost completely deserted except for one or two solitary men sitting on the benches or walking slowly down the paths. Even later, men from the countryside, drunk and sleepy, may find their way from the cheap bars surrounding the central market to sleep relatively undisturbed on the park benches until morning.

Plaza de la Cultura

In the Plaza de la Cultura the day also starts slowly. During the morning there are very few people, usually just a couple of men or male tourists reading a newspaper in the sun, and a group of green-uniformed plaza employees who sweep and empty the trash cans. Sunday is a little busier with the artisan market for the tourists, but even then there is little activity.

About noon the older North Americans appear in their baseball hats, sunburns, and smiles (figure 1.4a). They will stay for most of the afternoon, waiting for girls or watching those who walk by. Students, young office workers, and friends sometimes stop to have their lunch in the plaza or to buy ice cream at the nearby Pops Ice Cream Parlor and sit a moment to finish eating. Tourists are having lunch at the Gran Hotel, which fronts the plaza, or wandering in front of the National Theater, buying souvenirs and taking pictures.

By 2:00 PM the pace quickens as office workers return to work, walking through on their way from the bus stop. Young mothers and children stop to look at the fountain or to play with the pigeons. Students stop to meet friends while they are still in their school uniforms. On some afternoons a clown and his assistant or a Peruvian musical group may come by. Later an evangelical group with guitars, singing popular songs in praise of Jesus, might entertain a teenage crowd.

At 4:00 PM the gringos leave for their afternoon coffee and rest, and many families start on their way home (figure 1.4b). By 5:00 PM or so, however, teenagers in blue jeans begin to appear (figure 1.4c). They play music on portable radios or tape decks, dance, and even start soccer games on the far end of the main open space. They are the major occupants until the National Theater opens at 8:00 pm. Sometimes there are special evening events, such as a tribute to local high school bands or a radio

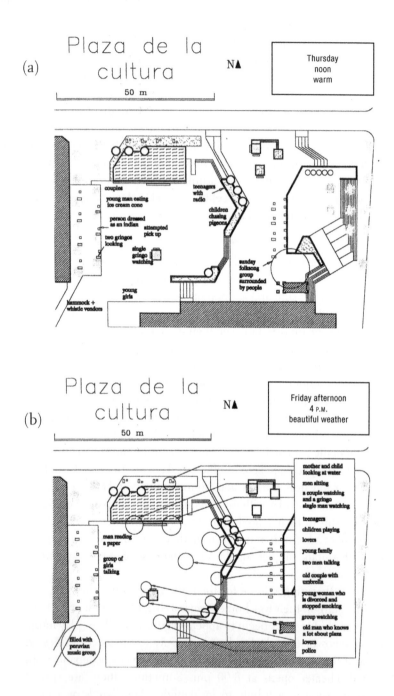

Figure 1.4. Plaza de la Cultura: Behavioral Maps: (a) 12 noon (b) 4:00 PM. Created by author.

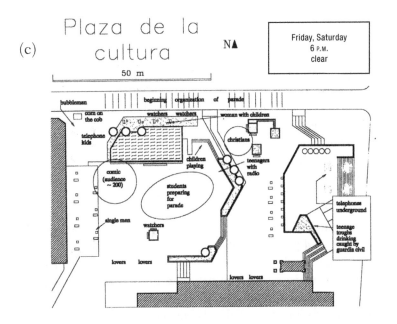

Figure 1.4. Plaza de la Cultura: Behavioral Maps: (C) 6:00 PM. Created by author.

interview of teenagers who are there. If there is no performance at the National Theater, the plaza becomes quiet by 8:00 PM as the teenagers leave to go on to their evening destinations. Later in the evening, after 9:00 PM, single men gather on the lower plaza near the theater's ticket window to meet and talk. Groups of young men often wander by or stop to smoke marijuana. In a few cases policemen arrested one of the young men either for drinking or having drugs on him.

It is apparent from these descriptions of Parque Central and the Plaza de la Cultura that the activities of reading, talking, eating, and meeting friends are quite similar. Both plazas are dominated by men and their related activities of reading, sitting, watching, and talking in the morning; the plazas accommodate women, families, children, and couples in the afternoon. They both have vendors who sell flowers, food, and trinkets; people who provide personal services; entertainers who sing or clown; and preachers of various denominations. They are both surrounded by cafés where users can go to get inside from the rain or sun or where nonusers can simply survey the scene. They both have a small number of people who want to lay claim to the space but who are considered by some to be undesirable occupants of the space, such as beggars, sex workers, homeless people, drug dealers, and gamblers. Police who patrol and maintenance people who clean up the trash are also there representing the municipal social order. But as discussed through the movement maps, the nature of those activities and movements and the spatiotemporal patterns are socially distinct.

The behavioral maps complete the time-space descriptions begun with the movement maps. While the movement maps describe paths that link individuals walking with gender segregation in Parque Central, the behavioral maps record individual projects such as men shining shoes, elderly pensioners meeting to talk, or teenagers playing soccer. The accretions of multiple paths and projects located in space and time link the individual activities to age, gender, and class differences found in the two plazas. Over time these differences become naturalized, as has been argued by Bourdieu, and perceived as social reality.[26] Thus, individual paths and projects are transformed—that is, spatialized—into cultural norms of behavior and action. These microgeographies demonstrate how plaza space is produced by the historically constituted social practices of walking, user behavior, and group activities. The paths and projects create distinct social worlds through embodied social practices of the people who inhabit these spaces.

Memories of Ritual Walking

Embodied space also includes the memories of walking and other bodily movements. Anyone who has spent time walking or dancing in a particular location has experienced "knowing" a space through their body, a sense that recurs each time they return, even if it is many years later. For example, Deborah Kapchan writes about the bodily intimacy created in a salsa dance club in Austin, Texas, where regulars claim space through dance competence and bodily contact with other dancers. Over time and through numerous repetitions of music and dance steps, participants create a space where dancers feel at home in what is otherwise perceived as a nomadic world.[27] This bodily belonging exists in many forms in different cultural contexts. For example, in Costa Rica there were a number of kinds of "strolling" that traditionally enabled young people to meet, talk, flirt, and court one another in San José public spaces. The most famous of these is the *retreta*, a clockwise and counterclockwise walking around the kiosk in Parque Central, with boys walking in one direction and girls in the other, after mass and the military band concert on Sunday morning and in the afternoon. A number of interviewees evoked memories of this ritualized walking and its accompanying sociability, again adding depth to the spatial experience of walking there now. The following is taken from a series of interviews with older Josefinos who remembered the retreta.[28]

Alvaro Wille spent time in Parque Central as a young man in the 1930s and 1940s. He is one of the few people I interviewed who remembers participating in the retreta.

A(lvaro): On Sunday afternoon young people would get together and walk around the park with the girls on the inside and the boys where they could see them. It was a way to meet someone. I did it; yes, I went sometimes.

S(etha): What year was this?

A: I do not remember exactly, but in the 1940s. I would have been at least fourteen years old in 1940.

S: And how was the experience? How did you feel about it?

A: Well, it interested me the first time—everyone told me that I had to do it because it was the custom. So I went after the three o'clock movie at Las Palmas. I went with my friends, and we would walk around. But this experience did not convert me into a regular [laughing]. I did not have a single girlfriend to look at, and would not have one; there was plenty of reason to attend only if you had a girlfriend. Thus, it was a park of teenage romance. And afterwards, I am sure, there were evening romances as we became more adult.

S: So this was in the afternoon?

A: In the afternoon about five o'clock. And we would stay until it got dark or a bit later. I went two, three, or four times; not much more than that.

Alvaro's wife is the well-known anthropologist Maria Eugenia Bozzoli de Wille. Although much younger than Alvaro, she also remembers walking in Parque Central, but the circuit she recalls included more of the downtown area, including a stop for snacks. Maria Eugenia remembers this walking as a paseo, a linear stroll, taken with her friends as a two-part event, the morning associated with the music from the military band, and the evening spent at the movies with her friends.

S(etha): When did you go to Parque Central?

M(aria Eugenia): For young people the idea was to stroll down the avenue past the movie theater, make a circle of the park, and then continue on to

Chelles. We would stop at the corner of Chelles because it was the bar with the best little pastries and *los arreglados* [flaky pastry shells filled with meat, vegetables, or cheese] . . . The people who went to Chelles, however, were more adult because it was a bar and people would go to drink. This trip to Chelles was part of the entire paseo in the early hours of the evening. Everyone would leave the movie theater about 5:00 PM, make a circle before going down to Chelles. Some people would enter the movies at 7:00 PM and leave about 9:00 PM, but even those that left at 9:00 PM spent a little time walking around. At other times the parade was down the avenue, and the boys and men would stop at the corner as the girls and women walked by: boys watching the girls and men watching the women. Some girls would come alone, but normally a girl would not come with a boy. She would meet him at the corner.

The retreta is a traditional form of courting that still occurs in small country towns throughout Latin America. Most descriptions of the retreta include groups of young men walking arm-in-arm around a plaza or square with groups of young women also walking arm-in-arm in the opposite direction so that the groups face each other as they pass by. The idea is to catch the eye of an admirer and then, in some cases, meet the person at the end of the ritual walking, which usually takes place on Sunday evening. Although the exact form varies from town to town and country to country, even when I arrived in Costa Rica in December 1985, young people would walk facing one another along the main street, which was closed for Christmas shopping, and throw confetti at one another as they passed by. Traditionally it seems that the bodily movements of the retreta created a ritual space where young men and women were allowed to flirt and talk to one another in what was traditionally a rather gender-segregated or chaperoned life, and yet some of this ritual walking is retained in other strolling contexts.

The paseo, on the other hand, is a more general term used for "taking a walk." Costa Ricans often talk about their Sunday paseo, which can mean anything from a Sunday stroll in the neighborhood to a picnic in the countryside. "Paseo" is also the word used in Spain for important streets that have wide, tree-shaded sidewalks that encourage walking. In my experience, a paseo is more of a leisurely walk than a ritualized movement sequence; however, in Maria Eugenia's story it is clear that the paseo she describes has taken on ritual form. In her story the paseo is a kind of personal inscription of the city, through the streets and with special places to stop, not unlike de Certeau's "tactics," in which citizens make the city their own through their everyday bodily practices. In the paseo, nodes of social interaction interrupt the linear movement creating new spaces and places inhabited by the strollers. The goal is the sociability of the walking and the sense that during the paseo the city is one's own, legible through bodily movement and at the same time a kind of placemaking to accommodate a realm for more intimate and relaxed social relations.

These descriptions, albeit drawn from Costa Rica, are similar to my experiences growing up in Westwood Village in West Los Angeles, where every Saturday I would meet my friends, stroll to the bowling alley to meet other friends, then stop at Baskin-Robbins for ice cream, and finally end up at the Bruin Theater to see the 2:00 PM matinee. These ritual strolls created a safe place for our friendship group to loiter, and they inscribed those spaces in my mind and body such that each time I return I can feel the person I was and the places I enjoyed through the rhythm of my walking.

This ethnographic exploration illustrates how embodied space and bodily movement produces different kinds of places. It locates the body, which has so often been overlooked, in the center of all placemaking activity, and it makes the body an important component of the social production of space. This has ontological as well as methodological implications for scholars of the built environment, who are more often concerned with recording and studying the material aspects of a site without seriously considering how users, as spatial mobile fields, materially create space and place as well. The movements and meanings of people are critical to understanding, reading, and representing space. This perspective solves many of the problems inherent in a solely material-culture approach that records the built environment and landscape as a container for people rather than a creation of their own bodies, movements, and activities.

Further, this new form of analysis allows us to theorize and imagine the body as a moving, speaking, cultural space in and of itself. This evocative and theoretically powerful conceptualization marks a radical shift in our thinking that previously separated the domains of material culture and human agency. It resolves many of the dilemmas that plague those of us who cross the micro/macro boundaries from individual body and embodied space to macro-analyses of social and political forces. This integrated notion of embodied space addresses both the metaphorical and material aspects of the body in space as well as space-time to communicate, transform, and contest existing social structures.

NOTES

1. Michel Foucault, *Discipline and Punish: The Birth of the Prison* (New York: Vintage, 1975); Michel Foucault, "Des Espaces Autres," *Architecture, Mouvement, Continuité* 5 (October 1984): 46–49; Michel Foucault, "Of Other Space," *Diacritics* (Spring 1986): 22–27; Pierre Bourdieu, *Outline of a Theory of Practice* (Cambridge: Cambridge University Press, 1977); Anthony Giddens, *The Constitution of Society: Outline of the Theory of Structuration* (Berkeley: University of California Press, 1984). See also Setha M. Low and Denise Lawrence-Zúñiga, *The Anthropology of Space and Place: Locating Culture* (Malden, Mass.: Blackwell, 2003).

2. Setha M. Low, "The Social Production and Social Construction of Public Space," *American Ethnologist* 23, no. 4 (1996): 861–79; Setha M. Low, *On the Plaza: The Politics of Public Space and Culture* (Austin: University of Texas Press, 2000).

3. Thomas J. Csordas, "Introduction: The Body as Representation and Being in the World," in *Embodiment and Experience: The Existential Ground of Culture and Self*, ed. Thomas J. Csordas (Cambridge: Cambridge University Press, 2004), 1–26, 12.

4. Setha M. Low, "Configuración Espacial de Cultura: Etnografía del Espacio y Tiempo en la Plaza," *Mesoamérica* 51 (2009): 158–67; Setha M. Low, "Claiming Space for Engaged Anthropology: Spatial Inequality and Social Exclusion," *American Anthropologist* 113, no. 3 (2011): 389–407.

5. On spatial orientation, see Nancy D. Munn, "Excluded Spaces: The Figure in the Australian Aboriginal Landscape," *Critical Inquiry* 22 (Spring 1996): 446–65; and Stuart Rockefeller, *Starting from Quirpini: The Travels and Places of a Bolivian People* (Bloomington: Indiana University Press, 2010). On mobility and movement see Tim Ingold, "Culture on the Ground: The World Perceived through the Feet," *Journal of Material Culture* 9, no. 3 (2004): 315–40; Tim Ingold, *Lines: A Brief History* (London: Routledge, 2007); Tim Ingold and Jo Lee Vergunst, eds., *Ways of Walking: Ethnography and Practice on Foot* (Aldershot: Ashgate, 2008).

6. Munn, "Excluded Spaces," 449.

7. Ibid., 448.

8. Ibid., 452.

9. Rockefeller, *Starting from Quirpini*.

10. Vishvajit Pandya, "Movement and Space: Andamese Cartography," *American Ethnologist* 17, no. 4 (1990): 775–97.

11. Allan Pred, *Place, Practice, and Structure: Social and Spatial Transformation in Southern Sweden, 1750–1850* (Cambridge: Polity,1986), 6.

12. Michel de Certeau, *The Practice of Everyday Life*, trans. Steven Rendall (Berkeley: University of California Press, 1984).

13. John Gray, "Open Spaces and Dwelling Places: Being at Home on Hill Farms in the Scottish Borders," *American Ethnologist* 26, no. 2 (1999): 440–60, esp. 449.

14. Rachel Thomas, "L'accessibilité des piétons à l'espace public urbain: un accomplissement perceptif situé," *Espaces et sociétés: architecture et habitat dans le champ interculturel* 113/114 (2004): 233–49.

15. Ingold, "Culture on the Ground" and *Lines: A Brief History*.

16. James Gibson, *The Ecological Approach to Visual Perception* (Boston: Houghton Mifflin, 1979).

17. Maurice Merleau-Ponty, *Le Primat de la perception et ses conséquences philosophiques* (1945; Lagrasse: Verdier, 1996).

18. Tim Ingold and Jo Lee Vergunst, unpublished manuscript, from their research project, "Culture from the Ground: Walking, Movement, and Placemaking," Economic and Social Research Council (ESRC), Swindon, U.K., http://www.esrc.ac.uk/my-esrc/grants/RES-000-23-0312/read. This project also informed their book, *Ways of Walking*.

19. Jo Vergunst, "Rhythms of Walking: History and Presence in a City Street," *Space and Culture* 13, no. 4 (2010): 376–88.

20. Low, *On the Plaza*.

21. Allan Pred, "Place as Historically Contingent Process: Structuration and the Time-Geography of Becoming Places,"*Annals of the Association of American Geographers* 74, no. 2 (1984): 279–97, esp. 286; emphasis in original.

22. A 2013 field visit determined that many of these patterns remain, but in a modified way; these patterns adapted to change in the surrounding streets and parks.

23. James Fernandez, "Emergence and Convergence in Some African Sacred Places," in Low and Lawrence-Zúñiga, *Anthropology of Space and Place*, 187–203, originally published in *Place: Experience and Symbol*, ed. Miles Richardson (Baton Rouge: Geoscience Publications, Louisiana State University, 1984), 31–42.

24. Low, *On the Plaza*.

25. Vergunst, "Rhythms of Walking"; and Gray, "Open Spaces and Dwelling Places."

26. Bourdieu, *Outline of a Theory of Practice*.

27. Deborah Kapchan, "Talking Trash: Performing Home and Anti-home in Austin's Salsa Culture,"*American Ethnologist* 33, no. 3 (2006): 361–77.

28. Low, *On the Plaza*.

2.

Visualizing the Body Politic

SWATI CHATTOPADHYAY

The concept of public space in modern political theory is remarkably impoverished. It largely ignores the material attributes of space—its architectonics and physical-sensorial dimensions that enable habitation—and the process of social production that creates the "publicness" of public space. Such imagination of public space is disembodied in keeping with the disembodied, abstract imagination of the modern state. When it does consider material attributes and the bodies of citizens at work in shaping public space, it assumes a particular delimited imagination of the Greek polis. Both ignore the possibilities of a political vernacular that might enable us to expand the imagination of public space and its attendant materiality.

"To be embodied," writes James Mensch, "is to be physically situated." By that logic it is also to "exclude other persons from the position that one occupies in viewing the world."[1] This produces a plurality of viewpoints that we must accommodate, because we are also "dependent" on others to inhabit this world. To be embodied is to be aware of the vulnerability of the flesh. An embodied understanding of politics and public space thus requires attention to the conditions of our physical situatedness in relation to other bodies and objects. It involves an understanding of our position in a given space, our movement and ability to access space, what we can see, hear, feel, and touch: our *vulnerability* as well as our *capacity* to manipulate and change the aforementioned conditions. These states of vulnerability and capacity that actualize our political freedom set the parameters of our relation to fellow subjects. These material conditions (and their limits) are the bases of our political subjectivity and enable our political imagination.

In this chapter I examine the recent prohibition of political wall writing in India as an instance of the ill-understood relation between political subjectivity and public space. I focus on the materiality of public space and on the relation among bodies, space, text, and the quest for political freedom that produced a political vernacular in the twentieth century. Before I turn to those examples, allow me to clarify the point about the imagination of public space that appears in Mensch's critique of contract theory.

Embodiment

The social contract theorists from John Locke to Jean-Jacques Rousseau have understood freedom as innate, a preexisting attribute of the individual, a priori to social formation. Thus, in contract theory "politics begins with the agreement to limit this original liberty."[2] In such form, liberty works as a dual move of an empty "I want" and the right to "our person and possessions." This is the basis of politics as the need to limit freedom and to secure private property. Mensch notes that the assumptions of contract theory invariably lead to equating political freedom with sovereignty—that is, self-sufficiency and mastery achieved through violence: "both the violence that establishes it and the violence that preserves it." The state is established through violence and arrogates to itself the right of self-preservation through violence. Given the original empty conception of freedom, in the hands of the state it takes the form of unlimited abstract freedom. This conjunction of violence and freedom implies that "politics consists not so much in expressing, as in containing freedom."[3]

Mensch opposes this notion of freedom by proposing a form of embodied political freedom: freedom as a "gift of others" that flows contrary to the idioms of mastery and self-sufficiency that drive contract theories. Working primarily from Maurice Merleau-Ponty's notion of "intertwining" of the world within and without, and Hannah Arendt's proposition of the political as the space of "appearance," Mensch describes the body politic as the bodily "I can," residing in our ability to act and change the world. He suggests that if we break the connection between sovereignty and violence, we open up a *space* between authority and physical power. Having proposed a space, here as an opening for inserting a different figure/trope, Mensch notes the difficulty of specifying the "architectonic of such thought." Jettisoning the position of an abstract disembodied point of view and authority, the new notion of freedom must be articulated through a crooked line of thought. These spatial and architectural analogies and metaphors are not accidental. It is fundamental to Mensch's view that freedom is something we gain by coming in contact with others, in the society of others.[4] Such freedom is always an expression "in context."

> Its content is formed by the ways of being and behaving that are shaped by the various projects of individuals and groups. To the point that these projects coincide, there is commonality in the content of freedom. To the point that they do not, interests will clash. Such a clash, however, is always in a context. Thus the excess of the other—the excess stemming from his interpretation of a given situation—involves an overlap. . . . The excess—the non-coincidence—is the other's freedom. It manifests the other's non-predictability and is the engine of newness in our encounter.[5]

The architectonics of such interaction cannot be predicated, outlined a priori, and must involve the risk of spatial imagination that has learned to negotiate and coalesce multiple and contradictory points of view. Politics is this art of accommodation. That the site of this accommodation and strife would be the city does not come as a surprise. But it is also a particular city imagination, that of the Greek polis, and its prime public space—the agora or marketplace—where the discussion of public space begins, ending up in spaces other than the marketplace, in the enclosed, bounded spaces of the council chamber, legislative assembly, and town hall.

I wish to question this assumption about the architectonics of public space and the attendant understanding of embodiment by reference to Mensch's point about opening up a "space" between freedom and violence. That is, I want to examine the spatial imagination that prompts our understanding of public space. The political posters and wall writings that I have chosen to serve as examples of a particular relation between the body, city space, and body politic turn on the *attempt* to open up a space between freedom and violence. They do so by crafting a spatial imagination that challenges the one associated with the modern state.

Spatial imagination is the process through which a given social group works out the relation between social and physical phenomena, establishing links between physical attributes of people and objects, other sensory attributes such as sound and smell, as well as the nonphysical dimensions of ideas and ideology. Every spatial imagination thus has a constitutive relation to the historical field of production.[6]

In his study of antebellum American cities, Dell Upton has argued that the republican spatial imagination, based on the dual desiderata of freedom and property, assumed the rectangular city grid to be the structure by which this dual desire would be objectified in the landscape. Political subjectivity would be acquired by placing the citizen-subject in an ordered space. This ordered space would enable the freedom inherent in the individual, at the same time constraining him (the subject was male) within the bounds of space and time. The ethics of freedom had to be *practiced* in such ordered and orderly space. Upton notes, however, that it is in the treacherous ground of practice that the order of the grid was turned upon itself; the intentions implicit and explicit in the republican spatial order were disobeyed. This disobedience was demonstrated visibly in the occupation of sidewalks by store owners and the appropriation of public space by the underclass populating streets, alleys, and squares with their excessive sensory presence. The grid, as a metaphor of republican virtue and an artifact of republican spatial order, relied on its transparency for its political effectiveness. This transparency demanded by the state and republican elite was challenged and the grid made opaque through inhabitation—by bodies challenging the existing spatial order—precisely because such a spatial order was disembodied, abstract, and imposed.[7]

The point about transparency is important because it implies conditions of legibility and recognition. Hannah Arendt, in line with ancient Greek thought, argued that the fundamental principle of public space is its "openness" to political action. The openness is indexed in the freedom of appearance. Freedom, Arendt noted, consists of "deeds and words which are meant to appear, whose very existence hinges on appearance."[8] But what is the form of this appearance? According to Arendt, public freedom is not "an inner realm" to which an individual could retreat; neither must it be equated with social freedom. Rather it could only appear in public space, where it could become "visible to all." Indeed, the goal of revolution was the establishment of the grounds of such a freedom: "founding of a body politic which guarantees the space where freedom can appear."[9] Upholding the Greek polis and its agora as the exemplary public space, Arendt argued that public freedom—that is, political freedom—could be achieved only in delimited spaces. In ancient Greece this translated as the walled polis and the council chamber and theater, where the Greek citizen was free to argue and debate among fellow citizens and be validated by their approbation. Given that the agora was not delimited in any conventional physical manner, and that it was the site of not just enclosed public spaces like the council chamber but also a vibrant marketplace in which citizens as well as noncitizens conducted business, it afforded other opportunities for exchange and contact that are not encapsulated within Arendt's theorization of freedom.

Arendt's connection between public space and freedom is based on two ideas that sometimes appear contradictory. She argues that one can be free only among equals. This argument recognizes the existence of noncitizens and slaves in ancient Greece who were by definition unequal and socially unfree, and one could not speak of political freedom as such in the "mixed" milieu of ancient Athens. Arendt's demand for circumscribed spaces where citizens are among fellow citizens who can be seen and heard proceeds from this specificity of the Greek polity. This move invalidates the idea of the polis as a physical space of political freedom, but not as a conceptual site in which freedom is instituted. The same move also tends to drive public freedom "indoors" to the interiors of public buildings rather than public open space to which citizens and noncitizens alike might have access.

Richard Sennett has argued in a different vein that the architectonics of the council chamber and theater "immobilized" each citizen in a fixed space where he was captive to rhetoric. Sennett makes a distinction between such enclosed spaces and the open space of the agora. In the "swirling crowds" of the agora, "conversations fragmented as bodies moved . . . and an individual's attention broke and shifted." In contrast, the enclosed centripetal space of the council chamber, and the theater with its back screen and contoured seating, created a directed emphasis between speaker and audience. These spaces "sustained a single voice" and at the same time produced "a regime of visual surveillance." The sloped seating enabled the councilors to be identified as to how they voted. The magnification of the speaker's voice was also the reason behind the division between "actor" and "spectator" in the Greek venue of theater and politics. In the sitting position the citizens took up a "passive and vulnerable posture." The vulnerability of exposure was tied to one's responsibility to the power of spoken words, one that took the form of not just a mental conduct but a bodily affirmation of their role as citizens. Sennett argues that in Greek thought rhetoric meant the body ruling the word, a process that "estranged men's power to live rationally through the unity of word and deed."[10]

The second crucial link between public space and freedom, according to Arendt, is the citizen's emergence into recognition. This she understood as the moment of freedom, and she sought support in John Adams's argument that what makes the poor man politically impotent is not his poverty but obscurity.[11] This point, however, might allow us to argue, contra Arendt, that the moment of emergence into freedom *enables* equality, consisting of the ability to bracket (rather than deny or relegate) one's social position to enter the political arena rather than the other way around. It entails a different order of space that cannot be circumscribed as an indoor venue where only some might convene. As outdoor space it must enable the presence of others, and as such it must contain room for refashioning, alteration, and maneuver, which would affect the content of freedom. Emergence from obscurity thus need not entail "exposure" in the sense discussed by Sennett. Here I am relying on Mensch's argument that something must appear "to be." From this it follows that the form in which it appears, and the specificity of its *siting* (situatedness), must have something to do with its content— that is, the content of political freedom. Needless to say, my point is not that indoor spaces of politics are useless. Rather I am suggesting that the *content* of freedom and politics relies on physical parameters of space and the degrees of openness it sustains, not as a determinant but as a contingency. Let me turn to the debate about political wall writing in India to elaborate on this point.

Legibility

Political wall writing has been prohibited in India. A law banning the writing of political slogans and election campaign messages on walls was formulated in 1992, invoking and extending the West Bengal Prevention of Defacement of Property Act of 1976.[12] Very little of these laws had been put into practice until March 2006, when the election commission sent out a new set of directives on the conduct of political parties before and during elections that banned political wall writing. This "Model Code of Conduct" has been reiterated since then.[13] The list of banned practices is long: posting notices; erecting flagstaffs; writing slogans; suspending banners; painting symbols of political parties on the land, building, or compound wall of any individual without his or her consent, or on any public building. It is also evident from the debates that ensued from this enforcement that wall writing is the key figure among these banned practices. What is it about wall writing that invokes such reactions?

The election commission observed that it has "received numerous complaints from the public to the effect that at the time of electioneering campaigns, workers of political parties and candidates indulge in defacement of walls of public and private buildings by pasting of election posters, writing of slogans, painting of election symbols, etc. All this is done without the permission of the owners of the buildings, much to their annoyance, which gives an ugly look not only to the buildings but also to the whole city."[14] It seems as if the election commission has two major concerns: the right of private property and the visual character of the city that ensues from such practices as wall writing and festooning streets and buildings with political banners and placards. Why would the election commission concern itself with the visual culture of cities? What indeed is the presumed relation in this case between visual culture, public space, and political rights of the citizenry, specifically the right of the franchise? The election commission noted that the law was meant to create an election environment "free of [the] tension and violence" that usually resulted from "wall capturing" by rival political parties.[15] Here a different set of relations is cited, one that views wall writing as insinuating violence not just by words but through the spatial appropriation against competing claims. This point of view explicitly recognizes the territorial implications of wall writing—the claim to and mode of "defending" one's turf—and thus construes wall writing as a sort of visual disorder, one that refutes the given order of the city. Political rivalry, visibly indexed in city space through wall writing, the election commission suggests, sets up improper kinds of political venue and wrong kinds of political subjectivity.

Whatever ambiguity remained in the election commission's articulation of the Model Code of Conduct, in its implementation in West Bengal the state government chose to abide by the more sweeping language of the 1976 act, thus banning all political wall writing, with or without the owner's permission.[16] Though widely opposed by political parties across the spectrum, there does not appear to be any consensus on the (de)merits of the act's wide-ranging provisions. The leader of the ruling communist party in West Bengal, the Communist Party of India (Marxist) (CPI[M]), pointed out that with the ban on wall writing, the two hundred and ninety-six thousand party members might need to "carry posters on their person"—after all, "the human body is none other's property which can suffer defacement."[17] The West Bengal chief minister, while affirming the usefulness of political wall writing to reach a mass audience, noted that perhaps wall writing should not be allowed on the walls of government offices: "Would we allow such things on Writers' Buildings for example?" Then he added, "No civilized country allows that." He hoped for a "balanced law" that would not infringe on the rights of property owners, and he wondered whether commercial billboards and political graffiti ought to be treated similarly.[18] The chief minister, no doubt, had in mind a large constituency of the middle and upper classes who wanted to see "cleaner" walls. The general secretary of the Pradesh Congress

Committee suggested that if the ban on wall writing went into effect, they would have to resort to distributing posters and handbills door to door and at street corners, but noted, "The positive side of the directive is that the walls of the city and districts will now be cleaned."[19]

The linking of cleaner cities with cleaner elections deserves closer attention. The irony of the 1976 act as a template for the election commission's directive is salient given that there has been no suggestion by the municipality or the state government to enforce the "defacement" law against commercial hoardings that have come to dominate the contemporary cityscape or the publicity for religious festivals that sprout seasonally. In cities such as Delhi and Bangalore, where laws have been passed to control the size, location, number, and content of billboards, the goal to minimize "visual clutter" ostensibly proceeds from concern for safety and revenue.[20] These regulations, then, are not just about protecting property rights. Private property is a justification for ends that signal an aesthetic-civic dimension of the body politic. It suggests a desire to reshape cities to encourage certain normative modes of visuality centered on notions of the consumer-citizen, one that also wishes to hide the messy process of mass participation in Indian democracy.

If the comments by politicians about the changing tactics for election campaigns suggest a reluctance to abandon tried methods of campaigning, from a willy-nilly acceptance of privatization of politics to substituting bodies for words, they signal the interchangeability of the bodies and words of citizens that constitute the materiality of public space in the political process. The burden of campaign publicity devolving on the individual person of the party cadre with the unavailability of walls and buildings as sites of publicity—the political mirror of Walter Benjamin's sandwich-board man—rather than doing away with the material artifacts of political competition, foregrounds the materiality of political space.

Partha Chatterjee has argued that the new law attempts to move democracy from the street to the drawing room, from public visibility to private contemplation mediated by the television screen. It thus privileges the middle and upper classes in the political process, altering the conceptual and material parameters of political rights and subjectivity.[21] A critic of Chatterjee's argument asked, "Why shouldn't voting be a private act of the private citizen?" and followed up by asking what is wrong with trying to "cleanse" the "public political arena." He insisted that the desire to rid the cities "of all the noise, smell and gaudiness of a publicly mobilized plebian [lumpen] culture" is not "a violation of Indian democracy."[22] A concern for "cleaner" elections appears as both a demand for removing from public space the sensorial excess of the underclass, and a desire for maintaining a strict separation between the private and the public, governed by a dominant aesthetic and spatial paradigm.

The simple response to those who ask, "Why shouldn't voting be the private act of the private citizen," is this: it contradicts the very basis of democratic politics and freedom because the essence of political freedom is freedom in public. But there is more to it in terms of the configuration and materiality of public space in which such freedom is exercised. The politics of materiality that sustains the debates over wall writing needs to be situated in the longer *durée* of the twentieth century, because it is evident from contemporary debates that political wall writing has calcified as a practice, and even those political parties that undertake it or those politicians who support it have forgotten, or would rather not acknowledge, the source of its strengths as an art and mode of communication.

Text Acts

The practice of graffiti—writing or scribbling on the wall—is ancient. I have chosen the term "wall writing" rather than "graffiti" to signal a key difference between the art form that we now commonly designate as graffiti and the modes of visual/textual communication that constitute the kind of political wall writing that I am discussing. As visual culture, political wall writing's peculiarity resides in its overlap of textual, visual, and spatial content; its mode is both permanent and ephemeral. In this respect it is similar to contemporary graffiti in American cities, for example. It differs from graffiti in one key aspect: graffiti's hallmark is "illegibility," cryptic or coded communication between members of a subculture. Political wall writing is starkly legible; its goal is to communicate across social groups and thereby build mass solidarity. The most effective wall writings accomplish this goal by crafting a political vernacular that is different from the proper language of the state or civil society. It is important to note that American-style graffiti is not a popular street art form in India and that political wall writing avoids or ignores the graphic style and textual conventions of graffiti, and therefore graffiti's connotation. If political wall writing posits a problem of recognition, it is not because it is illegible, but because to recognize it—both in the sense of understanding and accepting its import—is to accept its challenge to the materiality of public space. It is also different from the tradition of political murals in Northern Ireland, Mexico, South Africa, and the United

States. While many political wall writings exhibit artistry and compositional deftness, they are not marked by the vibrant and nuanced color schemes that are the hallmark of the more painterly tradition of the mural movements and the extensive artistic labor that in part validates this art form.[23] One reason for this difference is that even though post-independence political wall writing in India is not typically a secret practice of underground movements, being the preferred device for registered political parties, it is executed quickly and designed for short duration, carrying in its mode the forgotten trace of its beginnings under state persecution.[24] It does not preclude the great care often taken to display artistry. But the temporal factor is key to understanding how constraints of time affect the art and spatial execution of political wall writing.

In her study of the graffiti of the intifada in the occupied West Bank during the late 1980s and early 1990s, Julie Peteet points out the essential elements that give rise to the practice under temporal-spatial constraints.[25] Executed in a climate of strict censorship and violence (over fifteen hundred military orders regulated the everyday life of the Palestinians in the West Bank), political graffiti became a medium for debating tradition, envisioning competing futures, recording historical events and processes, and inscribing memory. As a political weapon they were "self-reflexive and critical," publicly registering a cacophony of dissenting voices in response to the denial of voice and claim to the public. The key importance of such wall writings is not that they conveyed messages or were "resistant" but that the "mere appearance" of such texts "gave rise to arenas of contest in which they were a vehicle or agent of power."[26] The walls were transformed by graffiti and became interventions in public space, speaking to an audience and forming audience communities by activating reading on the street. Peteet notes that in order to understand the meaning of such graffiti, one needed to understand the conditions and process of production—secret, swift, dangerous—as well as the "optics" involved in the process of reading. The power of Palestinian graffiti derived from the risk involved in their appearance, demonstrating to the occupying force its lack of territorial control. Reading the texts on the street was an active engagement in public space, irrespective of one's political stance, and involved a reflection on the power structures within which one's reading activity was situated. This is its primary difference from the solitary act of private reading. The threat of such "text acts" was that they had the potential of linking peoples and communities that had been fragmented by state power and of creating platforms of political debate.[27] And yet such platforms were not singular venues like a theater or council chamber; rather, they were dispersed across the West Bank. Such writing and reading took on the quality of a "live" performance that undermined hier-archical control and expanded the spatial parameters of the given order of public space.

It is useful to clarify here the link between public sphere, public space, and public texts. Discussing the public texts of early nineteenth-century New York—posters, handbills, news bulletins, sign boards, currency notes, and business cards—that were plied in the city, David Henkin has argued for a model of public sphere that takes into account the materiality of space and the reading practices in public space that produce a new public. Henkin relies on three aspects of Jürgen Habermas's notion of the public sphere: the rootedness of the public sphere in commercial life; the recognition that pub-licity is not simply an institution or concept but a form of subjectivity; and its link with print culture: "print form provided forums, subjects, and models for public discussion."[28] Yet Habermas was deeply ambivalent about the com-mercial sphere that gave rise to the bourgeois public sphere, and he sought to locate it not in the competitive domain of the marketplace, with its riot-ous array of signs and promiscuous exchange of words, but in the bosom of the bourgeois family, in the form of an audience-oriented subjectivity exem-plified by the eighteenth-century novel. The ideal bourgeois public sphere is thus grounded in certain kinds of reading and conversing practices: read-ing in private and rational critical debate of the salon and coffeehouse. It is based on the assumption that the bourgeois individual emerged from the pri-vate space of the family or home into public space with his subjectivity fully formed. He did not entertain the possibility that perhaps this subjectivity was acquired through the process of relating to others—negotiating the rau-cous Other—amid the socio-spatial dynamics of the pub and coffeehouse.[29] Henkin's goal is to provide a corrective to two aspects of Habermas's work: to bring "back" the discourse of publicity to the street as public space, rather than limiting it to the rational-critical debates in interior spaces, and to con-sider the importance of physical space in shaping forms of publicity. The two points are related and urge us to think about the relation between pub-lic sphere and public space, which is insufficiently theorized by Habermas, and about the kinds of reading that are made possible by different types of written texts and the contexts of their reading. Citizens of New York, Henkin argues, honed their political subjectivity in and through the process of navi-gating the multiple forms of the written word on the street.

The intersections of public space and the public sphere, where the physical/concrete and the discursive/abstract dimensions of spatiality meet, are historically specific.[30] The political wall writing of the 1970s and early

1980s in Calcutta offers us one such specific articulation. In the balance of the chapter I link these text acts with the political and visual culture of the anticolonial nationalist movement against British rule in order to ascertain their provenance and to locate the concept of freedom and the imagination of the body politic that animate these forms of writing. Political wall writing does something more than produce reading communities and political subjects; it does so by radically altering the materiality of the wall and with it the very meaning of public space.

Insurgent Bodies

On December 8, 1930, three young men walked into the offices of the Writers' Building in Calcutta and shot dead Col. N. S. Simpson, the inspector general of prisons, and wounded three others. Of the three assailants, Badal (Sudhir) Gupta committed suicide on the spot by swallowing potassium cyanide, Benoy Bose died in the hospital from a gunshot wound five days later, and Dinesh Gupta was hanged the following July. The Writers' Building, a nineteenth-century edifice built to house the British colonial bureaucracy, is located in Dalhousie Square (now renamed Benoy-Badal-Dinesh Bag), the heart of the administrative district of colonial Calcutta, which included Government House, the high court, the town hall, and the police headquarters on Lall Bazaar Street. The area had been brought under Section 144 of the Indian penal code following popular agitation against the 1905 Partition of Bengal, thus prohibiting any form of public gathering in the center of colonial power. As a heavily guarded premise, the ability of the three men to reach its inner precincts garnered much attention in the aftermath: dressed in tailored suits, they were able to pass as "gentlemen." The language of authority was turned on itself, disturbing the norms of recognition and the social character of public space. The state responded by intensifying police guard at the Writers' Building.

The day Dinesh was to be hanged in Alipore Jail, the Calcutta police took exceptional precaution to prevent a mass gathering of any sort.[31] The same day the Calcutta Municipality, under an Indian nationalist majority, passed a resolution mourning the death of Dinesh and honoring his sacrifice for the nationalist cause. The police had reason to be anxious. They were not only battling widespread unrest against British rule, but in the process they were also erratically coming to terms with newer modes of political agitation that challenged the very basis of public authority: those visible markers of state power inscribed in the landscape, and the assumption of state oversight in the everyday use of common space and the institutions marked "public." Schools, colleges, and libraries, even when not directly supported by the colonial government, and even when located within residential premises, were considered public space. Indeed much of the conflict between the colonial state and the nationalists may be seen as a long, protracted battle over the definition of the "public" and the limits of public space.[32] The nationalist movement was a challenge to the authority of the colonial state to inscribe meaning on the functions and use of state and community property and infrastructure, including parks and open space, roads, sidewalks, and the boundary between buildings and the street. Days before the Writers' Building shootout, posters had appeared in the city with red letters proclaiming: *rakte amar legeche aaj sarbanasher nesha* (today the intoxication for annihilation has touched my blood).[33] The day after Benoy died, posters declared: "Benoy's Blood Beckons for More Blood." More such leaflets appeared after Dinesh's execution.[34]

In hindsight it is easy to discern from the events and activities that preceded and followed the trio's suicidal act that between the agitation of the1905 Partition of Bengal and the heyday of armed attacks of the 1930s, a political vernacular had been established, one that would shape the contours of political engagement in public space in Calcutta. This involved both the use of public parks and the *maidan* (open green space that initially served as the firing field surrounding Fort William) for open-air meetings and processional routes, as well as the material culture of political agitation, including posters, bulletins, handbills, placards, and portraits of nationalist leaders and martyrs.[35] All of these practices have survived into the present and have been strengthened in many ways following independence, becoming norms of political performance.

Nationalist posters were among a long list of artifacts considered seditious by the colonial government, which included printed material such as newspapers, plays, novels, and poetry, as well as *swadeshi* (self-sufficiency) illustration and advertisement, banners, and placards, and clothing with nationalist texts and images.[36] Censorship of the written word is a prohibition of the act of communication and an assertion of the state's monopoly of the word: the law and the word become the same. It seeks to fragment the power of community—that is, the ability of the people to come together as a body through communication. In an environment of state censorship, the texts circulated by the state as propaganda combine the powers of physical and symbolic violence. Nationalist posters, as text acts, were a challenge to the colonial state's monopoly on modes and spaces of communication.

Nationalist bulletins, posters, and leaflets, both printed and handwritten, were usually pasted on buildings, lampposts, and trees and were torn off these sites by the police and found their way into the colonial archive. The police noted with alarm the appearance of revolutionary leaflets on public buildings—schools, colleges, public library, courthouse, town hall, bar library, and post office—where they could reach a wide reading public and would make the dare of these "secret" political associations visible to public authorities.[37] However, the removal of posters from their pasted locations did not merely seek to eliminate these seditious writings and images from public space, thus restoring the impress of colonial authority; as visible signs of an underground movement they also served as evidence and clue.[38] The state became the "collector" of these ephemera, hoping to read in the material traces of these fragile documents the specificities of insurgent authorship that would enable the police to construct the networks of political agitators, networks that linked Calcutta to nearby and distant provincial towns and villages. The posters and pamphlets recovered from police raids became the means to trace the public texts back to their authors, producers, and distributors—to punishable individual bodies.

Materiality

Early and mid-twentieth-century Calcutta, much like the New York landscape that Henkin describes, was saturated with the written word. Political posters were part of the readable landscape of the early twentieth-century city, where commercial billboards and advertisements jostled with public notices, as well as street and building names and numbers. They bore certain formal affinity with the latter and at the same time challenged the commercial character of written interventions both in public space and, in a larger sense, the commercial dominance of the colonial city. They disturbed the relative permanence of authorized city texts and their locational claims by introducing in that geography a clandestine, "ownerless," and mobile class of texts whose territorial effect depended on usurping the preexisting signs of permanence and stability. As a mode of insurgency, political posters expressed the lack of freedom and introduced into city space a different kind of reading practice aimed at ameliorating this loss of political subjectivity. They capitalized on a double effect. "Specific to time and location," they played with the transitory and provisional.[39]

Looking at these small posters on thin paper seven decades after they were produced, I am confronted by both their variety and fragility. They consisted of printed and handwritten notices; painted, stenciled posters; lithographed or cyclostyled bulletins, sometimes containing the plea "Please reprint, read and pass on."[40] Usually inscribed on newsprint, they could also be one-line warnings handwritten on ruled paper—easily accessible and easily disguised. Their small format, some as small as 5" × 7", ensured that as handbills hidden under a shawl they could be distributed in schools, railway stations, and street corners.[41] They could be dispatched from any location, carried without invoking suspicion. When used as posters, they could be quickly pasted on gates, walls, and notice boards. It mattered less that they were not readable unless one were up close, and very few could be posted at a time; they served as insinuation for revolutionary activities and to signify the reach of the revolutionary groups.

The compositional style of the posters was simple and unadorned and tended to follow the format of newspapers and commercial notices. Texts broken up in different columns and placed according to a hierarchy of importance assumed of its audience the same kind of reading competence as that required of newspaper readers. The most carefully designed posters, memorializing the death of nationalist heroes, included halftone photographs in oval frames (figure 2.1). The same photograph of Benoy Bose that was used by the police for "wanted" posters and notices in the *Criminal Gazette* was used by the Bengal revolutionaries to publicize his sacrifice and to serve as a counter-warning to the police.[42] In the latter the photograph was placed in an oval frame as was the norm for family portraiture, thus altering the connotation of the image. The texts next to the image—often a verse—emphasized the *affect* of the message as memorialization: it linked images with words. To paraphrase Johanna Drucker, the format was the rhetoric; it made the switch from the familial to the national, from a singular familial tragedy to a popular commemorative moment.

The drive toward the popular could be expressed in incandescent language. In 1931 a police raid in Calcutta retrieved a large number of leaflets advocating boycott of British goods and two stencils with the following inscriptions: *"thanay thanay agun jwalo"* (set fire to police stations) and *"saheb dekhlei thangao"* (beat up every *sahib* you see).[43] The incitement to violence, uttered in an untranslatable colloquialism, suggests a popularization of the vocabulary of revolution that exceeded the efficiency of the usual slogans such as "Long Live Revolution" or "Blood Calls for Blood."[44] Not all posters stated the name of the revolutionary group as a claim to authorship and responsibility; many were anonymous.[45] This popular dimension was not cynically fabricated. The sample of leaflets and posters in the colonial

Ram Krishna Biswas.

Birth—1911.   Age—20 years.

"ফাঁসির মঞ্চে আজিকে তোমারে হেরি অপরূপ বেশে
বীরবিদ্রোহী সৈনিকরূপে বারে বারে তুমি হেসে
অত্যাচারীর খঞ্জের তলে পাতিয়া দিয়াছ শির
আপন বুকের রুধিরে মুছালে কলঙ্ক জননীর।"

Accused in the Chittagong Armoury Raid—
sentenced to death in the Chandpur Inspector
Murder Case—1931.

Figure 2.1. Nationalist poster with Ramkrishna Biswas's family-style portrait. Courtesy West Bengal State Archives, Kolkata.

archive indicates the extremely wide domain of authorship and audience of this publicity, many of whom were barely literate. Posters written in crude handwriting but with carefully, if unskillfully, drawn images remind us of the singularity of these text acts and the humble abodes in far-flung towns where they were produced, which became connected to a larger political structure due to the sheer dint of political will.

The sites where the posters were pasted augmented their meaning. While posters could appear anywhere in the city, some locations near schools, colleges, and parks were favored, and their effect could be electrifying. These locations were singled out for police patrol so as to prevent the posters' appearance.[46] The police kept watch on houses where they suspected posters were kept for distribution; they routinely raided houses, clubs, offices, and presses, and patrolled railways and streets. Notwithstanding this active pursuit, posters showed up on school notice boards, on the gate of the district magistrate's bungalow, on corporation notice boards, and on the walls of the criminal court, indicating a tacit collaboration between revolutionaries and personnel in precincts of power.[47] Leaflets and posters gathered new meaning as they moved on, changed hands, and created a new community of readers.

The relation between posters and the sites of their emergence were mutually supportive in producing an insurgent landscape. The posters attributed significance to the sites on which they were pasted in excess of their normal expressive capacity. Ordinary, everyday elements of the landscape—walls, trees, lampposts—suddenly became conspicuous within the optical field of nationalism. They changed the materiality of the wall, and its claim to obdurate permanence, by showing up its susceptibility to reinscription and transformation. A poster fluttering on the gate of the district magistrate's bungalow was a citation—"the day has come"—that not only served as a warning to colonial authorities but was also a gesture of usurping the materiality of the state.[48]

The producers of the posters imagined a sympathetic readership, and their appearance in places marked by the authority of the state spoke of invisible links that constituted the body politic. The twin themes of sacrifice and memorialization played astutely on the problem of embodiment. The first was a warning to the colonial government—or, more specifically, to the police—that the revolutionaries planned on spilling blood, their own and that of their adversaries. Red stenciled letters on white paper—"without blood, o patriot, the country will not be free"—emphasized the materiality of blood, a reminder of the vulnerability of the flesh. A response to the colonial government's denial of political subjectivity to Indians, the thematic of bloody sacrifice challenged the state to spill more blood as a mode of confronting and acknowledging the insurgent bodies. At the same time, the memorial functions of posters, calling on the public to remember the sacrifice of the revolutionaries, insinuated a prolongation of the lost lives in stories, poetry, and songs. What is remarkable is that the Bengal government took to responding by printing counterpropaganda leaflets and posting them in public spaces, in effect legitimizing the practice of political posters.[49]

A Political Vernacular

Following independence from British rule, such political posters were augmented with political writing on walls, a different but allied mode of claiming public space.[50] Political wall writing, begun in the late 1950s, matured during the tumultuous political era of the 1960s and 1970s. Initially used by parties on the left for election campaigns to publicize the name and party affiliation of the candidate, it was turned into a sharp instrument of political critique by the Naxalbari movement, a mode soon adopted by the mainstream political parties.[51]

The wall writing of the Naxalbari generation focused attention on the failure of nationalism to deliver the promised freedom and began with a critique of the parliamentary system itself. The critiques were pithy, and they stuck in people's minds: "*parliament shuorer khnowar*" (the Parliament is a pig sty); "*pulish tumi jatoi maro, mayine tomar eksho baro*" (police, no matter how much you beat [us] your salary remains hundred and twelve). Humor was a tool of critique as well as self-reflexivity. The tongue-in-cheek playfulness and rhyming made such couplets easy to be cited and recited. Even when the goal of building solidarity was unambiguous—"*tomar nam amar nam Vietnam*" (your name, my name is Vietnam)—the rhythmic call for identification with a distant cause touched a popular chord.

In terms of both content and style, political wall writing made connections with political and artistic phenomenon in other parts of the globe and to other historical moments. Drawing inspiration from modernist typography, painting, book illustration, and political cartoons, it generated a global historical context to give form to the particular political events that were the focus of its address (figure 2.2). In this it was following larger trends in graphic art practices in Bengal. Indeed these writings assumed of the reader a certain awareness of political cartoons and commentary in newspapers and magazines and played off the visual possibilities pertaining to these forms

Figure 2.2. CPI(M) critique of Congress (I): Guernica. Courtesy of Chitrabani.

of print culture. The difference that ensued from the enlarged scale of wall writing, however, invoked a different viewing response than that of the small format of newsmagazines and political cartoons that had become popular as a mode of critique by midcentury.[52]

Wall writings of this period were executed by party cadres who were taught techniques of composing on the wall. It required a spatial savvy to gauge the size and type of the letters relative to the available wall space and the dimension of the street. The materiality of the words differed from anticolonial nationalist posters that had small format and small letters, were often handwritten, and were surreptitious and instigative. Political wall writing was confident and openly confrontational, with large handwritten letters. Their artistry and authority were apparent in the tone and humor used to command attention. They set the stage of political dialogue and were designed to persuade and propagate their vision of the body politic. Highly localized, as opposed to the clandestine, mobile posters, wall writing was made to configure to the site, emphasizing particular spectator effects, and were not constrained by the technological and cost limitations of print or paper. They could take up a large space, and their form—somewhere between typography and painting—could be varied with relative ease. We see the remaining effects of this phase in the wall writings from the early 1980s produced by the CPI(M), Indian National Congress (Congress [I]), and the Socialist Unity Centre of India (SUCI).

Wall writings of this era constructed a writing surface either by resonating the wall's formal properties or by selectively assembling the formal suggestions in the building's façade. Long, uninterrupted surfaces at eye level for a person walking on the street or passing in a vehicle were especially favored and were often marked off with inclusive arrows and the party name to claim the space for future use by the party. Font sizes were chosen for readability from across the street. For example, a long wall surface and a wide street would be addressed with larger lettering than would a wall on a narrow street. The "three dimensionality" of the fonts often echoed the building geometry—lintel and soffit lines, and windows that punctured the wall surface. The text would pick up and elaborate on the rhythm of the fenestration. In some cases wall writing might simulate the visual format of an open book, particularly when the writer was confronted by two walls at right angles, with its "pages" narrating a set of events and carrying the political message.[53]

By the 1990s texts on the walls had become purely propagandist and routine. Mostly executed by paid commercial painters who paint signboards, they demonstrate a uniformity across political parties.[54] In contrast, until the early 1980s the individuality of brush strokes, the idiosyncratic lettering, and insistent humor were noticeable, betraying the bodily trace. They focused on the play between image and text that supported political critique and brought out the potentiality of wall writing. At the very least, even in the case of conventional election campaign publicity, they worked to alert the reader or viewer to the relation between text, image, and wall. Consider the following example (figure 2.3).

The wall writing is a compositional sketch that assembles segments of whitewashed surfaces, and in the process it *creates* a space of reading. The sketchbook approach is a process of appropriating the wall by following its geometry of surfaces, solids, and voids. Resonating the patchwork plaster of the wall and the exposed brickwork, several spaces are whitewashed without regard to uniformity. On these white patches are then painted images and texts that are designed to be read as an assemblage of distinct parts. Each patch is composed separately, but they share a formal resemblance allowing them to be read in relation to each other. At the top, muscular workers carry the banner of the candidate. Below, the party symbol behooves the passerby to stamp on this sign at election time. Deftly executed, it is nevertheless commonplace in terms of its content. Its usefulness resides in the opportunity it affords to ask questions about the spatial relation that holds together the words, images, wall, and the act of reading.

Figure 2.3. SUCI poster promoting the candidacy of Professor Subir Basu Roy. Photo by Ardhendu Chatterjee. Courtesy of Chitrabani.

In the process of composition, the wall writing shows that the space of its inscription is not something inert and neutral, but is "a field in which forces among mutually constitutive elements make themselves available to be read."[55] Following Johanna Drucker, once we begin to see the wall as a field of force that assumes a certain form when intervened through "the productive act of reading," rather than an a priori construct, we recognize the importance of writing on the wall.[56] Political wall writing dematerializes the extant wall and creates a new condition of legibility with which the observer must acquaint oneself and in which he or she must participate.

The power of wall writing resides not merely in its artistry, nor even in the attitude of claiming territory; its most important role is expressing the wall's impermanence and malleability, its usability to bring forth new intentions and forge new readership and political agency with sundry effort and resource. In performing an act of creating space, it is a challenge to the privileged materiality of public space that flows from the spatial imagination of the modern state. Between the words, images, walls, and the reading subjects, it gives rise to a political vernacular that has the capacity to express and illustrate the logic of embodiment that is the basis of political subjectivity. If contemporary wall writing has lost its critical edge, it does not mean it has lost its inherent potential for generating conditions that allow us to imagine politics as spatial culture. Its historical role in creating a political vernacular is a reminder of the importance of the relation between the materiality of public space and political freedom.

Sounds strange? Drucker would say, "Not really, just unfamiliar as a way to think about 'things' as experienced."[57]

NOTES

1. James Mensch, *Embodiments* (Evanston, Ill.: Northwestern University Press, 2009), 5.

2. Ibid., 9.

3. Ibid., 10.

4. Ibid., 12.

5. Ibid., 95–96.

6. Dell Upton uses the term "spatial imagination" to describe the positing of ideal landscapes by the political elite. See Dell Upton, *Another City: Urban Life and Spaces in the New Republic* (New Haven, Conn.: Yale University Press, 2008). In William Glover, *Making Lahore Modern* (Minneapolis: University of Minnesota Press, 2007), Glover has argued that "spatial imagination works to translate these kinds of social and spatial metaphors into actual physical geometries" (31). (Glover emphasizes the concretization of ideas and plans.) This, however, does not exhaust the possibilities of spatial imagination or the numerous spatial imaginations at work in a given situation. After all, elite spatial imagination encounters other, often contradictory, sets of spatial imaginations that undo or expose the ideologies manifest in the physical organization of the city.

7. Upton, *Another City*.

8. Hannah Arendt, quoted in Mensch, *Embodiments*, 129.

9. Hannah Arendt, *On Revolution* (New York: Viking Press, 1963), 120, 121.

10. Richard Sennett, *Flesh and Stone: The Body and the City in Western Civilization* (New York: W.W. Norton, 1994), 53–55, 56, 57, 66.

11. "He feels himself out of sight with others, groping in the dark. Mankind takes no notice of him. He rambles and wanders unheeded. In the midst of a crowd, at church, in the market . . . he is as much in obscurity as he would be in a garret or a cellar. He is not disapproved, censured, or reproached, *he is only not seen*. . . . To be wholly overlooked and to know it, are intolerable. If Crusoe on his island had the library of Alexandria, and a certainty that he should never again see the face of a man, would he ever open a volume?" John Adams quoted in Arendt, *On Revolution*, 63–64; emphasis in original.

12. The West Bengal Prevention of Defacement of Property Act of 1976, applicable only within the municipal limits of Calcutta (Kolkata) and Howrah, defines defacement as "impairing or interfering with the appearance, beauty, damaging, distinguishing, spoiling or injuring in any other way whatsoever," any property, including huts, structures, walls, trees, lampposts, and poles. It states, "Whoever defaces any property in public view by writing or marking with ink, chalk, paint or any other

material, except for the purpose of indicating the name and address of the owner or occupier of such property, shall be punishable." "Writing," according to this law, includes decoration, lettering, ornamentation, and stenciling. The act is available from the website *Laws of India: A Project of the PRS Legislative Bureau*, http://www.lawsofindia.org/pdf/west_bengal/1976/1976WB21.pdf.

13. Election Commission of India, *Model Code of Conduct for the Guidance of Political Parties and Other Candidates* (New Delhi: Publication Division, Election Commission of India, 2007), available at http://ceo.uk.gov.in/files/handbooks/Model_Code_Conduct.pdf.

14. "Prevention of Defacement of Property," Election Commissioner's letter No. 3/7/94/J.S.II, dated January 5, 1994, addressed to the Chief Secretaries to the Governments of all States (except Jammu and Kashmir) and Union Territories, available through the website of the Election Commission of India, http://eci.gov.in/archive/instruction/compendium/defacement/dfac97.htm.

15. "Defacement of Walls," *Frontline* 23, no. 16, December 1, 2006.

16. "No Writing on the Wall Says Bengal Government," *Times of India*, February 26, 2006. The report noted that violation of the law is a "cognizable offence and violators could face six months imprisonment and/or a fine of Rs. 1000."

17. "The Writing Is on the Wall for Political Graffiti," *Hindu*, March 10, 2006.

18. "Buddha Firm on New Graffiti Law," *Telegraph*, June 16, 2006.

19. "Writing Is on the Wall."

20. Subhash Gatade, "Paste a Poster, Go to Jail," *Central Chronicle*, January 3, 2008. Gatade notes that in the case of Delhi, this was merely a "game plan of "beautification of the city" before the Commonwealth Games of 2010.

21. Partha Chatterjee, "Cleaning up Democracy," *Telegraph* (Calcutta, India), March 16, 2006.

22. Susanta Ghosh, "Against the Wall," Letters to the Editor, *Telegraph* (Calcutta, India), March 20, 2006.

23. For studies on public murals in Ireland, see Bill Rolston, *Drawing Support: Murals in the North of Ireland* (Belfast: Beyond the Pale, 1992).

24. Naxalite wall writing, as "subversive" politics, is the exception to the rule.

25. Julie Peteet, "The Writings on the Walls: The Graffiti of the Intifada," *Cultural Anthropology* 11, no. 2 (1996): 139–59.

26. Ibid., 141, 140.

27. See Adam Yeut Chau's argument in "An Awful Mark: Symbolic Violence and Urban Renewal in Reform-Era China," *Visual Studies* 23, no. 33 (2008): 195–210.

28. David Henkin, *City Reading* (New York: Columbia University Press, 1998), 9.

29. See Nancy Fraser, "Rethinking the Public Sphere: A Contribution to the Critique of Actually Existing Democracy," in *Habermas and the Public Sphere*, ed. Craig Calhoun (Cambridge: MIT Press, 1992); Kevin Heatherington, *The Badlands of Modernity: Heterotopia and Social Ordering* (London: Routledge, 1997), 81–82; Swati Chattopadhyay, *Representing Calcutta: Modernity, Nationalism, and the Colonial Uncanny* (London: Routledge, 2006), 16–18.

30. Rose Marie San Juan, *Rome: A City Out of Print* (Minneapolis: University of Minnesota Press, 2001).

31. "Official Precaution: Extraordinary Police Arrangement in the City," *Amrita Bazar Patrika*, July 8, 1931.

32. The increasing reach of the state in the space of the family and community was resented, and the state's desire to control the use of public space was resisted by the nationalists. The agitation against the 1905 Partition of Bengal had inaugurated a new and radical usurpation of the norms of public space and consequently blurred the distinctions between public and private.

33. This line, from a poem by Kazi Nazrul Islam, was also emblazoned on leaflets found pasted on the gates of the district magistrate's and superintendent of police's bungalows in Malda six days before the shootout. Intelligence Bureau (hereafter, I.B.) File No. 149/28. The poem was popular and appeared on several leaflets, including one that carried pictures of Santi Ghosh and Suniti Chowdhury, the teenage girls who shot District Magistrate Charles Geoffrey Buckland Stevens in December 1931 and received life imprisonment. The version of the poem that appears in the collection of Nazrul's work is worded as follows: *rakte amar legechhe abar sarbanasher nesha* ("The intoxication for annihilation *again* has touched my blood," emphasis added). *Kazi Nazrul Rachanasamagra*, vol. 3 (Calcutta: Bangla Academy, 2000).

34. Copies of the "Blood for Blood" leaflet were found in the town of Midnapore. Extract from I.B. Weekly Report for w/c 8.8.31. I.B. File No. 149/28. Another "Blood Calls for Blood" leaflet carried the following note: "For those who have murdered Dinesh Gupta in cold blood there can be only one reward: righteous retribution." I.B. File No. 149/31.

35. See, for example, the processions and meetings carried out in Calcutta after Dinesh Gupta's execution. "Hartal in Calcutta," *Amrita Bazar Patrika*, July 8, 1931. I elaborate on this process of claiming public space during the 1905 agitation against the Partition of Bengal in "Politics, Planning, and Subjection: The Town Hall as Public Space in Colonial Calcutta," in Swati Chattopadhyay and Jeremy White, eds., *City Halls and Civic Materialism: Towards a Global History of Urban Public Space* (London: Routledge, 2013).

36. For example, the Government of India's Ordinance No. VI of 1930 noted that an instigation against the government could include any word, "written or spoken," or any signs or "visible representation."

37. Instances are numerous. See, for example, I.B. File No. 20/30; I.B. File No. 149/28; I.B. File No. 225/40.

38. Most of these artifacts were referred to as "leaflets" by the colonial government and were seen as interchangeable with posters. On some occasions a distinction was made between leaflets (distributed without regard to location) and posters and placards that were found on specific institutional sites and derived their meaning partly from their pasted location.

39. San Juan, *Rome*, 23.

40. "An Appeal to the Students," Circular no. 2, June 1932. I.B. File No. 149/28.

41. Memo by Phanibhusan Roy Chowdhury, A.S.P., noted that a youth caught with handbills had them "kept concealed under a chadar." I.B. File No. 149/28. 3.2.32.

42. See the instruction to the Special Assistant DIG, I.B. Calcutta, dated September 4, 1930, accompanied by a photograph of Benoy Bose for the purpose of printing

a "large poster" with "black lettering," and photograph, and reward offer (I.B. File No 537/30). Also see in this connection the comments made by J. R. Phillips and I. P. Rajshahi about the prohibitive cost of printing the seventy-five copies of Bose's photograph at the local press, September 12, 1930. I.B. File No. 537/30.

43. The police translation: "assault sahibs where ever seen." I.B. Wk 28.2.31. File No 149/28.

44. Extract from I.B. Weekly Correspondence for w/c 14.11.31.

45. Those who declared authorship included Bengal revolutionaries. One signed "some students of Presidency College" was found being distributed in College Square (I.B. File 149/8, 2.8.30.

46. Some sites were specifically called out for vigilance: Kalighat Park, Mitra Institution, South Suburban School, College Square, Asutosh Building (Calcutta University), Presidency College, Bethune College, Harish Park. I.B. File 149/28. 12.8.31.

47. For example, I.B. File No. 149/28. Placards with the inscription "Din Agata" (the day has come) were found on the gate of the S.P.'s (superintendent of police) and D.M.'s (district manager) bungalow in Malda, 2.12.30. A revolutionary leaflet in red paint, heralding "Long Live Revolution," was found on the walls of the criminal court in Ghatal.

48. Ibid.

49. I.B. File No. 225/40, Appendix I. Note of chief secretary dated March 7, 1940, 7. The same note also acknowledged the failure of the police to curb the distribution of revolutionary leaflets.

50. According to contemporaries, the Communist Party used wall writing for election campaigning from 1958 onward, a mode soon adopted by the congress and normalized by the mid-1960s.

51. The Naxalbari movement began in 1967 as an armed struggle against landlord-moneylender-police oppression in rural Bengal under the leadership of Charu Majumdar, Kanu Sanyal, and Jangal Santhal. It derives its name from the small village in north Bengal, Naxalbari. The movement broke with the Communist Party of India (Marxist) and formed the Communist Party of India (Marxist-Leninist) in 1969.

52. For cartoons in Bengali newspapers, see Subhendu Dasgupta's discussion of cartoonists from the 1940s onward, including Rebatibhusan, Chittaprasad, Kafi Khan (Prafulla Lahiri), Chandi Lahiri, "Omio" (Amiya Ghosh), Bonoful (Balaichand Mukhopadhyay), and Somnath Hore, in "Takhan Jemon ekhon temon," *Ekdin* (2009–2010); as well as his "*1940 dashaker Bharat: cartoon'e sheyi dashak,*" *Banhik,* no. 3 (August 2010): 148–59.

53. For discussion of other examples of political wall writing, see Swati Chattopadhyay, *Unlearning the City: Infrastructure in a New Optical Field* (Minneapolis: University of Minnesota Press, 2012).

54. Only SUCI tends to retain some older stylistic variation.

55. Johanna Drucker, "Graphical Reading and the Visual Aesthetics of Textuality," *Text* 16 (2006): 271.

56. Ibid., 274.

57. Ibid.

3.

Inside the Magic Circle: Conjuring the Terrorist Enemy at the 2001 Group of Eight Summit

EMANUELA GUANO

The arena, the card-table, the magic circle, the temple, the stage, the screen, the tennis court, the court of justice, etc., are all . . . forbidden spots, isolated, hedged round, hallowed, within which special rules obtain. All are temporary worlds within the ordinary world, dedicated to the performance of an act apart.

—Johan Huizinga, *Homo Ludens:*
A Study of the Play-Element in Culture

Held in Italy shortly after the election of Silvio Berlusconi's second conservative government, the 2001 Group of Eight (G8) summit went down in history as the battle of Genoa due to the violent clashes and the extreme brutality of state repression. From July 20 through July 22 the leaders of the eight wealthiest countries in the world conducted their debates inside a militarized citadel—a magic circle—at the heart of downtown Genoa. In the meantime, the rest of the city became the theater of a guerrilla warfare and a police and army violence that had few antecedents in recent Italian history. While most protesters sought to hold their demonstrations peacefully, anarchists known as the Black Bloc carried out hit-and-run attacks on the police as well as on civilian targets, ravaging and burning down parked cars, banks, and small businesses. Instead of seeking to contain the Black Bloc's offensive, police and army corps responded by indiscriminately beating all of the protesters who happened to be in their way. Over three hundred of them were illegally detained; more than four hundred had to be hospitalized; and one young man, Carlo Giuliani, was fatally shot in the head.

The end of the violence coincided with the conclusion of the summit on July 22. By July 23 most protesters had left town; over the next several weeks, the devastated city slowly returned to a disconcerted normalcy. As cleaning crews moved in to pick up the burnt rubble and business owners began replacing their shattered shop windows, astonished local and global publics who had followed the events from afar wondered what on earth had happened in Genoa. Instigated by the media apparatus owned by Prime Minister Silvio Berlusconi, Italian conservatives blamed the social movements; progressives, instead, pointed the finger at the fascist undercurrents in Italy's newly elected government.

Even as Italian political factions kept accusing each other, myriad reports on the events materialized not just in newspapers and television broadcasts all over the world but also on the Internet. In a matter of weeks, countless sites documenting the battle of Genoa made their appearance on the web, while books and videos on the same topic piled up on the shelves of Italian bookstores. Borrowing from such testimonials as well as from ethnographic interviews, this chapter is yet another attempt to make sense of the battle of Genoa.[1] Rather than compiling an investigative report, however, I use the tools of anthropological, sociological, and geographic theory to examine the narrative and spatial dynamics that contributed to the collective enactment of a starkly polarized political imaginary: one that, populated by discordant representations of righteous selves and evil foes, played an important role in triggering state violence.

More specifically, this chapter engages recent sociological analyses of social dramas as collective enactments of crisis and resolution as well as geographic debates on the resistive spatialities created by protest movements—an approach it complements by drawing on current anthropological inquiries into the organizational and performative practices of global social movements.[2] However, while much of the anthropological and geographic literature on social movements focuses exclusively on the strategies enacted respectively by the protesters and by those seeking to police them, here I highlight the existence of yet another public, though one that was largely excluded from the event: that of Genoa's own residents, whose urban everyday was interrupted forcefully through the creation of a highly contested, though ephemeral, spatiality invested with antagonistic political worldviews.

Political imaginaries are culturally negotiated landscapes of power in which a "people"—that is, a collectivity sharing an enemy—entitles a sovereign agency to wage war in its name.[3] As they legitimize sovereign power, such Manichaean narrative schemata feed social dramas as public enactments of conflict and resolution.[4] I argue that the drama that took place in Genoa was precipitated by the inscription of a political imaginary into a peculiar spatiality: a magic circle where the elimination of normal social life and the spectacularization and militarization of political action enabled the performance of an "act apart" of epic proportions.[5] As on one hand the Italian police and the army took it upon themselves to protect the free world from its communist, anarchist, and Al-Qaeda-inspired enemies, on the other hand the social movements lashed out at the symbols of global oppression and exploitation. The epochal clash that ensued took place in the name of the "people" whose rights and freedom had to be protected.

A Spectacle for What Publics?

In the story I am about to tell, the "people" were in the first place the highly abstract signifier that emerged from the interpellations issued by Italy's media, the majority of which were (and still are at the time of writing) controlled by conservative leader and prime minister Silvio Berlusconi. An important condition for the hailing of such a "people," I suggest, was the almost complete erasure of those other populations who did not fit this abstract, hypothetical mold—Genoa's own residents in the first place.

The summit had been designed as a global spectacle to be watched on television rather than seen in person; its imperial placelessness was to be enforced through the threat of violence as well as through aesthetic intensification.[6] Being particularly concerned with the performative aspects of the first world summit he would ever host, newly elected Berlusconi took charge of even the most minute visual details of downtown Genoa. After all, this is where he would get his first chance ever to be immortalized next to the likes of George W. Bush and Vladimir Putin.

As a seasoned media tycoon, Berlusconi could not help fretting over a beautiful city that was seemingly not beautiful enough. He had flowerpots rearranged, ordered that lemons be hung from non-citrus trees, and had unsightly buildings covered with trompe l'oeil sheets featuring baroque façades.[7] His beautification measures included, among others, an embargo on drying laundry on window lines. Even as it drew much ridicule, this bizarre imposition became indicative of the intent to exclude Genoa's residents from the event; implicitly redefined as "matter out of place" that should not be seen, citizens' everyday lives were not an acceptable background to the summit.[8] By the same token, Genoa's residents were not an intended public of observers, either.

Little did it matter that the renovation of Genoa's downtown had been presented as a gift to the city and its residents; the Genoese would have to wait to enjoy the restored buildings and the freshly paved pedestrian areas.[9] Far from being exclusively symbolic, their exclusion was operated through fear. "Genoese, in the weekend from July 20 through the 22, if you are not on vacation yet and if you have a chance to, go to the beach or the countryside"—this was the message issued by Achille Vinci Giacchi, the ad hoc minister for the G8 summit, in order to encourage Genoa's residents to vacate the city.[10] In the meantime, the militarized citadel that was being built right at the heart of the city made it obvious that downtown Genoa was to become unlivable for whoever resided or worked in that area. As the barriers were being erected, police officers went from door to door, issuing passes and informing residents that they were expecting riots and, potentially, even terrorist attacks. Leaving the city, thus went the message, would be the most reasonable choice in view of the summit.

Many Genoese heeded the recommendation. By the time the event began, at least one third of the approximately six hundred thousand inhabitants had left.[11] Others sought to use their sense of humor to lighten up what was becoming an unbearably tense atmosphere in a city that was no longer their own. In this vein, a group of unionists residing in the downtown historic district tried to drag a mock Trojan horse through a gate, reciting poems to stone-faced police officers who, as one activist told me later on, "didn't find it funny." The presage of state violence inscribed unto the militarized cityscape—the metal fences, the massive presence of the army and the police, the sight of snipers on rooftops—was compounded by the worrisome news seeping in about the alleged plans of antagonistic social movements that were expected to ravage the city. This is how the owner of a small business in Genoa's historic district described his feelings at that time: "On one hand, we saw the rising threat of state violence; on the other, we were being told that the city would be invaded by deviant youth [spostati] keen on destroying everything." Dismayed at the realization that the very same event that was supposed to promote the city on a global scale had turned ominous, he decided to close and barricade his shop for the duration of the summit. Many of his fellow business owners did the same.

As an increasingly deserted Genoa took on the feel of a ghost city, some of those residents who had not left made a point of participating in the protests—at least until they figured out that it was not safe to be in the street. As one man told me,

> I went with my wife to the migrants' march [*corteo dei migranti*]; initially the atmosphere was festive, and there were a lot of people with their children . . . However . . . the police in anti-riot gear looked scary. I saw them, and then I saw some of those [anarchist] kids dressed in black with their somber faces . . . I figured that, if anything had happened, we could have been easily trapped between the two groups. Then I told my wife: let's go home, I don't like it here. And I was right.

Like many others, he eventually opted for following the summit from his own home, monitoring the events from his windows whenever he could, but mostly through television.[12]

Many fellow Genoese did the same. As they lost the right to their own city—to inhabit, use, and experience it as they pleased—the Genoese who withdrew to their homes had to join the summit's global audiences of television viewers.[13] They, too, became yet another atomized public in a public sphere that had been engineered as a consensus-making machine.[14] If the suspension of normal social life contributed to the onset of liminality in downtown Genoa, the justification for a state of exception whereby fear legitimized sovereign violence was provided by the narratives of danger that had engulfed the Italian public sphere (figure 3.1).[15]

Figure 3.1. Who is out of place? A resident of Genoa walks her dog while in the background the police prepare to attack the demonstrators. Photo courtesy of Federico Figari.

Conjuring the Terrorist Enemy

Even as many of Genoa's residents had been persuaded to vacate their city, a multitude of social movements grouped under the umbrella of the Genoa Social Forum (GSF) flocked to it for the sake of holding a counter-summit. Their goal was to question publicly and challenge the purposes and modalities of the summit while proposing an alternative model of globalization; "another world is possible" was their slogan. The GSF comprised a variety of movements ranging from environmentalists to feminists, from Catholics and unionists to indigenous groups, and from gypsies and migrants to anti-IMF (International Monetary Fund) activists.[16] Regardless of their heterogeneity, though, what the GSF-affiliated movements had in common was their critique of forms of oppression and exploitation imposed by dominating powers.[17] In an open letter to Genoa's citizens, the GSF summarized the multifarious ideals and purposes of its more than two hundred thousand affiliates who convened for the counter-summit as follows: "actions of international cooperation, environmental protection, valorization of citizenship and labor rights, the promotion of ethical and responsible economic models, development of forms of multi-ethnic coexistence and of intercultural exchange, affirmation of the principles of peace and struggle against injustice."[18] The overwhelming majority of social movements also shared peaceful intentions and nonviolent strategies. A few of those who planned on participating in the counter-summit, however, had pledged to carry out violent attacks in order to express their rejection of global capitalism. Prior to the summit, these groups obtained disproportionate attention in the Italian public sphere.

In the weeks preceding the event, the Italian media had launched a fear campaign that sought to inscribe and congeal a specific narrative of the GSF as the enemy of western civilization.[19] Conservative newspapers owned by, or aligned with, Berlusconi and his allies published daily reports on how the GSF movements were going to ravage the city and carry out indiscriminate attacks on civilians and police officers alike. Allegedly, the protesters would be armed with balloons filled with HIV-positive blood. They would also fling marbles full of a disfiguring acid; the most benign among them would use catapults to throw dung; and marginal youth groups such as the *punkabbestia* would unleash their pit bulls against the police.[20] As if this were not enough, rumors circulated about a possible Al-Qaeda attack. Osama Bin Laden himself was supposedly planning on instigating riots among the protesters in order to distract the police and the army while his drones and scuba divers would annihilate the leaders of the free world.[21]

Concerned with the potential of extremist violence, even much of the moderate Italian left led by the Democratici di Sinistra (Left-Wing Democrats) party distanced itself from the GSF.[22] This failure to provide a public counter-narrative in the mainstream media allowed conservative television channels and newspapers to shape and control the climate of growing anxiety. Little did it matter that the crowd of protesters spanned a highly heterogeneous multitude. Pacifists, human rights activists, migrants, environmentalists, feminists, and many other declaredly peaceful groups were all subsumed under the generic, and generically threatening, label of *no-global*: a somewhat English-sounding sobriquet that not only simplistically homogenized them as antagonists to globalization but also marked them as alien to local culture and society.[23] As such stark dichotomy of just selves and evil others became inscribed unto Genoa's physical territory, the tension was bound to escalate.

The Map Is the Territory

The officialdom's preemptive defense against the threat allegedly posited by the protesters had been the rearrangement of the area of the summit into a highly defendable citadel. In the days that preceded the summit, Genoa's airport, its railway system, and the port were sealed off, and two thousand people were turned away at the Italian border.[24] Following a strategy that had been implemented in Quebec City during the Free Trade Area of the Americas summit of April 2001, much of the city center was turned into a red zone (*zona rossa*) meant to protect the sacred ground of legitimate power.[25] This area was surrounded by a metal fence (and, in some cases, heaps of containers) that isolated the area of the summit and prevented any face-to-face engagement between the G8 leaders and the movements. Around the militarized red zone was yet another ring—a yellow zone (*zona gialla*) that included the remainder of the city center as well as adjacent residential neighborhoods.[26] Inside the yellow zone, social movements had been assigned thematic plazas (*piazze tematiche*): spaces for representation where they could not only hold their meetings but also performatively manifest their goals and express their critiques of dominant powers by directly addressing global publics instead of political referents.[27] As performative counterpoints to the theatricality of the summit, their banners, symbols, chants, music, and costumes sought to convey complex messages to their global publics.[28] By the same token, their carnivalesque antics criticized and mocked an ostensibly self-absorbed and self-referential establishment intent on discussing world poverty even as it played a major role in its perpetuation.[29] Commenting on the resistive quality of GSF practices in the yellow zone, one activist remarked: "There were two different cities. In [the yellow zone] there was an outdoor university with economists, pacifists, people like Rigoberta Menchú talking with the youth from other countries. On the other hand there was the police that kept pouring in, and the huge fences that created the ghetto of the powerful." For the protesters, the hierarchical separation between the red and the yellow zone constituted a ready-made physical and metaphoric terrain of resistance that lent itself to the spatialization of dissent.[30]

However, the protesters were also painfully aware of how they were being kept in their place, both spatially and metaphorically.[31] In the words of a Ya Basta (Enough Already) affiliate, the fence separating the red from the yellow zone was a material reminder of the "enormous wall" symbolizing the global conflict between the North and the South of the world: "Just as the symbol of the third world war was the Berlin wall, the symbol of [this war] is the enormous wall that starts at the Rio Grande and runs through to Turkey, passing Gibraltar and then north, leaving out Eastern Europe; it divides Australia and Japan from the rest of East Asia. This wall is an insult to humanity."[32] The fence, in this perspective, provided the ultimate evidence of how global political and financial elites sought to avoid a dialogue with the people they claimed to represent. Confined to the exterior of the citadel, the "people," in this view, were excluded from the process of making decisions that would impact them all. What many protesters had contemptuously dubbed "the cage" (la gabbia) symbolically reproduced the separation between the rich and the poor, the powerful and the dispossessed—or, as one activist put it, "the New World Order, the Global Empire, protected by 20,000 police and military, besieged by the new Global protest movement."[33] Signs displayed by the movements read: 8 stronzi in gabbia (eight shits in a cage), zona rossa di vergogna (the zone is red with shame), strada chiusa: muro della vergogna (dead-end road: wall of shame).[34] The fence effectively collapsed the global scale of inequality into a very tangible, very local, and very sizable symbol—one that posited an irresistible instigation to be torn down.

In her analysis of the spatial politics of standoffs, sociologist Robin Wagner-Pacifici observed how as state representatives and antiestablishment groups confront each other, their moral and ideological polarization is reinscribed—and exacerbated—through the physical boundaries that surround the central point of containment. Almost inevitably, such a binary organization of space increases tension and leads to violence.[35] On a similar note,

I suggest that by designing and building the fence the Italian government did not just prospect and seek to stave off a violation attempt; it *invited* it. Prying open the red zone, even though only symbolically, became a categorical imperative for the protesters, one that was matched only by the determination of the army and the police officers to prevent any trespassing.[36] To them, too, the fence was the boundary where the enemy began to manifest.

Some movements purported to violate the fence only symbolically—for example, by throwing flowers and balloons over it. Others braved the mace cannons to pin messages to its meshes, thus seeking to draw attention to that very same reciprocal acknowledgment and dialogic communication with political leaders that had been denied to them. Occupying the ambiguous space between the declaredly nonviolent movements and the extremist fringes, the White Overalls (*Tute Bianche*), affiliated with Ya Basta, instead decided to try to physically violate the fence.[37] A few weeks before the summit, their leader, Luca Casarini, added fuel to the fire by publicly declaring war on the G8 summit: "We shall block the G8 summit," he declared to the Italian media.[38] And yet the White Overalls' agenda was not quite as explicitly violent. Their strategy was characterized by a Gandhi-inspired passive resistance, with the caveat that, even as they professed restraint from proactively violent attacks, the White Overalls purported to use the weight of their mass to tear down the red zone barrier.[39] In the words of one member, "The aim was to shut down the G8. The strategy was to attempt to breach the fortifications from a variety of positions. The tactics were direct action. The first task was to break through the myriad fortified police lines."[40]

Like Gandhi's freedom fighters, however, the White Overalls also sought to expose themselves to police brutality in order to show the world the true colors of an essentially repressive state.[41] On July 20, movement members hosted in the Carlini stadium prepared for their march by taping Styrofoam sheets and empty plastic bottles to their bodies; while symbolizing the waste produced by consumer capitalism, these items were also meant to protect them from police attacks.[42] Hiding behind Plexiglas shields, the White Overalls set out for the fence. They never made it. Riot police and carabinieri corps (Italy's military police) attacked them when they were still in the yellow zone, about a mile away from the red zone fence.[43] As one eyewitness reported, "First [there was] a frantic barrage of tear-gas, lobbing over the front lines, deep into the heart of the demonstration. Nobody here had gas masks. The poisonous gas first blinds you, then hurts, and then disorientates you. It is immediate and devastating. The people, packed in tightly, panicked and surged backwards. The chaos was manic."[44]

Armed with the highly toxic CS tear gas that had been banned by the 1997 Chemical Weapons Convention, as well as with the T-shaped *tonfa* batons, known to produce deep wounds, the police pushed the protesters against a wall.[45] The protesters fought back, and mayhem ensued. By that evening, hundreds of civilians lay injured in local hospitals or detained in police stations and army barracks. One of them, Carlo Giuliani, was dead, shot in the head by a young carabiniere conscript under circumstances that were never fully clarified.[46]

The Black Bloc: Liminal and Elusive

The police attack had taken place in a yellow zone area for which the White Overalls' march had been authorized; the alleged trigger had been an incursion by Black Bloc anarchists.[47] Long before the summit, the Black Bloc had been singled out as a major security concern. Their participation at the 1999 World Trade Organization summit in Seattle, the 2000 International Monetary Fund and World Bank meeting in Prague, and the 2001 summit of the Americas in Quebec had been characterized by a high level of devastation.[48] Because of their declaredly violent intent, the Black Bloc were feared not just by the Italian defense apparatus but also by the majority of GSF movements who were concerned about the effects that their violence could have on their own efforts to promote their cause. As expected, the Black Bloc wreaked havoc in Genoa, too—and other protesters ended up paying the price for it.[49]

In what follows, I suggest that the Black Bloc played the role of mythological tricksters who, positioned betwixt and between, simultaneously violate and establish boundaries.[50] Frequently described as cunning deceivers and liars, tricksters are ambiguous and polyvalent.[51] Most importantly, they are shape-shifters, situation-invertors, and meta-players who break the rules only to reaffirm them.[52] Just like the tricksters of world mythology, the Black Bloc who took part in the 2001 G8 counter-summit used shape-shifting, chaos, and ambiguity to help crystallize representations of the terrorist enemy, thus escalating a repression they invariably eluded.

Surprisingly enough, the Black Bloc's participation in Genoa's counter-summit was characterized by their lack of interest in the very same fence that had monopolized everybody else's attention.[53] Instead of targeting the red zone, the Black Bloc made quick, unexpected appearances in the yellow zone, where they carried out violent attacks against what they described as the symbols of global capitalism. Their objectives supposedly included the destruction of luxury vehicles, banks, chain stores, car dealerships, and the city jail; however, apartment complexes, small shops, and cheap cars were also hit in the process.[54] Black Bloc targets included journalists, photographers, and—although from a safe distance—army and police officers.[55] In the words of one of them, "Firstly the Black Bloc did a lot of property damage, some of it sensible: banks, porn shops, petrol stations, expensive cars, supermarkets; some of it stupid: traffic lights, bus shelters, cheaper cars; and some of it lunatic: starting a fire in an office above which was an apartment bloc."[56]

Whenever they launched an attack, the Black Bloc donned their peculiar attire: black clothes, hoods, and surgical or gas masks. On some occasions they also enacted a ceremony of their own, waving black flags and marching in circles to the sound of their drums before lashing out at their targets. This visibility, however, was restricted carefully in time and space. The Black Bloc always materialized out of nowhere and left behind no evidence. They disappeared immediately after their attacks, either by dispersing through Genoa's maze of shortcuts or by changing clothes and blending in with the crowds. Even their weapons were improvised out of materials that were quickly harnessed and just as swiftly discarded. The stones they hurled at the police were ripped from flowerbeds, and their Molotov cocktails were concocted out of bottles picked from recycling bins and filled with gas removed from parked vehicles. Masters of elusiveness, the Black Bloc met attempts to photograph or film their raids with violent attacks, during which cameras and camcorders were routinely destroyed (figure 3.2).

Best described as a tactic of urban guerrilla warfare rather than a movement, the Black Bloc groups roaming Genoa's yellow zone were open to anyone willing to wear black clothes and join them in their attacks.[57] Through the use of masks, the Black Bloc sought to deny the existence of subjectivities for the sake of becoming, as Edward Avery-Natale put it, an undetermined "anything."[58] By the same token, however, donning a black mask allowed *anyone* to become part of the Black Bloc. For example, a man acting as a member of a Black Bloc group self-identified as a British Nazi, and when interviewed by a journalist declared, "I don't give a dime about the G8 . . . I am here to wreak havoc and I am having a hell of a good time."[59] The uncertainties about the Black Bloc's political affiliation also contributed to raising questions about the real purposes of their attacks. This was especially the case since the latter took on the same modality again and again: after positioning themselves in front of a group of nonviolent protesters, the Black Bloc would lash out at the police, pelting them with stones and Molotov cocktails. Then the police would attack—but never before the Black Bloc

Figure 3.2. Immortalized during an attack, Black Bloc threaten the photographer. Photo by anonymous.

had vanished into thin air.[60] Each time, peaceful protesters were left to bear the brunt of the repression: the blows, the tear gas, and the arbitrary arrests, which the Black Bloc invariably escaped (figure 3.3).

Along with their elusiveness, the Black Bloc's organizational fluidity and their lack of a consistent, and consistently identifiable, public persona gave way to competing readings of their strategies and real identities.[61] For the police and the military who had been bombarded with warnings about the terrorist threat, the Black Bloc were the proof that all GSF movements were essentially violent and that, as such, all of them had to be repressed by using all means available.[62] Many GSF members, instead, were irked by the police officers' lack of responsiveness to the Black Bloc. Eyewitness reports—but also films and photographs—proved how the police consistently failed to contain the Black Bloc, targeting peaceful protesters in their stead. Black Bloc were also spotted and even photographed as they socialized on the roof of a carabinieri barrack.[63] Others were seen as they filmed journalists and reporters at a checkpoint; interacted collegially with carabinieri and police officers; and walked freely in and out of police precincts and army barracks, carrying guns under their black clothes.[64] The suspicion thus arose that the Black Bloc had been infiltrated by police officers keen on delegitimizing dissent and providing an alibi for state repression.[65]

Figure 3.3. After positioning themselves at the front of the protest, the Black Bloc attack the police. They will vanish before the police retaliate. Photo by anonymous.

While answering the question of the Black Bloc's real identity is beyond the scope of this chapter, here I wish to highlight their pivotal contribution to precipitating the drama of just selves and terrorist others inscribed unto the G8 summit. By holding a revolving mirror to the political fantasies of all parties involved, and, most importantly, by exacerbating the fear of an elusive, if dangerous, enemy, the Black Bloc enabled the sovereign violence that was exercised through police retaliations.[66] As folklorists have observed, tricksters are made sacred by their violations; in turn, this sacredness separates them from society and puts them in the condition of those who can be killed with impunity.[67] Just like mythological tricksters, however, the Black Bloc also held the ability to divert the consequences of their actions unto others; hence, their sacredness was transferred to the other protesters, who consistently paid the price for the Black Bloc's raids.[68]

Spaces of Death

The disruptive ambiguity that the Black Bloc injected into the battle of Genoa contributed to the creation of sinister liminalities: "spaces of death in the land of the living," where illegally detained GSF affiliates were stripped of their rights and subjected to a brutal repression, even as fellow activists, lawyers, and families were prevented from intervening.[69] In a plot that kept repeating itself throughout the duration of the summit, the alleged presence of the Black Bloc provided the pretext for the violent police incursion in the Armando Diaz school complex, which hosted the Independent Media (Indymedia) Center as well as several GSF members and journalists. On July 21, at about 11:00 PM a police commando irrupted into the school. Unidentifiable because of their antiriot gear, the police officers who broke into the Diaz school that night beat up and severely injured sixty-two of the ninety-three journalists and GSF members who were staying there.[70] The police reportedly walked around the rooms screaming, "Where is Carlo? [Giuliani, who had been killed earlier that day]," and savagely attacking people still in their sleeping bags. By the time they were finished, the rooms of the Diaz school were splattered with blood, and sixty-two people had deep wounds and fractured bones.[71]

During the incursion a crowd amassed in front of the school: concerned GSF members, physicians and nurses, journalists, and even politicians, none of whom was allowed to enter the premises as the massacre went on.[72] All they got to see was the bleeding bodies of the wounded who were carried away, to be taken into custody. As legality was restored a few days later, Italian magistrates cleared all of the apprehended: none of them, they found, was a Black Bloc member. The two Molotov cocktails that were exhibited as evidence turned out to have been planted by an officer during the raid.

The plight of many of the Diaz school victims did not end with their arrest, though. Seventy-five of them were taken to the police barracks in Bolzaneto. Along with the other detainees, they were to be subjected to physical and psychological abuses in an environment where legality had been suspended. Jailers would confiscate or even rip prisoners' identity documents as they told them, "See? Here you are nobody, you have no rights."[73] One detainee reported, "I requested a lawyer, and all I got was more blows."[74] Reduced to bare life that could be disposed of with impunity, the detainees were deprived of sleep, water, and food and were not permitted to use the restrooms.[75] Many prisoners, regardless of their injuries, were forced to lean against walls as they stood on their toes, their arms spread-eagled, for hours on end. As a Bolzaneto detainee later reported, "Those who showed signs of weakness and let their arms down were invariably slapped on their neck, kicked on their feet or shins, punched on their belly or hips . . . As to myself, I was in that position . . . for about 15 hours."[76]

Signs of perceived deviance were removed forcefully from bodies: piercings were ripped away, and long hair was summarily shaven. Earlier on, the protesters' colorful clothes, costumes, and hippie garb had mocked the dark uniforms of the police as well as the black suits of politicians; their upbeat music and improvised dances had challenged army discipline and the stiff formality of the officialdom.[77] In the Bolzaneto barracks, however, the same unruly bodies that had made fun of the establishment were punished through degradation and violence. Women were molested and threatened with rape; prisoners were made to walk through two rows of soldiers who spat and urinated on them.[78] Often the blows were administered on existing wounds so that the victims' bodies would bear no additional evidence.[79] Even such distortion of the concern with legality was not consistent, though. At times the viciousness of the abuses betrayed a bold confidence in the victimizers' impunity: "all of a sudden, a policeman . . . took my hand, spread my fingers apart and pulled them violently, thus tearing my flesh and splitting my hand."[80]

The space of exception that had emerged inside the barracks—one whereby state powers dealt with the threat of terrorism by suspending legality in the name of the law—dissolved with the end of the summit, when prisoners were eventually released.[81] The injuries, however, persisted. Their signs scarred the violated bodies of the victims; they also lingered in the collective psyche of those publics who still grappled to come to terms with the events.[82] In the aftermath of the battle of Genoa, much was said and written about the seemingly inexplicable brutality of police and army corps. Persistent rumors surmised that Gianfranco Fini, vice president of the council of ministers and leader of the post-Fascist Alleanza Nazionale party, had taken a trip to Genoa during the summit. A Genoese woman who had watched the events from the safety of her home told me: "I see a motorcade enter the barracks, and shortly after that I hear this loud chanting and applauses, so many applauses. Then, the following day I hear that Fini was in town. It must have been him; he came here to incite the violence [metterli su]. Who knows what he promised them."

On the other hand, apologetic explanations for police brutality singled out the conspicuous presence of inexperienced young conscripts along with that of corps who had never been trained in peaceful crowd-control methods and worked only with dangerous detainees; such tenuous circumstances were further compounded by the lack of nonlethal weapons in police and army equipment.[83]

On a deeper level, however, the repression of dissent at the 2001 G8 summit shed light on the extent to which the military machinery activated by the government was, in fact, a self-standing political player capable of embodying and performing its own version of the state, one that owed less to utilitarian rationalism than to a highly abstract Manichaean worldview.[84] As this political imaginary was being called forth, it became appropriate for soldiers and police officers to chant hymns to Mussolini and Pinochet as they abused their victims, often even forcing them to sing along.[85] A fantasy was at work that not only exceeded functional rationality but also activated a sedimented fascist repertoire—a root paradigm of "symbols, archetypal characters, and rhetorical appeals" that is still known to haunt the conservative Italian imaginary.[86] As soldiers and police officers inscribed their discursive, yet absolute Other (communist, anarchist, terrorist, queer, hippie, etc.) unto the humiliated and brutalized bodies of their detainees, their personal enactment of the dominant narrative became thicker, more intimate, and also more extreme. It became a rapt, and deadly serious, deep play where everything was at stake, and whose bloodbath was simultaneously highly symbolic and very real.[87]

By then captive GSF members had become anonymous blank screens onto which a dangerous alterity could be not only projected but also punished by means of the same brutality that had been imputed to it.[88] Given the enormity of these Others' imaginary crimes, their retribution could reach above and beyond legality. Thus, in the magic circles drawn around the Bolzaneto barracks and the Diaz school, the summit that had begun as a ceremony meant to illustrate and celebrate the global world order turned into a ritual of elimination of the chaotic Other.[89] Blending the mode of the "world *as if*" with that of real actions with tangible consequences, the sovereign violence that was applied to the defeated bodies of the protesters enacted the pretense of an epochal victory over its absolute, if multifarious, enemy.[90] The fiction of this victory, however, did not outlast the end of the heterotopic spatiality that had been created for the summit.[91] As soon as the summit reached its conclusion on July 22, the magic circle of the Bolzaneto barracks was lifted, too. This is when the spell broke, and news about the abuses committed during the summit erupted in the global media.

The End of the Drama

While Italy's conservative television channels and newspapers had had a considerable impact in framing the anti-G8 protests for the public opinion before and during the event, theirs was not the only gaze on the G8 events.[92] The summit was characterized by an intense participation not only of international journalists but also of independent and amateur reporters and photographers who generated an alternative flow of information. Following

Indymedia's advice, "don't hate the media, become the media," hundreds of protesters armed with camcorders and cameras produced a mass of evidence of police and army brutality, thus assembling a counter-narrative that challenged the official version of the events.[93]

Once they flooded the media, the images of bruised, lacerated bodies and the myriad reports of police repression, torture, and violence generated a global spectacle of horror that cast a deep shadow on the G8 summit as well as Italy's conservative government. In the aftermath of the summit, the public confidence in the police and carabinieri corps reached its lowest levels ever. As one Genoese woman told me, "The presence of the police used to make me feel safe. Now when I walk by them I get nervous." Formal investigations began of the abuses of the Diaz school and the Bolzaneto barracks, followed by trials and appeals that often failed to give the victims the closure they expected.[94]

The loss of trust in the Italian state was just as stark on a global level. If the official narrative of the government had posited the need to defend western civilization, globally circulating tales of a repression that was unheard of for a European Union country opened up a crevice in Italy's claims to the status of western democracy. After the events of the Diaz school, even conservative media around the world began condemning the brutality of the repression; furthermore, that such violence had taken place in twenty-first-century Europe made things even worse.[95] Leading European and U.S. newspapers called Italy a "Chilean," "Argentine," "East European," or "Cuban" dictatorship, thus activating a transnational imaginary whereby the Italian state's attempt to confirm its membership in an ideal western civilization had produced the opposite result.[96] As it became clear that the violence that had been imputed initially to the social movements had been committed by representatives of the Italian state, what had been regarded as the solution to the terrorist problem was singled out as the problem itself. In the weeks that followed the end of the summit, Silvio Berlusconi's legitimacy as a G8 leader and as Italy's prime minister became the object of intense, and intensely critical, debates, both at home and abroad. For much of the summer, Berlusconi's government seemed to be heading for a quick demise. All of a sudden, however, a highly dramatic event took place that provided a formidable validation for Italy's conservative government, its fear campaigns, and its violent repression of protesters.

On September 11, 2001, two hijacked airplanes rammed into New York's World Trade Center, destroying the towers and killing thousands; a third plane hit the Pentagon in Arlington, Virginia; and a fourth one crashed in Pennsylvania while presumably en route to the White House.

Western civilization was indeed under attack. Now that the terrorist enemy had turned out to be every bit as dangerous as expected, the state of exception became a welcome—and permanent—necessity.[97] As concerned citizens around the western world stockpiled canned food and duct tape, the global indignation over the abuses committed in Genoa faded in a splashing of orange alerts. Berlusconi's government lasted until the end of its five-year mandate.

Conclusions

Rather than being a merely physical gesture, the act of drawing a magic circle and assigning meaning to it makes it possible to create a "sphere of activity with a disposition of its own."[98] By virtue of being "apart together," participants in this circle enter a shared imaginary world where normality is interrupted.[99] In this chapter I argued that the tragic events that transpired from the G8 summit—the guerilla warfare as well as the violent repression—were at least in part a product of the creation of a sui generis magic circle, one that inscribed an ideological map unto a cityscape that had been transformed for the occasion. The suspension of normal social life, the crystallization of official narratives, and, above all, the creation of a militarized citadel inside the city were pivotal to turning a highly abstract and starkly dichotomic political imaginary into lived experience.

Rather than being an attempt to improve residents' own lives, the restoration of Genoa's built environment prior to the summit was only the first stage of a deadly serious deep play in which the creation of a peculiar placelessness went hand in hand with the need to claim and defend territories at all costs. What had begun as a constellation of camera-ready vignettes (of world leaders celebrating themselves, and of GSF movements debating, marching, and performing in their thematic plazas) thus unfolded into a full-fledged social drama. The stakes were high for all of those involved. What, for the officialdom, was the epochal clash between the free world and its terrorist enemies, for the protesters epitomized the chasm between humankind and the agents of global oppression. While these imaginaries differed radically from each other, they both shared the same Manichaean organization of righteous selves and evil enemies. Hence, both the protesters and the state representatives respectively sought to enact their own narrative even as they recruited each other in the role of the "familiar stranger": the blank screen for projections of "predictable but unreasonable, unaccountable, deeply flawed, possibly immoral" alterity.[100]

By skillfully blending violence and shape-shifting, the Black Bloc intensified the polarization, thus contributing to precipitating the events. Not only did their transgressions enable the Italian state to reclaim its monopoly over violence, but they also made it easier for it to suspend the law in the name of legality.[101] Death spaces thus emerged where the terrorist enemy could be punished or even eliminated, in an exercise in magical thinking whereby attacking the part became equivalent to vanquishing the whole.

After the end of the summit, as normality was reinstated, the realization of the brutality of the repression sent shock waves through the very same western world whose defense had supposedly been at stake. Only a few weeks later, however, the lingering indignation was upstaged by the 9/11 attacks. What followed was a decade of grappling with enemies who were sometimes real and often imaginary. The battle of Genoa had been but a dress rehearsal; eventually, the magic circle had gone global.

NOTES

I am deeply indebted to my anonymous reviewers, as well as Jennifer Patico, Katherine Hankins, Faidra Papavasiliou, and Megan Sinnott for their comments. A version of this article was presented at the Embodied Placemaking in Urban Public Spaces symposium of the Center for 21st Century Studies on April 29, 2011. I am grateful to my fellow presenters as well as the audience and the colleagues of the center and the University of Wisconsin–Milwaukee for their comments on my essay. Any errors and omissions are entirely my own.

1. Unless otherwise noted, the reports and testimonials used in this article are drawn from ethnographic interviews conducted from 2002 through 2010 with individuals who lived in Genoa, and in several cases resided or worked inside the red zone.

2. Robin Wagner-Pacifici, *The Moro Morality Play: Terrorism as Social Drama* (Chicago: University of Chicago Press, 1986); Robin Wagner-Pacifici, *Theorizing the Standoff: Contingency in Action* (Cambridge: Cambridge University Press, 2000); Ron Eyerman, *The Assassination of Theo Van Gogh: From Social Drama to Cultural Trauma* (Durham, N.C.: Duke University Press, 2008); Don Mitchell, *The Right to the City: Social Justice and Public Space* (New York: Guilford Press, 2003); Paul Routledge, "Critical Geopolitics and Terrains of Resistance," *Political Geography* 15, nos. 6/7 (1996): 505–31; Kurt Iveson, *Publics and the City* (New York: Wiley-Blackwell, 2007); Jeffrey S. Juris, *Networking Futures: The Movements against Corporate Globalization* (Durham, N.C.: Duke University Press, 2006); Jeffrey S. Juris, "Performing Politics: Image, Embodiment, and Affective Solidarity during Anti-corporate Globalization Protests," *Ethnography* 9, no. 1 (2008): 61–97; and David Graeber, *Possibilities: Essays on Hierarchy, Rebellion, and Desire* (Oakland, Calif.: AK Press, 2007).

3. Susan Buck-Morss, *Dreamworld and Catastrophe: The Passing of Mass Utopia in East and West* (Cambridge: MIT Press, 2007), 12; Michael Hardt and Antonio

Negri, *Multitude: War and Democracy in the Age of Empire* (Cambridge, Mass.: Harvard University Press, 2004), 16.

4. For Manichaean narrative schemata, see Bruno Gullí, "Beyond Good and Evil: A Contribution to the Analysis of the War against Terrorism," in *Implicating Empire: Globalization and Resistance in the 21st Century World Order*, ed. S. Aronowitz and H. Gautney (New York: Basic Books, 2003), 83–94; and James Wertsch, "The Narrative Organization of Collective Memory," *Ethos* 36, no. 1 (2008): 120–35. For social dramas as public enactments of conflict and resolution, see Eyerman, *Assassination of Theo Van Gogh*; Victor Turner, *Dramas, Fields, and Metaphors: Symbolic Action in Human Society* (Ithaca, N.Y.: Cornell University Press, 1974); and Wagner-Pacifici, *Moro Morality Play*.

5. Johan Huizinga, *Homo Ludens: A Study of the Play-Element in Culture* (Boston: Beacon Press, 1955), 10.

6. Michael Hardt and Antonio Negri, *Empire* (Cambridge, Mass.: Harvard University Press, 2000); Retort (Iain Boal, T. J. Clark, Joseph Matthews, and Michael Watts), *Afflicted Powers: Capital and Spectacle in a New Age of War* (London: Verso, 2005).

7. Mizio Ferraris, *I silenzi della zona rossa: G8 e dintorni* (Genoa: Fratelli Frilli Editori, 2001).

8. The "matter out of place" quotation is from Mary Douglas, *Purity and Danger* (New York: Routledge, 1966), 33. Berlusconi's request did not sit well with many (traditionally left-leaning) Genoese, who reacted to this imposition by hanging underwear from their window lines for the duration of the summit.

9. Genoa's renovation cost was 70 billion lire (approximately 35 billion euros); see Marietto Chiesa, *G8/Genova* (Torino: Einaudi 2001), 6. Its reconstruction after the end of the summit cost another 8 million euros. Donatella Della Porta and Herbert Reiter, *Polizia e protesta: L'ordine pubblico dalla Liberazione ai "no global"* (Bologna: Il Mulino, 2003), 5. For a detailed list of the restorations, see the Speciale G8 issue of *Arkos* 1 (2001).

10. Genoa Social Forum (GSF), *Genova: Il libro bianco* (Milano: Nuova Iniziativa Editoriale, 2001), 16.

11. In the days preceding the summit, electrical consumption and waste disposal reportedly dropped by 40 percent. Della Porta and Reiter, *Polizia e protesta*, 3.

12. Continuous coverage at the local level was offered by the Genoese television station PrimoCanale. Broadcasts on the event were provided by Italy's three public television channels (Radiotelevisione italiana, RAI) along with Berlusconi's own Canale 5, Rete 4, and Italia Uno. While RAI 1 and RAI 2 were controlled tightly by Berlusconi's government, RAI 3 is traditionally closer to the Italian left. At that time, however, the latter was still critical of the Genoa Social Forum.

13. Henri Lefebvre, *Writings on Cities* (Oxford: Basil Blackwell, 1996).

14. As prospected by Jürgen Habermas in *The Structural Transformation of the Public Sphere: An Inquiry into a Category of Bourgeois Society* (Cambridge: MIT Press, 1991), his well-known 1989 theorization of an ideally democratic public sphere as one comprising face-to-face dialogic engagements among members of culture-debating publics, contemporary television and print media are indeed characterized by a lack of participation in the process of opinion formation. And yet

this monologic quality does not have to be an insurmountable obstacle to democracy, provided that the pluralism and the accountability of information channels are guaranteed. On this topic, see J. B. Thompson, "Social Theory and the Media," in *Communication Theory Today*, ed. David Crowley and D. Mitchell (Stanford, Calif.: Stanford University Press, 1994), 27–49. Unfortunately, both of these conditions were denied in the organization and official coverage of the 2001 G8 summit.

15. Giorgio Agamben, *State of Exception* (Chicago: University of Chicago Press, 2005); Hardt and Negri, *Empire.*

16. Della Porta and Reiter, *Polizia e protesta*; Juris, *Networking Futures.*

17. Donatella Della Porta et al., eds., *Globalization from Below: Transnational Activists and Protest Networks* (Minneapolis: University of Minnesota Press, 2006); Juris, *Networking Futures*; Routledge, "Critical Geopolitics."

18. GSF, *Libro bianco*, 41.

19. For the Italian media's fear campaign, see Stefano Cristante, *Violenza mediata: Il ruolo dell'informazione nel G8 di Genoa* (Rome: Editori Riuniti, 2003). On the GSF as the enemy of western civilization, see Della Porta and Reiter, *Polizia e protesta*, 6. On the role of the media in crystallizing narratives, see Eyerman, *Assassination of Theo Van Gogh*, 17.

20. Andrea Colombo, *Storia politica di un disastro: Il caso Genova: da piazza Alimonda alla scuola Diaz* (Rome: Manifestolibri, 2002); Cristante, *Violenza mediata*; Antonio Sema, "Limoni e sangue: a che servivano gli scontri di Genoa," *Limes* 4 (2001): 17–28. The *punkabbestia* are members of a youth group who live on the streets and breed large dogs.

21. Sema, "Limoni e sangue," 22.

22. Della Porta et al., *Globalization from Below*, 148.

23. The movements were critical of neoliberal and corporate globalization rather than globalization as a whole; see Della Porta and Reiter, *Polizia e protesta*, 12.

24. Della Porta et al., *Globalization from Below*, 3.

25. Juris, *Networking Futures*, 55.

26. For the GSF map of Genoa's red and yellow zones, see the website of the Genoa Social Forum, "Red Zone/Yellow Zone," http://www.processig8.org/GSF/redz.htm.

27. For spaces of representations, see Mitchell, *Right to the City*. On the performative aspects, see Graeme Chesters and Ian Welsh, "Rebel Colours: 'Framing' in Global Social Movements," *Sociological Review* 52, no. 3 (2004): 314–35; Graeme Chesters and Ian Welsh, *Complexity and Social Movements: Multitudes at the Edge of Chaos* (London: Routledge, 2006); Graeber, *Possibilities*; Juris, "Performing Politics"; Juris, *Networking Futures*; Della Porta and Reiter, *Polizia e protesta*.

28. Graeber, *Possibilities*; Chesters and Welsh, *Complexity and Social Movements*, Chesters and Welsh, "Rebel Colours."

29. Graeber, *Possibilities*; Juris, *Networking Futures.*

30. Routledge, "Critical Geopolitics," 517–20.

31. Tim Cresswell, *In Place/Out of Place: Geography, Ideology, and Transgression* (Minneapolis: University of Minnesota Press, 1996), 3; Stef Jansen, "The Streets of Beograd: Urban Space and Protest Identities in Serbia," *Political Geography* 20 (2001): 35–55.

32. "Who Are Ya Basta?" http://www.struggle.ws/global/about/yabasta.html.

33. Ramor Ryan, "Death and Terror in Genoa," http://struggle.ws/global/genoa/ramor.html.

34. GSF, *Libro bianco*, 61, 37, 17.

35. Wagner-Pacifici, *Theorizing the Standoff.*

36. Ibid., 8.

37. Lucio Caracciolo, "Editoriale: Da Marx a Matrix," *Limes* 4 (2001): 7–14; Emily Vanderford, "Ya Basta!—'A Mountain of Bodies that Advances, Seeking the Least Harm Possible to Itself,'" in *Representing Resistance: Media, Civil Disobedience, and the Global Justice Movement*, ed. Andy Opel and Donnalyn Pompper (Westport, Conn.: Praeger, 2003), 16–26.

38. Fabrizio Ravelli, "Dichiariamo guerra al G8: Le tute bianche a Genova: saremo in 200.000," in *La Repubblica*, May 27, 2001, available at http://www.lamia terraan.it/pdf/ng27_05_01c.pdf.

39. On the strategy of passive resistance, see Francesco Vitali, "La rete della sconfitta," *Limes* 4 (2001): 67–70. On their desire to tear down the red zone barrier, see Alex Callinicos, "The Anti-Capitalist Movement after Genoa and New York," in Aronowitz and Gautney, *Implicating Empire*, 133–50; Juris, *Networking Futures*, 44.

40. Ryan, "Death and Terror in Genoa."

41. Caracciolo "Editoriale," 12.

42. Vanderford, "Ya Basta."

43. As Mike Zajko and Daniel Béland point out, the role of the police at recent international summits has increasingly become that of enforcing a territorial form of state power that is asserted through the creation of no-protest zones. See "Space and Protest Policing at International Summits," *Environment and Planning D: Society and Space* 26 (2008): 719–35.

44. Ryan, "Death and Terror in Genoa."

45. GSF, *Libro bianco*, 24, 108. The *tonfa* is a baton with a handle, often used in martial arts.

46. On July 20 Giuliani had joined the White Overalls march toward the red zone. In the clashes that ensued after the police had attacked the White Overalls, an army Land Rover Defender got cornered in nearby Piazza Alimonda. Giuliani approached the jeep holding a fire extinguisher in his hands. From inside the jeep, carabiniere conscript Mario Placanica fired two shots, one of which hit Giuliani in the head and killed him (see GSF, *Libro bianco*, 80–91). In the ensuing trial, Placanica claimed he had acted in self-defense; he also argued that he had aimed in the air but a falling stone had deflected the bullet, causing it to hit Giuliani. Placanica's line of defense was accepted, and his acquittal drew much discontent from the GSF and Giuliani's parents. By then, however, Giuliani had become an icon of the movement. In 2006 a room of the Italian Parliament was dedicated to his memory. On July 20, 2011, a memorial stela was erected on the site where Carlo had been killed.

47. Della Porta and Reiter, *Polizia e protesta*, 161.

48. GSF, *Libro bianco*, 164.

49. Juris, *Networking Futures*. This is what happened, among others, to Rete Lilliput movements (mainly pacifists and feminists) assaulted by the police in Piazza

Manin on July 20, as well as to the protesters who were attacked in the Foce neighborhood on July 21 (see Chiesa, *G8/Genova*; see also Juris, *Networking Futures*).

50. Barbara Babcock-Abrahams, "A Tolerated Margin of Mess: A Trickster and His Tales Reconsidered," *Journal of the Folklore Institute* 11, no. 3 (1975): 147–86.

51. Laura Levi Makarius, "Le trickster," chap. 5 in *Les sacré et la violation des interdits: Chapitres V á VII* (Paris: Éditions Payot, 1974), 4–58, electronic edition, http://classiques.uqac.ca/contemporains/makarius_Laura/sacre_violation_interdits/sacre_violation_interdits_2.pdf; William J. Hynes, "Mapping the Characteristics of Mythic Tricksters: A Heuristic Guide," in *Mythical Trickster Figures*, ed. William J. Hynes and William G. Doty (Tuscaloosa: University of Alabama Press, 1997), 33–45.

52. William J. Hynes, "Inconclusive Inconclusions: Tricksters as Metaplayers and Revealers," in *Mythical Trickster Figures*, 202–18; Hynes "Mapping the Characteristics," 37–38.

53. As Juris pointed out, small pack actions are synonymous with a commitment to "diversity, de-centralization, and self-management." *Networking Futures*, 8.

54. Della Porta and Reiter, *Polizia e protesta*, 137.

55. If violent acts committed by protesting crowds are guided typically by a rationality of their own, the question of how the Black Bloc selected the targets of their attacks contributes to raising issues about this group's real affiliation and purposes. See David Waddington, "The Madness of the Mob? Explaining the 'Irrationality' and Destructiveness of Crowd Violence," *Sociology Compass* 2 (2008): 675–87.

56. "With the Black Block in Genoa," http://www.struggle.ws/freeearth/genoa.html.

57. Franz Gustinchic, "Anatomia del Black Block (con una scheda di Emmanuela C. Del Re; Facciamo che io ero un antiglobalizzatore violento)," *Limes* 4 (2001): 41–50.

58. Edward Avery-Natale, "'We're Here, We're Queer, We're Anarchists': The Nature of Identification and Subjectivity among Black Blocs," *Anarchist Developments in Cultural Studies*, Post-Anarchism Today, 1 (2010): 95–115, http://www.anarchist-developments.org/index.php/adcs/article/view/7.

59. GSF, *Libro bianco*, 68.

60. Chesters and Welsh, *Complexity and Social Movements*, 84.

61. Gustinchic, "Anatomia del Black Block," 45.

62. Sema, "Limoni e sangue."

63. GSF, *Libro bianco*, 118–19.

64. Ibid., 119–21.

65. Caracciolo, "Editoriale," 9.

66. Giorgio Agamben, *Homo Sacer: Sovereign Power and Bare Life*, trans. Daniel Heller-Roazen (Stanford, Calif.: Stanford University Press, 1988), 85; Callinicos, "Anti-Capitalist Movement"; Juris, *Networking Futures*.

67. Babcock-Abrahams, "Tolerated Margin of Mess," 164; Makarius, *Le sacré et la violation*, 37. Not to be confused with the contemporary definition of "sacred" as "holy," the sacredness of tricksters is akin to the condition of those ancient Romans who, after committing a forbidden act, were deprived of their rights and could be killed by anyone. See Agamben, *Homo Sacer*, 82–84.

68. Babcock-Abrahams, "Tolerated Margin of Mess."

69. The "spaces of death" quotation is from Michael Taussig, *Shamanism, Colonialism, and the Wild Man: A Study in Terror and Healing* (Chicago: University of Chicago Press, 1987), 4. Also drawing on Taussig, in his ethnography of anticapitalist global movements, Juris called Genoa in its entirety a "space of terror" brought about by "blurring the line between law and violence, order and chaos (*Networking Futures*, 167–68). While I agree with Juris's argument about the liminality that emerged within this city's boundaries during the July 2001 events, here I prefer to maintain Taussig's definition of "space of death in the world of the living" for the sake of emphasizing the victims' experience of the disconnect between what was happening to them and the discourse of legality and rights that continued to regulate to varying degrees the "world of the living" just a short distance away, both within and without the city limits. It is important to note that the repression peaked at specific locations, and not all of Genoa was directly and homogeneously subjected to the terror of police violence.

70. Italian police and carabinieri officers are not required to wear visible identification.

71. GSF, *Libro bianco*, 281.

72. Ibid., 129–31.

73. Ibid., 146.

74. Ibid., 143.

75. Agamben, *Homo Sacer*.

76. GSF, *Libro bianco*, 142.

77. On the sartorial politics of social movements and the officialdom, see Graeber, *Possibilities*, 329.

78. GSF, *Libro bianco*, 142.

79. Ibid., 143.

80. Ibid., 144.

81. Agamben, *Homo Sacer*; Agamben, *State of Exception*.

82. Historically, the practice of violently suppressing public protests culminated with mid-twentieth-century *scelbismo* (named after Christian Democratic Prime Minister Mario Scelba) and became considerably less prevalent in the late 1900s (Della Porta and Reiter, *Polizia e protesta*).

83. See Andrea Nativi, "Militari e poliziotti: Le lezioni da imparare," *Limes* 4 (2001): 51–58. This is certainly not to say that all the police officers and soldiers deployed in the G8 summit participated in the repression. In fact, throughout the battle of Genoa there were several outstanding cases of officers who succored the victims of their own colleagues' brutality. GSF, *Libro bianco*.

84. Giorgio Agamben, *Il regno e la gloria: Per una genealogia teologica dell'economia e del governo. Homo Sacer II, 2* (Vicenza: Neri Pozza, 2007), 303; Begonia Aretxaga, "Maddening States: On the Imaginary of Politics," *Annual Reviews of Anthropology* 32 (2003): 393–410; Taussig, *Shamanism, Colonialism, and the Wild Man*.

85. GSF, *Libro bianco*, 142–43.

86. Wagner-Pacifici, *Moro Morality Play*, 7.

87. Della Porta and Reiter, *Polizia e protesta*, 172; Clifford Geertz, *The Interpretation of Cultures* (New York: Basic Books), 1973.

88. Taussig, *Shamanism, Colonialism, and the Wild Man*.

89. As Victor Turner suggested in his "Social Dramas and Stories about Them," *Critical Inquiry* 7, no. 10 (1980): 141–68, ceremonies have illustrative purposes; rituals, instead, have transformative effects.

90. Ibid., 163.

91. Here I draw on Michel Foucault's notion of heterotopia as an "other" place—that is, a segregated spatiality that helps compensate a society's needs, crises, and desires. Michel Foucault, "Of Other Spaces," in *The Visual Culture Reader*, ed., Nicholas Mirzoeff (New York: Routledge, 1998), 237–44.

92. David Perlmutter and Gretchen L. Wagner, "The Anatomy of a Photojournalistic Icon: Marginalization of Dissent in the Selection and Framing of 'A Death in Genoa,'" *Visual Communication* 3, no. 1 (2004): 91–108; Nancy Snow, "Framing Globalization and Media Strategies for Global Change," in Opel and Pompper, *Representing Resistance*, 108–14.

93. Della Porta and Reiter, *Polizia e protesta*, 113. Aside from beating whomever they encountered, the police who irrupted into the Diaz school also destroyed all of the Indymedia computers, camcorders, and equipment that contained images and testimonials of the abuses perpetrated throughout the summit, a behavior that critics interpreted as the attempt to eliminate evidence of state repression.

94. In 2010 the conservative government, led once again by Silvio Berlusconi and Gianfranco Fini, refused to ratify the suspension of the high-ranking police officers who had been found guilty at the trial for the raid on the Diaz school. In 2012, however, twenty-five police officers were found guilty by the Court of Cassation, and the victims were entitled to damages. Yet the latter were to be paid not by the perpetrators, but rather by the state on the basis of a recently approved ad hoc law. As to the tortures in the Bolzaneto barracks, forty-four defendants were found guilty during the appeal. These crimes, however, may become statute-barred before the final Corte d'Assise trial is held.

95. Jeffrey S. Juris, "Violence Performed and Imagined: Militant Action, the Black Bloc, and the Mass Media in Genoa," *Critique of Anthropology* 25, no. 4 (2005): 413–32.

96. Federico Fubini, "Il prezzo di Genoa lo stiamo pagando anzitutto in Europa," *Limes* 4 (2001): 85–99; Matteo Colombi, "L'Italia intravista dagli Usa: piuttosto illiberale e totalmente ininfluente," *Limes* 4 (2001): 99–106.

97. Agamben, *State of Exception*.

98. Huizinga, *Homo Ludens*, 8.

99. The "apart together" quotation is from Huizinga, *Homo Ludens*, 12. To some extent the placelessness imposed on Genoa by the Italian state was mirrored by the degree of abstraction that this city took on in the collective imaginary of global social movements. In post-2001 resistive narratives, "Genoa" frequently became a time-space coordinate fully defined by state repression (see, for example, Juris, *Networking Futures*, 194, 169). Many of the Genoese I interviewed, however, take exception to this categorization. Not only do they resist the reduction of the spaces of their everyday life to a theater of brutality, but they also find that such a designation complies with the conservative government's intent to mar Genoa's image as a traditionally left-wing city. As one man put it:

When I say I am from Genoa people look at me and say "oh, that's awful!" I had friends [from another city] visit a couple of months ago, and all they wanted to see was Piazza Alimonda [where Carlo Giuliani was killed] and the Diaz school. This makes me very angry. . . . At the end of World War II, Genoa was the only Italian city that did not need to be liberated from the Fascist, because it liberated itself, and this is why it earned a Gold Medal for Anti-Fascist Resistance [*medaglia d'oro alla resistenza*]. The 1960 Genoa riots caused the [conservative] Tambroni government to fall after it had permitted a neo-Fascist rally here. Tambroni wanted to stick it up to the Genoese, but we didn't allow him to. What happened with the 2001 G8 [repression] has been a revenge of the Italian right against a city that has always been on the left [di sinistra].

While more research is needed on this topic, the ethnographic component of this essay is meant to acknowledge those publics who, living in locations that become theaters of highly divisive events, feel stifled by how dominant and resistive narratives coalesce in defining their cities.

100. Cheryl Mattingly, "Reading Minds and Telling Tales in a Cultural Borderland," *Ethos* 36, no. 1 (2008): 145.

101. On the state reclaiming its monopoly over violence, see Max Weber, *Politics as a Vocation* (Minneapolis: Fortress Press, 1965). On suspension of law, see Agamben, *Homo Sacer*; Agamben, *State of Exception*.

4.

Eating Ethnicity: Spatial Ethnography of Hyderabad House Restaurant on Devon Avenue, Chicago

ARIJIT SEN

In 2006 an item in the *Chicago Tribune* announced the closing of Hyderabad House, an ethnic restaurant located on Devon Avenue, a popular and crowded retail street on the northern edge of the metropolis. The heart of a diverse and ever changing immigrant community, Devon Avenue is well known for its Indian, Pakistani, and Bangladeshi stores. Frequent visitors know that ethnic restaurants appear and disappear with regularity on this retail strip, so the only remarkable thing about the *Tribune*'s report was its vivid description of the health hazards in the establishment:

> A restaurant on Devon Avenue, a stretch well-known for its global cuisine, was closed Thursday after inspectors found insects, mouse droppings and food held at dangerous temperatures.
>
> The city's Dumpster Task Force visited the Hyderabad House, 2225 W. Devon Ave., after receiving complaints about rodents, but soon found it was a "minefield" of food safety problems, said Matt Smith, spokesman for the Department of Streets and Sanitation.
>
> In addition to finding more than 60 mouse droppings in the kitchen food prep area, inspectors found more than 200 live and dead flying insects, many of them on the front windows and in the dining area.[1]

Following the Dumpster Task Force's visit, the restaurant remained closed for a few days. But soon it was back in business, and not much had changed in 2011 when Misty Tosh and her friend celebrated the dive in the online Chicago magazine *CenterStage*:[2]

We both strolled into Hyderabad full of trash-talkin' attitude. If the cabbies loved it, then so would we. We silently screeched to a halt, inhaling the no-frills, paint-peeling atmosphere, and I quickly scanned the menu written on a dry erase board (and partially erased). What did it all mean? Every dish contained a new word, and we quizzed each other on what everything could possibly mean. The prices were so low, though, so I just set to ordering. . . .

We watched a steady stream of traffic—traditionally dressed families, neighboring auto repair customers and downtrodden degenerates alike—make their way to the front counter to order, while we scooped up big spoon-fuls of fragrant *biryani*. So, this is the world famous *biryani*, eh? Something like a poor man's paella.[3]

Hyderabad House's "no-frills, paint-peeling atmosphere" doesn't sur-prise the regular customers. Many associate its interior ambience with its less well-to-do customers and cheap food. The restaurant is well known as a cabbie hangout. As one visitor observed, "If you're not a cab driver don't bother visiting. I was there once and was waiting for an order and [a] violent argument broke out between waiter and one customer, though no punches were thrown. . . . The place caters to cab drivers, not families."[4]

The three descriptions of Hyderabad House listed above—as a health risk, an ethnic dive, or a cabbie haunt—render three popular images of this restaurant. The account of the health inspectors paints a picture of unsan-itary conditions and is part of the city of Chicago's constant struggle to enforce orderliness and cleanliness in immigrant-owned restaurants along Devon Avenue. This struggle has led the city to create laws against food carts and sidewalk sales of food, as well as intensive oversight of ethnic restau-rants.[5] The city's enforcement attempts against Hyderabad House and other restaurants reflect a desire to maintain surveillance, order, and health in these privately owned spaces.

A focus on the battle over the restaurant's hygiene, however, obscures more interesting inquiries that might be made regarding the restaurant as a public space. What role does the restaurant serve in maintaining the culture and cultural memory of its immigrant clientele? How does the space cre-ate different experiences for in-group and out-group members? Can the very characteristics that make some visitors uncomfortable serve to make others feel at home?

Hyderabad House is one of many Muslim-owned South Asian ethnic res-taurants in the West Ridge and West Rogers Park neighborhoods. Reviews of this restaurant on culinary websites reiterate that most customers experience the interior ambience of this space as very different from other mainstream restaurants in the city. Some immigrants review it nostalgically, as a space that reminds them of home, while others find it exotic, cluttered, and filthy.[6] This restaurant serves local South Asian residents and practicing Muslims. Muslim cab drivers of all national origins know that they can get halal food in this restaurant.[7] By serving regional cuisine, Hyderabad House claims a particular clientele within the larger South Asian immigrant population, but at the same time additional storefront signage attracts customers belonging to other regional and ethnic groups by advertising more generic Indo-Pak cuisine.[8] In addressing such a diverse constituency Hyderabad House mediates the expectations of its regular clients even while responding to the need to diversify as dictated by the marketplace.

Hyderabad House is part of an everyday landscape of working-class men in the neighborhood and also a gendered space where single men and families eat in separate locations. Misty Tosh's description posits the ethnic restaurant as an experience that goes beyond the gastronomic. Being in an "ethnic dive" is an edgy, urban encounter of a world that is very different from her world. Hyderabad House holds different meanings for different individuals and different social groups and reproduces multiple worlds inside a single space.

Visitors' experiences of Hyderabad House represent what B. Joseph Pine and James H. Gilmore call an experience economy.[9] The rationale for studying the experience economy of such a place lies in its banality. Hyderabad House is neither an extraordinary example of architecture nor a unique urban restaurant. Yet the experience of being in this place is unlike that of being in any so-called mainstream restaurant. This simultaneous commonplaceness (as a typical, cramped, ethnic cabbie dive) and exoticness (ethnic, South Asian, "Every dish contained a new word") makes Hyderabad House an important case study; this place tells us how "difference" is reproduced and consumed in American cities.

Ethnic places such as Hyderabad House are more than brick-and-mortar buildings that can be described easily with unanimous agreement. Understanding such a site is a hermeneutic act that demands a careful disentangling of the complicated material, experiential, psychological, social, cultural, political, and economic readings of this place. Even though the location is the same, these varying descriptions paint a range of images of place. Understanding Hyderabad House, then, requires that we interpret how users perceive the restaurant. That is a methodological task.

This chapter explores how a method called "spatial ethnography" can help us read places like Hyderabad House. Spatial ethnography is an interpretive method that combines analysis of artifacts (buildings, streets, furniture, and other forms of material culture) with ethnographic and observational accounts of how people use and give meaning to these artifacts. Spatial ethnography allows us to explore aspects of human culture that may not be available only through written, material culture, or oral evidence. Much of my current and previous research involves detailed documentation and spatial ethnographies of immigrant spaces.[10] Through observations, some based on my personal familiarity with such spaces, I seek to document these locations. I also conduct interviews with immigrant store owners, South Asian–born and native-born customers, community leaders, and local residents. I pose questions to them about their experiences and interpretations of these spaces.[11] I scan discussions and reviews in newspapers and on websites.

For instance, when employed at the intimate scale of an individual body and near environment, this method focuses on a study of corporeal and embodied experiences and affective responses of humans to their physical environment. Such a focus opens up a world of meanings and symbolisms that may not be immediately visible and obvious. This microscopic case study of Hyderabad House tests spatial ethnography as a useful method to study multicultural spaces. It seeks to uncover how the varied experiences of this restaurant by individuals from different backgrounds sustain many social worlds in a single location. Spatial ethnography seeks to shed light on the many creative and agile ways in which individuals reproduce culture. It allows us to examine how individuals maintain complex identities and backgrounds but also retain the freedom to move between them.

Hyderabad on Devon: A Restaurant on a Street

A study of Hyderabad House has wide implications. This restaurant represents a node within multiple intersecting and expansive systems of ethnic restaurants, businesses, and social spaces that crisscross the world, marking places where the South Asian diaspora has arrived. It is a node within a complex "foodway," a term that Patricia Harris and her colleagues define as "everything about eating—including what we consume, how we acquire it, who prepares it and who's at the table . . . a form of communication rich with meaning. Our attitudes, practices and rituals around food are a window onto our most basic beliefs about the world and ourselves."[12] This discussion of Hyderabad House is part of a larger urban investigation of Muslim ethnic landscapes along Devon Avenue.[13]

Devon Avenue is a perfect example of a multiethnic retail street.[14] Typically such streets include dense rows of multistoried, mixed-use buildings occupied by subsequent waves of new immigrants, for whom this street becomes the initial launching pad into American society. Compact in scale, Devon Avenue is characterized by narrow sidewalks and long and thin lot sizes. One- or two-storied buildings with residences on the upper floors and stores at street level line these thoroughfares. The stores sell ethnic wares and display a profusion of signage, unique smells and sounds, and a cacophony of colors, advertisements, and imagery on their storefronts. The streets are crowded and lack parking. So powerful is this image of an ethnic retail street in American culture that neighborhood organizations and merchant groups have actively reproduced this image in order to encourage tourism.[15] Although the visual character of Devon Avenue is not as exotic and touristic as Chinatown, local merchants and the West Ridge Chamber of Commerce advertise this street as Chicago's "international marketplace." They sell street banners inscribed in many languages spoken in the area, such as Hebrew, Arabic, Urdu, Hindi, Assyrian, English, and Korean.[16]

To call this street an "international marketplace" or "Little India" is to reduce the complexity of this environment and popularize a single story of this place. The buildings and the street stand as testimony to a more diverse history. German and Irish immigrants built many of the stores, restaurants, and other buildings on this street.[17] Jewish families moved into the area after World War II to the neighborhoods between Damen and Kedzie Avenues, and by 1963 there were approximately forty-eight thousand Jews in the West Rogers Park area.[18] Advertisements and painted signs of old Jewish delis still exist on side walls of buildings as spectral remains of a long-gone past. Since the late 1980s the now-aging Jewish residents and their children began moving to suburban locations such as Skokie, Buffalo Grove, Highland Park, and Deerfield and newer immigrants moved in. The newcomers were immigrants of South Asian origin: Indians and Pakistanis who set up businesses that catered to an ethnic clientele.[19] These stores were interspersed amid preexisting Jewish and nonethnic businesses, creating a checkered multicultural street fabric. Although the South Asian stores are denser between California and Western Avenues, this heterogeneous ethnic geography made up of interspersed South Asian, Jewish, Anglo-American, and Latino-owned stores continues to define the character of this street.[20]

By the 1990s the initial wave of South Asian immigrants moved out.[21] Many store owners who lived in the neighborhood or above their stores rented out their residences and moved to middle-class suburbs. Recent arrivals moved into these rental apartments, changing the ethnic demography of the street. During the late 1990s Muslim immigrants from Bangladesh,

Pakistan, and India began settling in this neighborhood.[22] New stores and services catering to the new residents appeared on the scene. In proximity to Devon Avenue, centers of Islamic worship developed to cater to residents.[23] Other services catering to local Muslim residents, including legal firms, Islamic bookstores, Islamic schools, halal produce stores, women's and children's services, and restaurants with prayer spaces, appeared in the neighborhood.[24] Applying the misnomer "Little India" to Devon Avenue therefore renders invisible this demographic and historical diversity.

Chinatown is like Disneyland in comparison—tourists in Chinatown know what to expect and aren't confused; store owners neatly package cultural diversity for consumption by tourists. Devon Avenue doesn't allow for that neat, preprogrammed experience, which is why a careful reading—"thick description," as Clifford Geertz would characterize it—of the visual, textual, and experiential cues is key to understanding the street.[25]

"Thick Description": Spatial and Behavioral Analysis of Hyderabad House

Across the street from the original Hyderabad House restaurant is Hyderabad House Family Dining restaurant, which caters to women, children, and families. Although belonging to the same owner, the two restaurants communicate distinct messages to their different customers. The physical separation of one restaurant into two separate buildings in order to serve very different kinds of customers provides a perfect opportunity to compare the nuanced spatial order within each restaurant and see how they produce different worlds. A comparison at this near-environment level allows us to see how the kinesthetic, experiential, multisensory, and affective qualities of place produce myriad senses of being and belonging in this space.

The original Hyderabad House restaurant is a typical example of an inventive reuse of a preexisting building along Devon Avenue (figure 4.1).[26] In the past this building was used as a gas station and auto repair shop. The interior layout, building structure, and material details closely follow gas station prototypes across the Greater Chicago region. The building has a chamfered entrance to a convenience store located in one wing of the building, while the auto repair shop is entered through another door. Today the convenience store part of the building has been converted into the restaurant; the auto repair area remains as it was in the past. The buildings overlook an elongated concrete parking lot across the entire block. A low wall currently separates the parking lot of the auto repair shop from that of the restaurant. Customers of

Figure 4.1. Original Hyderabad House restaurant, view from Devon Avenue. Photo by author.

the repair shop use both parking lots, but Hyderabad House customers and cab drivers get priority access to the parking spaces in front of the restaurant.

The Hyderabad House Family Dining restaurant across Devon Avenue from the original Hyderabad House occupies a corner storefront of a three-storied apartment building (figure 4.2). The storefront has a diagonal (typical corner store) entrance. The interior space occupies two adjacent premises—the corner store and an adjacent mid-lot retail space. The two upper stories of the building, above the restaurant, house rental apartments. A glass door in the middle of the block serves as an entrance to the upstairs apartments. At the very end of the block is the Youmax liquor and grocery store, an odd neighbor to a Muslim-owned family restaurant.

A common refrain from many I interviewed was that the interior of the original Hyderabad House is "cluttered" whereas the Hyderabad House Family Dining décor is appropriate and clean.[27] Shoppers explain the term "clutter" in different ways. For some it is the cacophony of signage and visual images, while for others the term refers to things out of place—garbage, plastic bags, and objects left on sidewalks.[28] Others mention the stacking of furniture, cheap silverware, crowded interiors, and piled-up objects. Some equate clutter with a lack of cleanliness and health, stained interiors, greasy food, and health inspector reprimands. Almost all agree that the original

Figure 4.2. Hyderabad House Family Dining restaurant, view from Devon Avenue. Photo by author.

Hyderabad House interior is cluttered; however, not everyone finds it disorderly. To male immigrants from the subcontinent, the interior ambiance is informal, familiar, and therefore preferred. Some appreciate the "cacophony of information" on the façade walls and are attracted by the graffiti; others fondly remember similarities with low-cost, roadside restaurants (*dhabas*) in the Indian subcontinent.

Much of the following interpretation of the two restaurants depends on observable human behavior and spatial rhythms. In Hyderabad House I examined how customers experienced the interior spaces, how they walked through them, and what they saw and felt. I carefully observed the kinds of customers who used the restaurant at different times of the day and interviewed them to find out how they occupied and understood this place.

At early dawn, when most neighbors are fast asleep, the original Hyderabad House restaurant opens its doors to serve piping-hot breakfast to middle-age and elderly Muslim men returning from their morning prayers. A bit later, after sunrise, early-shift cab drivers park their cabs and scurry into the restaurant to pick up tea and some food. Occasionally newcomers, all bachelors, emerge from nearby rental apartment buildings in search of breakfast. Fried dumplings in lentil soup (*vada sambar*), sweet cream-of-wheat puddings (*shira*), and other South Indian breakfast food not on the regular menu are served to these morning customers. During Ramadan, the holy month of daytime fasting, the use and rhythms of the restaurant change.[29] Crowds gather for late dinner, and *suhoor* breakfast is served before dawn. During the rest of the year, the family restaurant really fills up during dinnertime on weekends, while the original Hyderabad House remains open all day and night long for hungry cab drivers.

A careful study of human engagement with objects in these restaurants shows us that immigrants appropriate buildings they inherited from the past in creative and culturally inflected ways. They mark their stores and communicate with their customers using signs, banners, pamphlets, and posters. They transform the interiors, sometimes momentarily, through visual markings, framed images, air conditioning or noisy fans, and through transient behavior, protean performances, and momentary activities. By merely changing the signage, visual and spatial order, layout and interior sequence of spaces or by altering behavior, immigrants seamlessly transform the nature and character of these spaces. The following sections compare the experience of encountering, entering, and ordering food in the two Hyderabad House restaurants in order to understand how individuals interact with the building in three sequential acts.

Locating the Building

The name Hyderabad House and the signboards on the building façade send diverse messages to different constituencies. The name of the restaurant—Hyderabad House—points toward a regional subculture within the South Asian subcontinent. The city of Hyderabad is in the southern province of Sind in Pakistan. There are two settlements named Hyderabad in India, too: a metropolitan city in the southern state of Andhra Pradesh and a small town in the northern state of Uttar Pradesh. The restaurant on Devon Avenue is known among local South Asians as a place where one may get the regional specialties of the Andhra Pradesh metropolis. The name of a restaurant may be the first draw for customers and certainly a way to advertise the business. There are potential drawbacks, however, if the food doesn't rise to the expectations based on name recognition. As one unhappy customer complained, "The only reason I tried this place [was] because the sign said 'Hyderabad' biryani. Any biryani connoisseur will agree that Hyderabad biryani is the best. I was totally disappointed."[30]

Identifying the variety of signs can be informative for researchers. Pylon signs are tall, freestanding signs. Monument signs are shorter freestanding signs, rare on Devon Street. Projecting signs, pylon signs, and monument signs are generally permanent, indicating a business that has been there for a long time. Wall signs are located on the storefronts and façades and they change often. In general wall signage includes awning signs, wall posters and window signs, flat acrylic store names and board signs, and projecting signs.

The façade of the building is often the first thing a potential customer sees. But what one sees depends on point of view. Pedestrians encounter this restaurant differently from people driving by. Like neighboring stores, the original Hyderabad House and the new Hyderabad House Family Dining sport large storefront signage. The pylon sign for the original Hyderabad House is a remainder from the past. It communicates to those traveling in automobiles, as the large print on the pylon signs and on the wall stating, "Hyderabad House Restaurant" and "Dankha Auto-Repairs," are easy to read.

The original Hyderabad House has smaller wall signs, too, certainly many more than those found on the new Hyderabad House Family Dining façade. Wall signs produce a more fine-grained reading. Wall signs are one of the most popular types of signage on Devon, and they communicate best with pedestrians. They are not big enough to be legible from a fast-moving automobile. Hyderabad House has a smaller, acrylic sign, too. That sign says that the restaurant serves Indian and Pakistani cuisine—a more generic characterization of the cuisine aimed at wider non–South Asian customer base.

Window signs immediately below and beside the acrylic sign communicate more to those who are conversant with regional Indian cuisine. A brightly colored window sign lists a daily menu with regional delicacies not found in other North Indian and Pakistani restaurants. The section titled *meetha* advertises sweets and desserts while the section *parata* offers an inventory of flatbreads.[31] On the top, painted along the parapet—ostensibly for local residents and those returning from morning prayers mentioned earlier—is another sign that lists South Indian delicacies such as *idli, vada, dosa, upma,* and *puri* served 8 to 11 AM for breakfast.[32]

For those who may not be familiar with South Asian regional food, the poster on the door—lowest in the visual frame—borrows from fast-food franchises by listing numbered meals (#1–#10) with a photograph of the food accompanying the prices. These sign menus are hardly visible from the street; they are meant for customers standing in the parking lot.

The façade of Hyderabad House Family Dining restaurant serves as an exercise in total contrast. A series of formal green awnings has "Hyderabad

House Family Dining LLC" written in bold sans serif font. The narrow band below carries the words "Dine-In, Carry-Out & Catering" and a phone number. A potential customer driving by doesn't need to stop. She can remember the carry-out phone number and dial in at her leisure.

In contrast to the cluttered signage on the entrance to the original Hyderabad House, the new family restaurant is marked by a lack of signage on its windows. The only prominent sign is one posted on top of the entrance door located on the chamfered street corner wall; it says *Bismillahir Rahmanir Rahim* (in the name of Allah the most beneficent, the merciful). All may not understand this intricate Arabic script, but it stands out, signifying difference and Islam, even to outsiders. The sign is not immediately visible from the automobile, but is clearly seen by pedestrians entering the restaurant. On both sides of the inscriptions are quotes *mash'a Allah* (all praise to Allah, written in both Arabic and English). The entrance sign placed symmetrically over the door sanctifies, marks, and identifies the restaurant space, its Islamic credentials clearly communicated to the customers. Its prominent, yet odd, location makes the customer crane her neck up to see it, an unrehearsed momentary act of looking up and reading a verse in praise of God. Then as the customer steps through the double doors, a brightly lit and clean interior grabs her attention.

The distinction between the first sight of the original Hyderabad House and Hyderabad House Family Dining speaks to the different clientele the two restaurants attract. The working-class men and cab drivers frequent the original Hyderabad House restaurant, making this a more male space. They move in and out with speed and efficiency. The filled parking lot of the original restaurant, the prominent signs of the auto repair store, and the high metal fence are visible from passing automobiles. In contrast, pedestrians find the family restaurant easily. The green awnings, the closeness to the sidewalk, and the long frontage render Hyderabad House Family Dining highly visible and certainly more accessible from the street.[33]

Entering the Restaurant

A door at the center of the original Hyderabad House front wall is not the main entrance. This door opens directly into the kitchen. Often the cooks emerge from this door to hang out, socialize, and smoke with cab drivers and those waiting to pick up food. The plethora of images on the wall and two doors make these entrances invisible to a new customer approaching the restaurant on foot. Instead, the main entrance, with its makeshift frame

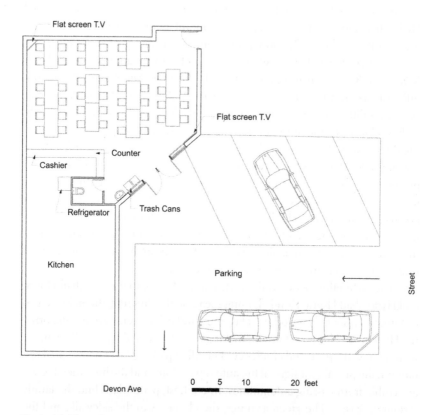

Figure 4.3. Floor plan: Original Hyderabad House. Line drawing by Sohail Kurram.

covered in maroon-colored canvas, stands out. One enters it sideways, barely slipping into the harshly fluorescent-lit interior. A second entrance located at the far end of the restaurant (along the chamfered entrance of the original gas station) opens directly into the car repair shop parking lot, allowing direct entry options for cab drivers (figure 4.3).

Irrespective of the time of day, the canvas entrance into the original Hyderabad House restaurant produces a sharp transition. As they step into the dining space, customers find a jarring contrast from the outdoors because of the harshness of the fluorescent interior lights. To some cab drivers I spoke with, the fluorescent lights remind them of cheap dining rooms in India.[34] One customer remembers the flickering fluorescent lights in low-cost Mumbai restaurants depicted in many Bollywood movies. Most South Asian–born customers felt an uncanny sense of familiarity that affectively produced a bodily and emotional response of recognition.[35] Interviewees used spatial metaphors—Bollywood movie set, a cheap dhaba, or "Indian Railways canteen"—as they described what they felt.[36]

Only later, during further probing, was I able to associate specific spatial descriptors to these evocative imageries. The customers were not using terms such as "scale," "light," or "layout" to describe the restaurant. Indeed, they neither experienced nor remembered places via those categories. They were describing a more holistic sensorium that could be rendered only through comparisons and metaphors. Their engagement with the building was more affective and less cognitively deciphered. For instance, in order to understand their references—such as the one about restaurants in Mumbai—one has to actually experience such a place, either in real life or in cinematic representations. One needed no words to recognize these spaces. A common affective experience defined who belonged to an in-group. But along with these images, respondents also remembered associated events and emotions—"the time I went to the movies with my mother"; "the scene when an actor kissed his beau in such a restaurant." Thus descriptions were not just spatial but also memorable, anecdotal, and episodic.

The original Hyderabad House is no fancy sit-down restaurant and it certainly feels different. The missing ceiling tiles; the damp, stained patches marking water leakage; the old wallpaper strip along the ceiling; the pickle containers lining the front counter; the flat-screen television looping loud Bollywood movie songs; and the plastic covers over fabric tablecloths can be intimate and familiar to some but tacky, dirty, noisy and "low-class" to others.[37] A white board above the counter lists a handwritten menu, difficult to read. A large red sign directs clients to order at the counter. The first response for a South Asian middle-class woman is that this is a cheap restaurant not appropriate for a formal dinner and an "unhygienic" one, too.[38] Another customer reflected in an online review, "This place is absolute cheap—Plates, water and ambience is unhygenic, would say this restaurant is disgrace on name of Hyderabadi biryani."[39]

There is a complex sense of time inside the restaurant. On the one hand is the hurried and immediate nature of transactions: cab drivers rushing in between shifts; carry-out customers waiting on the edge of the seats, not quite comfortable; and waiters making quick rounds to pick up the used plates.

On the other hand, the framed images on the wall are strategically chosen to display what Michael Herzfeld calls "monumental time."[40] Large images of architectural sites from South Asia adorn the walls. One can't help but scrutinize these images as he waits. Minarets, domes, and scalloped arches mark the Islamic architectural styles. Many of these images are those of mosques and tombs, official forms of national architecture. They perform mnemonic acts connecting individuals to a national memory. But these images are more than officially sanctioned references to a nation. Here they act as imagery that reproduces a sense of the familiar. Ensconced in the heart of Chicago, these images recreate an alternative safe space for members of the Pakistani community.

Writing about a set of images of "the Turkish House," Carel Bertram describes how visual imagery reproduces a "spiritually symbolic space of collective memory" that "as a sign that encoded what was felt to be at risk in this changing universe . . . became a memory-image charged with carrying old, outdated, and even forbidden ideas into the present, and even into the future."[41] Within the context of America, these Islamic monuments may not be recognizable to all, but their architecture is familiar. For a South Asian immigrant, crossing over into the dining hall of the original Hyderabad House and seeing these framed images is akin to stepping into a recreated safe, familiar, and informal space—a home turf of an imagined community, intimately encouraging a spontaneous remembering of homeland.

The spatial characteristics described above can make the restaurant interior seem unappealing to clients like Krsna V. from Chicago, who writes, "Dirty place and mediocre food. The only reason I tried this place because the sign said 'Hyderabad' biryani . . . I think the dept. of public health closed this place a while ago for health code violations. They may have reopened after that incident but, I will stay away."[42] To cosmopolitans slumming in culinary dives, this edginess was a draw: "i think across the street, there's a cleaned up version of this place. my friends, because we're all adventurers, chose the dirty, ramshackle option."[43] These different interpretations of the same space are central to reproduction and maintenance of social boundaries. Recognition or alienation allows users to actively align themselves as members of in- or out-groups. Belonging is experienced and performed in embodied forms.

Hyderabad House Family Dining, across the street, provides a different experience of time and place (figure 4.4). Upon stepping into the restaurant one confronts a tidy space that is brightly lit with natural light from the windows and warm filament light fixtures on the ceiling. The parquet

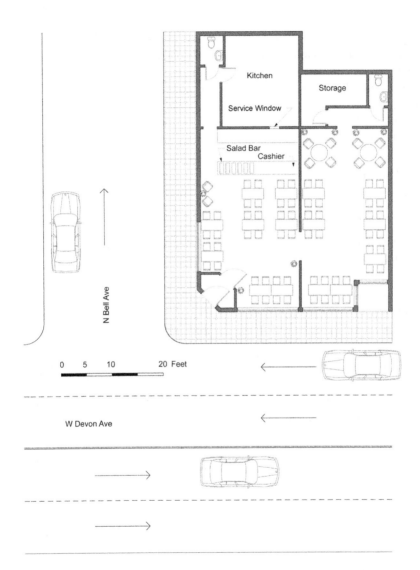

Hyderabad House Family Restaurant

Kitchen

Storage

Service Window

Salad Bar
Cashier

N Bell Ave

0   5   10   20 Feet

W Devon Ave

Figure 4.4. Floor plan: Hyderabad House Family Dining. Line drawing by Sohail Kurram.

floors are shiny, as are the cushioned chairs. The tables, spaciously laid out, have white tablecloths, metal silverware, and glass tabletops. The glass adds to the reflective quality of the space ("a little too shiny, reveal[ing] its cheapness," as one customer muttered to me). The framed images on the wall are modern abstract artwork of flowers, leaves, and plants. One sees the buffet containers on the front counter at the far end of the room. Menus, interior plants, and a bowl of anise seed mouth freshener are the only objects on the uncluttered counter. An attendant manning the counter welcomes a newcomer and takes reservations. Those who ordered takeout may choose to wait in the front room, while those wishing to be seated are usually taken into the back room if there is space.

The Hyderabad House Family Dining restaurant interior combines two adjacent spaces. A front room is separated from the back room by a portal. The back room is cozy and narrow. It is visually inaccessible from the front room, creating a sense of intimacy and privacy that is appreciated by large families.[44] The back room fits ten tables for families with children. The women's restroom is located at the back of this room.

A family restaurant is not merely a space where women, children, and families eat. In the context of Hyderabad House, the family restaurant is a space that appeals not just to women but also to middle-class customers, a place where one need not share space with the cab driver. Most importantly, this is not a space that carries the embodied and affective connotations of the dhaba or the Mumbai stalls described earlier, and it certainly does not impose the memories and events that, for the in-group, are inextricably linked with those locations. Saleem from Miami explains, "If you've got a wife/girlfriend, do not take her here [the original Hyderabad House], take her across the street to the family-oriented Hyderabad House. You'll know what I'm talking about when you do yourself a favor and hook it up with that masala chai."[45] Taking a wife and girlfriend out on a date and then "hooking" it up with the taste of *masala chai* allows Saleem to be cosmopolitan and ethnic at the same time.[46] It allows customers to participate and move among multiple worlds simultaneously, a condition that is comparable to one that Sharon Zukin refers to as "consuming authenticity."[47] This experience is important because it creates a controlled and sanitized space where users can experience just enough ethnic difference (eating food) without being corporeally present with a sensorium that is marked by signs of class, gender, and taste.

Ordering and Eating

Seating is first-come, first-serve at the original Hyderabad House. But before a customer seats himself, he has to order at the counter. The ordering process is usually difficult for those who are not familiar with the food, since the menu is handwritten on a white board with no descriptive explanation of the dishes. A customer notes: "The menu is relatively short, though also difficult to make out as it is scribbled out (and partially erased) on a white board behind the cash register. Each meal comes with an extensive array of plates and bowls. Five came out with my chicken masala ($8): a plate with sliced cucumber and onion, a bowl of large greasy chunks of chicken, a bowl of soup, a heaping pile of long rice and a side of what looked and tasted like wheat tortillas."[48]

The clerk at the counter is busy, constantly serving takeout customers at the back door, chatting with the kitchen staff, or directing the server to tables. He has less time to explain or chat with new customers, especially when it is crowded, often seeming surly and unsocial as a result. Cathy B. from Illinois reported: "Went with Indian friends I know. (And, please keep in mind that I am pretty familiar with Indian food, having eaten much of it on the sub-continent itself.) This place was not the bomb it was presented to me as being. Surly staff. Mysterious ordering system . . . I was glad to leave."[49] The "mysterious ordering system" and "surly staff" comment suggest that Cathy found the dining experience of the original Hyderabad House strange and certainly undesirable. But unlike the host in a regular restaurant, who may only take orders and seat customers, the person at the counter in Hyderabad House actually does more: he takes orders, remembers who ordered what, and mentally maps where they are seated. At the end of the meal customers walk up to the counter to pay for what they ate. The clerk always, without fail, remembers the order and the owed amount. Angelo explains, "Once you eat here a few times the staff will warm up to you and treat you like family. Definitely recommended for a late night bite!"[50] It is a kind of sociability that Cathy B. fails to recognize.

Food is served with paper napkins, cheap silverware, white ceramic ware, pebbled heavy plastic tumblers, and foil-wrapped baskets. The slightly sticky plastic cover on the tables reveals the grease that collects. Roughly cut onions and cucumber that accompany the food are typical extras for meat dishes, but unlike Hyderabad House Family Dining, here they are not garnished and arranged aesthetically.

At Hyderabad House Family Dining the customer is given a bill, and the payment ritual preceding the customer's leaving of the restaurant resembles that of any other restaurant. Food served in wicker baskets lined with paper, cloth napkins, and heavy clear glass tumblers make the dining experience distinct from that of the original Hyderabad House. Since the same person owns both restaurants, the two forms of presentation and sociability are intentionally reproduced to recreate varying spatial ambience.

A visit to the restroom in the original Hyderabad House is a reminder that distinct cultural practices influence the sense of place. Many South Asians use the plastic watering pot with a long spout for ablutions. The restroom floor in Hyderabad House is often wet. South Asian immigrants talk of an affective response to this space—it reminds them of restrooms in South Asia. The space also reminds them of shared cultural practices, even if they do not use the watering pot. In comparison, the restrooms at the Hyderabad House Family Dining restaurant do not produce the same affective response. They have the same objects, but the employees keep the neatly tiled floors clean and dry. Ensuring that the floor is dry is necessary because the Family Dining restaurant is designed to cater to a more general and wider clientele, and wet restroom floors would not be acceptable to non–South Asians.

A Pakistani customer at the Hyderabad House Family Dining restaurant complains, "We went to their new family resturant right across from the orignal one . . . The place have a weired smell too, but may be thats was the 'new resturant smell.'"[51] What he calls a "new resturant smell" was that of an odor-removing agent that the owners use in order to get rid of the very spice (cumin) smell that makes the restaurant on the other side of the street seem so informal and homelike to some.

At the original Hyderabad House one will find many patrons washing their hands in the wash sink placed outside the restroom, fully visible from the dining room. Since many of the customers eat curries and flatbread with their hands, as is customary and efficient with South Asian food, hand washing is a common practice. As a result the restaurant owner set up the sink outside the restroom, in a transition space near the entrance. Publicly washing one's hands at the end of the meal is a habitual ritual for many South Asians clients. The very visibility of this ritual in this space serves as reminder and reiteration of such habitual cultural practices. The affective responses and reactions of the customers to the interior environment of the original Hyderabad House and Hyderabad House Family Dining restaurant set the two spaces apart—like stages set up for specific embodied place experiences.

We Make Place and Place Makes Us

Urban sociologists have argued that a sudden popularity of ethnic restaurants reflects a search for an authentic experience of cultural diversity in the contemporary metropolis. Studies in New York, Cairo, Brussels, Quebec, and San Francisco have shown that we can observe a variety of social activities and a diversity of spaces inside ethnic hole-in-the-wall restaurants.[52] However, merely reading restaurants like Hyderabad House as spaces of culinary difference, as a locus of bootstrapping ethnic enterprise, or as working-class meeting spaces tells us a partial story. In addition to mere interpretive differences, the built environment accommodates multiple simultaneous worlds. These multiple worlds are not evident to all, because they are not always visible. Sometimes they are experienced by nonvisual cues.

As discussed above, embodied experiences of place help maintain these many simultaneous worlds inside Hyderabad House. Individuals experience the architecture of this ethnic restaurant through their senses, emotions, and prior cultural knowledge. Users respond to interior layout and spatial organization, façade decorations, architectural style, the processional and sequential experience of the interiors, and volumetric qualities of space with their bodies. A customer's response to sounds, smells, and kinesthetic engagement creates a sense of place. Touch, texture, and prior memories remind users of worlds that lie waiting to be discovered. Their reactions are framed by associated and incorporated memories triggered when they see familiar cultural practices or smell recognizable odors. They display surprise, curiosity, and even alienation when they see something they do not recognize. They experience unique rhythms of bodily movement, what Pierre Bourdieu calls "tempo," as they use and interact with the physical space and other humans inside such spaces.[53] In other words, spatial order is cognitively deciphered by the users and affectively experienced by their corporeal bodies.

Restaurant users and owners strategically deploy these experiences in order to mark spatial and social boundaries inside the establishment. Boundary-marking strategies include using signs to mark building façades, laying out interior spaces in order to produce unique processional and sequential experiences, and reproducing legible front and invisible rear zones.

These spatial experiences inside Hyderabad House in turn influence the way we think of culture and identity. For instance, the repeated experiences of class and gender difference in the original Hyderabad House and the Hyderabad House Family Dining restaurant became habitual—we expect family dining spaces to look a particular way and a working-class dive to look differently. Abstract impressions become corporeal and incarnate. We expect authentic South Asian restaurants to smell, feel, and look a particular way. Even insiders—Muslims, Hyderabadis (people from Hyderabad), women, middle-class South Asians—agree on spatial conventions. As Nigel Rapport argues, such conventions provide a well-recognized syntax and cognitive structure for all—"a source of consistent, expectable, broad and immediate ways of knowing of the social world; a ready means by which to embody and express a multitude of complex emotions; a shortcut to generalities, to future possible regularities and uniformities."[54] The importance of Hyderabad House and restaurants like it lies in reproducing such conventions within our everyday world. This is the reason why ethnic South Asian restaurants along Devon Avenue—and indeed across the world—look, smell, and feel the same: cluttered and overwhelming.[55]

But these conventions are not static.[56] Rather they change over time and are often manipulated by individuals. Elsewhere I describe "creative dissonance," a creative and purposeful strategy used by immigrant store owners in order to reproduce stereotypical interiors and storefronts as branding, making their stores identifiable to a large body of customers.[57] The architectural features are fronts and props that trigger instant recognition and expectations, but back zones and unexpected uses and activities in these interiors are rendered invisible. Elsewhere I have shown how some restaurants double up as prayer spaces for practicing Muslims, yet most customers neither know nor see these spaces, because they don't expect to find them inside a restaurant.[58]

By focusing on the cognitive and emotional exchanges of the human body with material worlds we can add to our knowledge of the built world. In the past the dominant metaphor of language, grammar, and codes served useful in the so-called linguistic and sociolinguistic models of analysis. An added focus on the individual and the performative will help us understand the reflexive relationship between living subjects and their worlds.

Hyderabad House: An Example of a Multicultural Public Space

Why is it important to focus on the ephemeral and experiential qualities of ethnic spaces? First, such concerns often escape the critical gaze of scholars who study buildings and cultures.[59] Many tend to focus on authorship by documenting who built these.[60] Others focus on building types and formal patterns, thereby ignoring accounts of how individuals interpret and engage with the material world. Much of the scholarship on immigrant and ethnic landscapes in America consists of voluminous material on the identity of builders, technologies of construction, and building materials.[61] Scholars of the built environment use diffusion theories, theories of performance, or morphology to demonstrate how buildings are constructed and changed by cultural groups.[62] These scholars do not address what happens when the building's occupants change and new tenants use old sites.[63] There are few accounts of temporary transformations of buildings that, once users leave, revert to what was there before. Few analyze the embodied and affective qualities of placemaking.[64]

Second, the lens of embodied placemaking allows us to focus on these less examined aspects of how place influences one's sense of community and belonging. For instance, many interviewees suggested that the phrase "Family Dining" in the title of the newer Hyderabad House restaurant implied its status as an appropriate space for women and families.[65] The original Hyderabad House caters to bachelor, and predominantly working-class, male clients. "Family Dining" acts as a code suggesting where different social groups and genders should congregate. Most South Asian clients understand this code, and by subscribing to it they maintain culturally appropriate behavior and social boundaries. But many non–South Asians miss the message. For instance, Eric S. wrote about his embarrassment at Hyderabad House Family Dining: "We brought a couple of Kingfisher pint bottles with because we had read online that it was BYOB. Whoever wrote that is a jerk, because the place appears to be operated by Muslims—no alcohol allowed. I felt like a dumbass and apologized profusely, but all my embarrassment was washed away in the wake of the yummy food to follow."[66] Indeed, the "yummy food" and the sense of "feeling out of place" becomes the central attraction of this place for many non–South Asians. Anthropologist Miles Richardson notes in his studies of Costa Rican plazas that this "sense of being-in-place" and "being-out-of-place" are primal experiences that help humans reproduce identity and belonging.[67]

Third, the methods described in this chapter help us understand how banal places like Hyderabad House can become new forms of urban multicultural public spaces.[68] A true public space, borrowing from Hannah Arendt, displays two central qualities: appearance or visibility and a common shared nature.[69] As a meeting ground for a variety of people, Hyderabad House is an example of a truly public marketplace. It is a place where individuals belonging to different social groups and constituencies meet, see, and interact with each other. Yet as Arendt describes, "Though the common world is the common meeting ground of all, those who are present have different locations in it, and the location of one can no more coincide with the location of another than the location of two objects. Being seen and being heard by others derive their significance from the fact that everybody sees and hears from a different position."[70]

At Hyderabad House the notion of public space is very different from one that assumes commonality and unanimous identification by all—the so-called plazas and polis. Rather, public space takes the form of a ground of exchange where people sharing a common world also share this common "space of appearance," but from different perspectives.[71] Various social stakeholders come face-to-face with one another; customers and servers get to know each other at a more personal level as regular customers, friends, and neighbors. People coming from different social backgrounds of class, gender, language, religion, or ethnicity meet, see, and interact with each other. During such interactions, they participate in a public process of alignment and realignment, distinction, and differentiation. They delineate and maintain social boundaries and social belonging. Meeting members of the in-group reproduces a sense of communion and intimacy through the sharing of memories, behavior, cultural practices, experiences, and emotional responses to this place. But meeting strangers plays an equally important role: these public interactions sustain differences through alienation and alterity. By its very nature Hyderabad House becomes an example of a twenty-first-century urban multicultural public space.

NOTES

I thank Dr. Marcia Hermansen and Maribeth and Greg Brewer for help during my research. Funding from the University of Wisconsin–Milwaukee's Graduate School made the fieldwork possible. I am grateful to Chelsea Wait, Jennifer Morales, Marta Gutman, Louis Nelson, and anonymous readers who read and commented on multiple drafts of this article.

1. News Services, "Devon Ave. Eatery Closed for Safety Violations," *Chicago Tribune*, September 1, 2006, http://articles.chicagotribune.com/2006-09-01/news/0609010376 _1_safety-violations-inspectors-mouse-droppings.

2. Throughout this chapter, the original spelling, capitalization, and punctuation of visitors' informal restaurant reviews have been retained.

3. Misty Tosh, "Messing about at Hyderabad," *CenterStage Chicago*, April 7, 2008, http://www.centerstagechicago.com/restaurants/articles/raving-dish-hyderabad.html; italics in original. *Biryani* is a rice dish made of layers of cooked rice, meat, spices, and vegetables.

4. Zabihahtaster, Zabihah Restaurant Reviews, March 26, 2007, http://www .zabihah.com/d/Chicago+1242+Hyderabad-House.

5. No author, "Putting the Brakes on Food Trucks," *Chicago Tribune*, July 25, 2012, http://articles.chicagotribune.com/2012-07-25/news/ct-edit-trucks-20120725 _1_food-trucks-gps-spaces.

6. See reviews in Metromix.com and Chicagoreader.com: http://chicago .metromix.com/restaurants/indian/hyderabad-house-west-rogers-park-west/reader-review/136633/view#4c98feed0c407a062f0ac20b9039b073; http://www.chicago reader.com/chicago/hyderabad-house/Location?oid=1023789

7. Halal food is food that is permitted under Islamic dietary guidelines.

8. "Indo-Pak" is an abbreviated term referring to food originating from India and Pakistan.

9. B. Joseph Pine and James H. Gilmore, *The Experience Economy* (Boston: Harvard Business School Press, 1999).

10. Arijit Sen, "From Curry Mahals to Chaat Cafes: Spatialities of the South Asian Culinary Landscape," in *Curried Cultures*, ed. Tulasi Srinivasan and Krishnendu Ray (Berkeley: University of California Press, 2012), 196–218; Arijit Sen, "Creative Dissonance: Performance of Ethnicity in Banal Space," *InTensions* 2 (Spring 2009), http://www.yorku.ca/intent/issue2/articles/arijitsen.php; Arijit Sen, "Decoding Ethnicity in the Jackson Heights South Asian Shopping Strip," lecture presented at the Vernacular Architecture Forum Conference, New York City, June 2006; Arijit Sen, "Ethnicity in the City: Reading Representations of Cultural Difference in Indian Storefronts" in *City, Space + Globalization: An International Perspective. Proceedings of an International Symposium*, ed. Hemlata C. Dandekar (Ann Arbor, Mich.: College of Architecture and Urban Planning, 1998).

11. Interviews with community members of the South Asian community, February-March 2009. Also, I collected information during the "Devon Avenue Needs Assessment: A Smart Growth Strategy," a community workshop organized by West Rogers Park Community Organization and the South Asian American Policy and Research Institute (SAAPRI) on June 19, 2008, at the Indo American Community Center, Chicago.

12. Patricia Harris, David Lyon, and Sue McLaughlin, *The Meaning of Food* (Guilford, Conn.: Globe Pequot Press, 2005), viii-ix.

13. In 2009 I planned collaborations with Marcia Hermansen, director of the Islamic World Studies Program and professor in the theology department at Loyola University, Chicago. Hermansen studies mosques and prayer spaces in basements of stores, back rooms of restaurants, and makeshift spaces in residential units along Devon Avenue, Chicago. I was interested in the spatial order of the South Asian Muslim immigrant cultural landscape—and more particularly, the diverse lifeworlds reproduced by customers and clients of South Asian origin using these spaces. My examinations of how the built environment has the capacity to accommodate multiple lived worlds, coupled with Hermansen's oral histories, constitute the larger and ongoing "Muslim Devon Project."

14. Examples of such streets include those in New York's Lower East Side and Chicago's Lower West Side. There are similar streets in cities such as Los Angeles, Philadelphia, and Boston. These streets have catered to waves of multiethnic immigrant residents.

15. The best example can be seen in Chinatowns. Spatial markers with architectural features such as pagoda roofs, lantern-shaped ornaments, babel of "foreign" languages, crowded stores, and colorful storefronts with exotic merchandise have literally "branded" Chinatowns as archetypical spaces of difference. See Kay Anderson, *Vancouver's Chinatown: Racial Discourse in Canada, 1875–1980* (Montreal: McGill Queens University Press, 1995); Kay Anderson, "Otherness, Culture, and Capital: Chinatown's Transformation under Australian Multiculturalism," in *Multiculturalism: Postmodernism, Image, and Text*, ed. G. Clark, R. Francis, and D. Forbes (Melbourne: Longman Cheshire, 1993), 58–74; and Marilyn Halter, "Tourists 'R' Us: Immigrants, Ethnic Tourism, and the Marketing of Metropolitan Boston," in *Tourism, Ethnic Diversity, and the City*, ed. Jan Rath (New York: Routledge, 2007), 199–215.

16. The concept originated from Amie Zander, now the executive director of the chamber of commerce. She thought of it around 2005 when she began work in the organization. Soon local organizations and bodies came on board and the idea became popular. These banners are available for sponsorship by local businesses. They cost between $250 to $300 with a modest renewal fee. See West Ridge website at http://www.westridgechamber.org.

17. Jacque Day Archer and Jamie Wirsbinski Santoro, *Images of America: Rogers Park* (Charleston, S.C.: Arcadia, 2007); Peter d'Alroy Jones, *Ethnic Chicago: A Multicultural Portrait* (Grand Rapids, Mich.: Wm. B. Eerdmans, 1995); John P. Koval et al., eds., *The New Chicago: A Social and Cultural Analysis* (Philadelphia: Temple University Press, 2006).

18. Irving Cutler, *The Jews of Chicago: From Shtetl to Suburb* (Chicago: University of Illinois Press, 1996); Adam Langer, *Crossing California* (New York: Riverbed Press, 2005); Jones, *Ethnic Chicago*.

19. In 1965 the passage of a new immigration act made it possible for highly skilled South Asians to immigrate to the United States. Until very recently the 1952 McCarran-Walter Act had eased the earlier restrictive immigration laws that prohibited immigrants from South Asian countries to emigrate and seek citizenship in the United States. Although the 1965 law lifted all geographical and racial quotas and let in only skilled immigrants, it was only in the 1980s that the family reunification clauses brought in less-skilled South Asian immigrants families to join their more educated and skilled compatriots. See Urmila Minocha, "South Asian Immigrants: Trends and Impacts on the Sending and Receiving Societies," in *Pacific Bridges: The New Immigration from Asia and the Pacific Islands*, ed. J. T. Fawcett and B. V. Carino (Staten Island, N.Y.: Center for Migration Studies, 1987), 347–74.

Ann Kalayil, who works at the University of Chicago, grew up in this neighborhood and worked in the Sari Palace when she was in high school. Ratan Sharma stated that the owner's decision to locate in this neighborhood was intentional. He wanted to make use of existing customers in northern suburbs of Chicagoland. The store website claims that the store was part of a larger transnational business of dress and saris. It started with Indian Emporium Ltd., founded by Mr. Manghanmal Hiranand in Hong Kong in the early 1930s. Interview with Ann Kalayil, March 2009, Devon Bank; website of "India Sari Palace," http://www.india-sari-palace.com; Gabriel Spritzer (Chicago Public Library), "Immigration on Devon Avenue," audio interview and transcript, WBEZ radio, March 6, 2007, http://www.wbez.org/episode-segments/immigration-devon-avenue.

20. The area of this study is very diverse. According to the 2000 census, this area has 49.7 percent white residents, 6.78 percent black, 15.5 percent Hispanic, 22.3 percent Asians, and 5.65 percent counted as "others."

21. Economic advancement allowed the purchase of property elsewhere, and many South Asian immigrant store owners and now-absentee landlords chose relocation to suburbs such as Lombard, Oak Brook, Naperville, Libertyville, and Northbrook. Nevertheless, growing numbers of South Asians regularly return to shop, worship, and socialize on Devon Avenue. Many South Asian elderly individuals continue to live in the immediate vicinity of West Ridge and West Rogers Park neighborhoods. Devon Avenue also serves as a point of entry for many less skilled or poorer immigrants. They rent affordable apartment housing on the eastern end near Ridge Avenue or apartments above the stores along Devon Avenue.

22. Because the U.S. census doesn't collect information on religious groups, the exact numbers of Muslim immigrants are not documented (except in the membership rolls of local cultural and religious bodies that in the recent political climate are difficult to obtain). Interview with GB/5/09, AZ/2/09, MH/2/09. (These alphanumerical codes refer to the names, dates, and file record numbers of oral history interviews. The names have been coded to ensure anonymity of those interviewed.)

Many new and growing South Asian Muslim residents of this area work in low-paid and unstable jobs. But not all are unskilled; for instance, I interviewed skilled plumbers who, because of their low English-language skills or unstable immigration status, cannot find regular and well-paid jobs.

23. This trend was reflected in the Greater Chicago region. Paul Numrich documented the increase of mosques in the Greater Chicago area from pre-1965, when only a handful served various groups and locations, to more than sixty in 1997. By 2008 there were more than one hundred religious centers, and many newly established ones serving the second and third generations of the community. Paul D. Numrich, "Recent Immigrant Religions in a Restructuring Metropolis: New Religious Landscapes in Chicago," *Journal of Cultural Geography* 17 (Fall/Winter 1997): 55–77; Paul D. Numrich, "Muslims," Electronic Encyclopedia of Chicago, Chicago Historical Society, 2005, http://www.encyclopedia.chicagohistory.org/pages/865.html; Fred Kniss and Paul D. Numrich, *Sacred Assemblies and Civic Engagement: How Religion Matters for America's Newest Immigrants* (New Brunswick, N.J.: Rutgers University Press, 2007); Hermansen, personal communication, March 2009; Garbi Schmidt, *Islam in Urban America: Sunni Muslims in Chicago* (Philadelphia: Temple University Press, 2004).

24. Worship spaces ranged from the Jama Masjid mosque, which holds thousands for regular Friday services, to a dozen basement gathering places that may each attract as many as several hundred male worshippers on Fridays, while functioning as schools and community centers through the rest of the week. Hermansen, 2008 email; Hermansen, personal communication, March 2009. Hermansen recently completed a study of basement mosques in the region with Dana Elborno. The children of the new immigrants enrolled in local public schools, making these schools more multicultural and diverse. Interview with GB/5/09, 5/15/2009, Chicago Public Library, Northtown Branch.

25. Clifford Geertz, "Thick Description: Towards an Interpretive Theory of Culture," in *The Interpretation of Cultures* (New York: Basic Books, 1973), 3–30.

26. Contemporary immigrant users did not construct most of the buildings on Devon Avenue. A majority of South Asian store owners along Devon Avenue occupy buildings that were built in the past by German and Jewish immigrants. Recently, however (since 2008), newer buildings built by first-generation South Asian entrepreneurs and developers have reinvented the visual and physical fabric of this street with newer architectural styles. Stores such as Sahil Boutique, Raj Jewels, Tahoora, and Patel Brothers have opulently redone their building exterior and interiors.

27. Much of this ethnography was conducted between February and March 2009. My students and I did informal oral history interviews with store customers and attended community workshops organized by the South Asian American Policy Research Institute (SAAPRI) and the West Rogers Park Chamber of Commerce. We also interviewed Maribeth Brewer, Greg Brewer, Marcia Hermansen, board members of the Indo-American Heritage Museum, Amie Zander of the West Ridge Chamber of Commerce, Ann Lata Kalayil, Padma Rangaswamy, and K. Sujata.

28. Littering was a big point of contention between the Devon merchants and the local non–South Asian residents. Local organizations such as the West Ridge Chamber of Commerce have started garbage removal and awareness drives to respond to neighbor complaints. Interviews, "The Devon Avenue Needs Assessment: A Smart Growth Strategy," workshop organized by West Rogers Park Community Organization and SAAPRI, June 19, 2008, at the Indo-American Community Center, Chicago. Amie Zander, West Ridge Chamber of Commerce, in interview with the author, February 2009.

29. *Suhoor* is the morning meal consumed before the onset of daytime fasting during the Islamic holy month of Ramadan.

30. Elite' 11, review, Yelp.com, June 9, 2007, http://www.yelp.com/biz/hyder abad-house-chicago. Or as S. G. of Alpharetta, Georgia, complained: "Don't even think of comparing this to the real Hyderabad House back in Hyderabad. Don't go by the name, this is a fake one . . . I was visiting Chicago and was hoping to get some delicious food on Devon and was so disappointed by the quality and taste of the food. How terrible it that to see the same exact gravy for a chicken and vegetarian curry. Long story short, if you are really craving for the Hyderabad House style food please avoid this place." S. G., Alpharetta, Georgia, review, Yelp.com, June 7, 2011, http://www.yelp.com/biz/hyderabad-house-family-dining-chicago.

31. *Meetha* literally means sweet; the word *paratha* refers to unleavened flat breads from South Asia.

32. *Idli* refers to a steamed rice cake; *vada* is savory fried doughnut made of graham flour or lentils; *dosa* is a fermented cake made from rice, lentil, or semolina batter; *upma* is breakfast dish made of roasted semolina; and *puri* is a deep-fried unleavened bread.

33. Customer interviews with the author, Chicago, February-March 2009.

34. South Asian customers in interviews with the author, Chicago, April-May 2011.

35. Customer interviews with the author, Chicago, February-March 2009.

36. South Asian customers in interviews with the author, Chicago, April-May 2011.

37. Class difference was a recurring theme that emerged during the interviews with Hyderabad House users and general shoppers along Devon Avenue. To many South Asian shoppers the interior ambience of the original Hyderabad House was more low-brow than the newer Hyderabad House Family Dining restaurant.

38. Customer interviews with the author, Chicago, February-March 2009.

39. Ricey, review, Google Reviews, March 29, 2009, http://maps.google.com/maps/user?uid=21823698978077098050&hl=en&gl=US&ved=0CIgBEIUK&sa=X&ei=HevSTfv1FIn2NOOF0awG.

40. Michael Herzfeld, *A Place in History: Social and Monumental Time in a Cretan Town* (Princeton, N.J.: Princeton University Press. 1991), 10. Herzfeld refers to multiple experiences of temporality that are often contested. In that context he describes monumental time as that temporal framework seen in the imaginings of the bureaucratic nation-state. Monuments, national icons, histories, and narratives of the nation-state come under the purview of this term. Herzfeld then contrasts monumental time to the everyday experiences of "social time."

41. Carel Bertram, "Architecture, Memory, and 'the Felt Real,'" in *Memory and Architecture*, ed. Eleni Bastéa (Albuquerque: University of New Mexico Press, 2004), 166.

42. Krsna V., Yelp.com reviews, June 9, 2007, http://www.yelp.com/biz/hyderabad-house-chicago.

43. Imran K., Yelp.com reviews, January 18, 2009, http://www.yelp.com/biz/hyderabad-house-chicago.

44. See http://www.youtube.com/watch?v=Oy5xuS6fp9k.

45. Saleem U., Yelp.com reviews, May 29, 2010, http://www.yelp.com/biz/hyderabad-house-chicago.

46. *Masala chai* is a tea that is infused and boiled with spices and herbs.

47. Sharon Zukin, "Consuming Authenticity: From Outposts of Difference to Means of Exclusion," *Cultural Studies* 22 (September 2008): 724–48.

48. Zach Freeman, editorial review, *CenterStage Chicago*, http://centerstagechicago.com/restaurants/hyderabadhouse.html.

49. Cathy B., Yelp.com reviews, July 3, 2010, http://www.yelp.com/biz/hyderabad-house-chicago.

50. Angelo P. from Saint Louis, Missouri, Yelp.com reviews, April 5, 2010, http://www.yelp.com/biz/hyderabad-house-chicago.

51. ChapliKabab from Peshawar, Pashtunistan, September 3, 2009, review, *Zabiha* website, http://www.zabihah.com/d/Chicago+1242+Hyderabad-House.

52. Sharon Zukin, *The Culture of Cities* (Berkeley: University of California Press, 1991); Anouk de Koning, *Global Dreams: Class, Gender, and Public Space in Cosmopolitan Cairo* (Cairo: American University in Cairo Press, 2009); Fernando Herrera Lima, "Transnational Families: Institutions of Transnational Social Space," in *New Transnational Social Spaces: International Migration and Transnational Companies in the Early Twenty-First Century*, ed. Ludger Price (New York: Routledge, 2001), 87; Sen, "Curry Mahals"; Christian Kesteloot and Pascale Mistiaen, "From Ethnic Minority Niche to Assimilation: Turkish Restaurants in Brussels," *Area* 29 (1997): 325–34; Laurier Turgeon and Madeleine Pastinelli, "'Eat

ARIJIT SEN

the World': Postcolonial Encounters in Quebec City's Ethnic Restaurants," *Journal of American Folklore* 115 (2002): 247–68.

53. Pierre Bourdieu, *Outline of a Theory of Practice*, trans. R. Nice (Cambridge: Cambridge University Press, 1977), 6–7.

54. Again Rapport explains, "The individual can be seen adopting and yet adapting stereotypes, developing his own routine relations with them, posing one against another, personalising what they purport in his own image. It is not that stereotypes contextualise their individual uses, then, but that they serve as a vehicle by which the migrating individual can continue consistently to contextualise himself and others. In an original and personal fashion, he very much speaks through his stereotypes; and the context they permit him to construe, for others and for himself, is as original and as personal." See Nigel Rapport, "Migrant Selves and Stereotypes: Personal Context in a Postmodern World," in *Mapping the Subject: Geographies of Cultural Transformation*, ed. Steve Pile and Nigel Thrift (London: Routledge, 1995), 267–82, esp. 279.

55. See Sen, "Creative Dissonance." For literary accounts of clutter and sensory overload in Indian stores, see work by Chitra Banerjee Divakaruni and Kirin Narayan. Purnima Mankekar's research on Indian stores shows that much of the interior spatial ambience is carefully reproduced by store owners. Chitra Banerjee Divakaruni, *The Mistress of Spices: A Novel* (New York: Anchor, 1998); Kirin Narayan, *Love, Stars, and All That* (New York: Pocket Books, 1994); Purnima Mankekar, "'India Shopping': Indian Grocery Stores and Transnational Configurations of Belonging," *Ethnos: Journal of Anthropology* 67 (2001): 75–97.

56. Recent theories of transculturation have suggested that immigrants "switch codes" of language, behavior, and cultural practices in order to negotiate cultural identities and operate in diverse social and cultural contexts. Much work on immigrant transculture follows from the initial scholarship on transnationalism. Arjun Appadurai, "Global Ethnoscapes: Notes and Queries for a Transnational Anthropology," in *Recapturing Anthropology: Working in the Present*, ed. Richard G. Fox (Santa Fe, N.M.: School of American Research Press, 1991), 191–210; Linda Basch, Nina Glick-Schiller, and Cristina Blanc-Szanton, *Nations Unbound: Transnational Projects, Post-Colonial Predicaments, and Deterritorialized Nation-States* (Amsterdam: Overseas Publishers Association, 1994); Nina Glick-Schiller, Linda Basch, and Cristina Blanc-Szanton, *Towards a Transnational Perspective on Migration: Race, Class, Ethnicity, and Nationalism Reconsidered*, Annals of the New York Academy of Sciences, vol. 645 (New York: New York Academy of Sciences, 1992); Ulf Hannerz, *Transnational Connections: Culture, People, Places* (London: Routledge, 1996); Aihwa Ong, *Flexible Citizenship: The Cultural Logics of Transnationality* (Durham, N.C.: Duke University Press, 1999). Many of my references to transculture come from Mary L. Pratt, "Arts of the Contact Zone," *Profession* 91 (1991): 33–40; Mary L. Pratt, *Imperial Eyes: Travel Writing and Transculturation* (London: Routledge, 1992); and Donald M. Nonini, "Situated Identities, Positioned Imaginaries: Transnational Traversals and Reversals by Malaysian Chinese," in *Ungrounded Empires: The Cultural Politics of Modern Chinese Transnationalism*, ed. Aihwa Ong and Donald M. Nonini (New York: Routledge, 1997), 203–27.

57. Sen, "Creative Dissonance."

58. Arijit Sen, "Transcultural Placemaking: Intertwined Spaces of Sacred and Secular on Devon Avenue, Chicago," in *Transcultural Cities: Border-Crossing and Placemaking*, ed. Jeffrey Hou (New York: Routledge, 2013), 19–33.

59. For an overview of such scholarship, see Anna Vemer Andrzejewski, "*Perspectives in Vernacular Architecture*, the VAF, and the Study of Ordinary Buildings and Landscapes in North America," *Perspectives in Vernacular Architecture* 13, no. 2 (2006/2007): 55–63.

60. Kenneth A. Breisch and David Moore, "The Norwegian Rock Houses of Bosque County, Texas: Some Observations on a Nineteenth-Century Vernacular Building Type," in *Perspectives in Vernacular Architecture*, ed. Camille Wells (Columbia: University of Missouri Press, 1986), 2:64–71; Fred W. Peterson, "Anglo-American Wooden Frame Farmhouses in the Midwest, 1830–1900: Origins of Balloon Frame Construction," *Perspectives in Vernacular Architecture*, vol. 8, *People, Power, Places*, ed. Sally McMurry and Annmarie Adams, (Knoxville: University of Tennessee Press, 2000), 3–16; Allen G. Noble and Hubert G. H. Wilhelm, "The Farm Barns of the American Midwest," *Barns of the Midwest*, (Athens: Ohio University Press, 1995), 1–23; Michael P. Conzen, "The European Settling and Transformation of the Upper Mississippi Valley Lead Region," in *Wisconsin Land and Life*, ed. Robert C. Ostergren and Thomas R. Vale (Madison: University of Wisconsin Press, 1997), 163–89; John M. Vlach, "The Shotgun House: An African Architectural Legacy," in *Common Places: Readings in American Vernacular Architecture*, ed. Dell Upton and John M. Vlach (Athens: University of Georgia Press, 1986), 58–78; Thomas C. Hubka, "The New England Farmhouse Ell: Fact and Symbol of Nineteenth-Century Farm Improvement," in Wells, *Perspectives* 2:161–66; Thomas C. Hubka and Judith T. Kenny, "The Transformation of the Workers' Cottage in Milwaukee's Polish Community," in McMurry and Adams, *Perspectives* 8:33–52; Thomas C. Hubka, *Big House, Little House, Back House, Barn: The Connected Farm Buildings of New England* (Lebanon: University Press of New England, 2004); Anne Vernez Moudon, "Getting to Know the Built Landscape: Typomorphology," in *Ordering Space: Types in Architecture and Design*, ed. Karen A. Franck and Lynda H. Schneekloth (New York: Van Nostrand Reinhold, 1994), 289–314; Fred Kniffen, "Louisiana House Types," *Annals of the Association of American Geographers* 26 (December 1936), 170–93; Richard Longstreth, "Compositional Types in American Commercial Architecture," in Welles, *Perspectives* 2:12–23.

61. Fred Kniffen and Henry Glassie, "*Building in Wood in the Eastern United States: A Time-Place Perspective*," in Upton and Vlach, *Common Places*, 159–81; William H. Tishler, "Stovewood Architecture," *Landscape* 23 (1979), 28–31; Christopher Tilley, "Metaphor, Materiality, and Interpretation," *The Material Culture Reader*, ed. Victor Buchli (New York: Berg, 2002), 23–55; Ritchie Garrison, "Carpentry in Northfield, Massachusetts: The Domestic Architecture of Calvin Steams and Sons, 1799–1856," in *Perspectives in Vernacular Architecture*, ed. Thomas Carter and Bernard L. Herman (Columbia: University of Missouri Press, 1991), 4:9–22; Ritchie Garrison, *Two Carpenters: Architecture and Building in Early New England, 1799–1859* (Knoxville: University of Tennessee Press, 2006); Gabrielle M. Lanier, "Samuel Wilson's Working World: Builders and Buildings in Chester County, Pennsylvania, 1780–1827," in Carter and Herman, *Perspectives* 4:23–30; Catherine Bishir, "Jacob W. Holt: An American Builder," *Winterthur Portfolio* 16 (1981): 1–31.

62. Bernard L. Herman, "Time and Performance: Folk Houses in Delaware," in *American Material Culture and Folklife: A Prologue and a Dialogue*, ed. Simon J. Bronner (Ann Arbor, Mich.: UMI Research Press, 1985), 155–75; Dell Upton, "The Preconditions for a Performance Theory of Architecture," in Bronner, *American Material Culture*, 182–85; Dell Upton, "Toward a Performance Theory of Vernacular Architecture in Southeastern Virginia," *Folklore Forum* 12 (1979): 173–96; Mary Corbin Sies, "Toward a Performance Theory of the Suburban Ideal, 1877–1917," in *Perspectives in Vernacular Architecture*, ed. Elizabeth Collins Cromley and Carter L. Hudgins (Columbia: University of Missouri Press, 1991), 5:197–207; Fred Kniffen, "Folk Housing: Key to Diffusion," in Upton and Vlach, *Common Places*, 3–26.

Folklorists have suggested an alternate focus on process; they call it the ethnography-of-speaking approach. Dell H. Hymes, "The Ethnography of Speaking," in *Anthropology and Human Behaviour*, ed. T. Gladwin and W. C. Sturtevant (Washington, D.C.: Anthropology Society of Washington, 1962); Michael Ann Williams and M. Jane Young, "Grammar, Codes, and Performance: Linguistic and Sociolinguistic Models in the Study of Vernacular Architecture," in Cromley and Hudgins *Perspectives* 5:40–51.

63. Although many of the recent immigrant spaces fall under this category, there are few studies on "reused" sites. Sen, "Curry Mahals"; and Christopher L. Yip, "Association, Residence, Shop: An Appropriation of Commercial Blocks in North American Chinatowns," in Cromley and Hudgins, *Perspectives* 5:109–17.

64. There are exceptions. Dell Upton, *Another City: Urban Life and Urban Spaces in the New American Republic* (New Haven, Conn.: Yale University Press, 2008); Gerald L. Pocius, *A Place to Belong: Community Order and Everyday Space in Calvert, Newfoundland* (Montreal: McGill-Queens University Press, 2000); Jennifer Nardone, "Roomful of Blues: Jukejoints and the Cultural Landscape of the Mississippi Delta," *Perspectives in Vernacular Architecture*, vol. 9, *Constructing Image, Identity, and Place*, ed. Alison K. Hoagland and Kenneth A. Breisch (Knoxville: University of Tennessee Press, 2003), 166–75.

65. Interview with Bashir Bozai of Ghareeb Nawaz, April 2011.

66. Eric S., Oak Park, IL, Yelp.com reviews, August 6, 2009, http://www.yelp .com/biz/hyderabad-house-chicago. See also Dukenelson1, review, DisneyFamily .com, December 14, 2008, http://198.105.193.76/travel/places-to-eat/illinois/chi cago/poi-353224-hyderabad-house/reviews/review-7277-avoid-this-place. Or Jake V., who got everything wrong on his first visit: "The best part was after taking a bite each, laughing about it and then moving on to my order of chicken wings and hot sauce or 'Chicken Chili' as they called it, the waiter got around to asking us if we wanted a box for our full bowl of 'butter chicken.' When we said that we'd rather not, he first asked if we were from around here and then went on to insist that it was extremely good curry as if that would change our mind." Jake V., Philadelphia, PA, Yelp.com reviews, September 13, 2010, http://www.yelp.com/biz/hyderabad-house-chicago.

67. Miles Richardson, "Being-in-the-Market versus Being-in-the-Plaza: Material Culture and the Construction of Social Reality in Spanish America," in *The Anthropology of Space and Place: Locating Culture*, ed. Setha M. Low and Denise Lawrence-Zúñiga (Malden, Mass.: Blackwell, 2003), 74–91.

68. For references to the term "publics," see Jürgen Habermas, *The Structural Transformation of the Public Sphere: An Inquiry into a Category of Bourgeois Society*

(Cambridge: MIT Press, 1991); Mary Ryan, "Gender and Public Access: Women's Politics in Nineteenth-Century America," in *Habermas and the Public Sphere*, ed. Craig Calhoun (Cambridge: MIT Press, 1993), 259–88; Geoff Eley, "Nations, Publics, and Political Cultures: Placing Habermas in the Nineteenth Century," in Calhoun, *Habermas*, 289–339; and Nancy Fraser, "Rethinking the Public Sphere: A Contributing to the Critique of Actually Existing Democracy," in Calhoun, *Habermas*, 100–42.

69. Hannah Arendt, *The Human Condition* (Chicago: University of Chicago Press, 1989).

70. Ibid., 57.

71. Public history scholarship uses such a framework. See, for instance, Low and Lawrence-Zúñiga, *Anthropology of Space and Place*; Dolores Hayden, *Power of Place: Urban Landscapes as Public History* (Cambridge: MIT Press, 1997); Setha Low, *On the Plaza: The Politics of Public Space and Culture* (Austin: University of Texas Press).

5.

Urban Boundaries, Religious Experience, and the North West London Eruv

JENNIFER A. COUSINEAU

On the Jewish Sabbath of Saturday, February 23, 2003, a woman carrying her infant child walked out her front door, through her yard, and into the street.[1] This seemingly unremarkable occurrence was an unprecedented act among Sabbath-observant Jews in London. After centuries of Jewish life in London, why should such a mundane gesture mark a significant departure in the experience of the Jewish Sabbath? The catalyst for ritual innovation in this case was a spatial device called an *eruv* (plural, *eruvim*). An eruv is a space whose disparate areas are regarded as forming a single domain by virtue of the contiguity of its boundaries. An eruv can be built in a single street, uniting several dwellings on that street, or on a much larger scale, uniting many streets, households, and even neighborhoods. All eruvim, however, require real, physical boundaries. These boundaries tend to be minimalistic and are usually well integrated into the urban built environment. It is often difficult, even for eruv users, to detect the boundary by sight.[2] Where possible, preexisting features of the urban environment deemed acceptable according to Jewish law, such as fences, row houses, hedges, railway lines, embankments, major roads, and bridges, can be borrowed imaginatively to create a contiguous boundary for the eruv. Where preexisting urban features are not fully contiguous, under certain circumstances Jewish law can allow for the boundary to be "completed" by erecting poles and wires to close gaps. The erection of some eighty poles in this way permitted the creation of an eruv that now encompasses an area of 6.5 square miles in North West London, including large parts of Hendon, Golders Green, Finchley, and the Hampstead Garden Suburb, and encircling the majority of the Jewish population of North West London. This eruv is known as the North West London Eruv.

Even though eruv boundaries do not limit the actions of those who do not make use of eruvim, the construction of such boundaries in cities across North America and in England has proven fertile ground for urban conflict. Encounters between eruv supporters and their detractors have been well documented in the scholarly literature.[3] For the purposes of this chapter, it will be sufficient to state that the construction of the North West London Eruv was unusually protracted because the objections to it were so vociferous, causing repeated delays in construction. Many people, including significant parts of the Sabbath-observant Jewish community in London, did not accept the North West London Eruv as legitimate, either for the purposes of carrying on the Sabbath or as a means of advancing the religious practices of a small segment of London's population. Some claimed that any urban area enclosed by an eruv would become a type of Orthodox Jewish "ghetto" in which both secular Jews and non-Jews would be unwelcome. Though irrational (because in all documented cases the implementation of an eruv has been *preceded* by the settlement of significant numbers of Jews in the area), this argument appears to have had broad appeal and has been a feature of urban conflict in places as disparate as Palo Alto, California; Outremont, Québec; and Westhampton Beach, New York, as well as in other communities in England. Eruv users, who have almost always lived in heterogeneous urban environments, however, have never made claims to ownership or exclusive use of the space within an eruv, and Jewish law does not require it.

The essays in David Chidester and Edward Linenthal's edited volume, *American Sacred Space*, chart a variety of conflicts that seem almost inevitably to accompany the establishment and practice of sacred space by individuals and groups.[4] This chapter turns away from urban conflict even while it acknowledges the inherent multiplicity of meaning of any urban space. Instead, it presents a study of urban religion from the perspective of religious practitioners. I am interested in the ways that urban places designated for religious practice alter the lives of those who use of them.

Historian of religion Robert Orsi has defined urban religion as "the dynamic engagement of religious traditions with specific features of industrial and post-industrial cityscapes and the social conditions of city life," and his work on the American religious landscape lays the groundwork for my work on the eruv.[5] Orsi's research differs from mine in two ways. First, for historical reasons that are beyond the scope of this article, British public culture in recent decades has shown itself to be less receptive to the open practice of religion than its American counterpart. Second, my research foregrounds gender and prioritizes the religious practices of women. Although I have considered both men's and women's experiences of the Sabbath, my focus in this chapter is on women's experiences. The establishment of the eruv changed the way many Jews thought about and practiced the Sabbath, but it was clearly most transformative for women. Men spoke about how the eruv improved their experiences of the day of rest, making it more convenient for them to carry necessary objects from place to place. For women, however, the eruv was revolutionary. I was also drawn to analyzing women's experiences of the Sabbath because the rabbinic tradition—by which I mean the content of Jewish law and its application in practice—has not prioritized it. Feminist scholars have spent nearly three decades excavating the ways in which women have been marginalized or excluded by rabbinic Judaism, but the literature on how traditional Judaism has served and even nurtured the spiritual lives of women is scant.[6] Women have nonetheless appropriated elements of Jewish law to serve their religious needs. Indeed, the eruv is a compelling example of how women's experience has been advanced by the application of Jewish law to the urban environment and can be understood as a prism through which to read deeply gendered, spatial experiences of the Sabbath.

One challenge to those investigating the spatial dimension of the Sabbath is that the Jewish Sabbath has been understood (both within and without the tradition) as a temporal phenomenon, generally untouched by concerns over space. Philosopher and theologian Rabbi Abraham Joshua Heschel examined the temporal nature of the Sabbath, deemphasizing space as a controlling paradigm for Judaism in his celebrated characterization of the day as a "palace in time."[7] While time has been a central theme of the Sabbath and its conscious manipulation has been vital to the creation of heightened significance around the Sabbath, my research among Sabbath-observant Jews, and women in particular, reveals that the characterization of the Sabbath as a recurring temporal refuge was partial and gendered. For many Jewish women in London, there was a gap between the idea of the Sabbath as a time of rest and their experience of it as restrictive. For women who felt this way, the gap was a function of space: the Sabbath, prior to the eruv, was connected to a sense of spatial confinement, while the other six days of the week signified spatial freedom—freedom that should rightly have belonged to the Sabbath day and those who observed it.

Methodology

The methods used to study the North West London Eruv included a combination of archival research and fieldwork conducted in the neighborhoods of Hendon, Golders Green, Finchley, and the Hampstead Garden Suburb over the course of several years. During the fieldwork phase, I collected twenty-seven oral histories and a series of hand-drawn mental maps of my informants' Sabbath experiences, through which I encouraged users to tell their own stories about the Sabbath with an eruv. Mental maps can be defined as images that represent an individual's perception of their relationship to place. They are a methodological tool pioneered by geographers and popularized by Peter Gould and Rodney White's 1974 landmark study, *Mental Maps*. The concept has been revised considerably since its publication.[8] Given that the North West London Eruv would directly affect the way women perceived and used space, it made sense to employ a method that had the potential to capture the real and perceived changes in the use of space brought about by the implementation of an eruv.

In the interviews, mental maps were referred to as "Sabbath maps," and interviewees were asked to delineate the spaces in which they might typically circulate, socialize, worship, eat, play, or entertain on the Sabbath. Neither the maps nor the interviews purport to represent a generalized Sabbath experience, for such a thing does not exist. The eruv, and indeed representations of it, are ever changing. British anthropologist Tim Ingold has argued that mental maps do not represent a description of experience produced in the mind and reproduced on paper. Rather, they are volatile, situationally informed, and culturally bound inscriptions.[9] Mental maps can be read as representing a moment in the spiritual life of an individual, subject to change over time. The places shown and the routes traveled across the maps might change from Sabbath to Sabbath, month to month, or year to year. Each religious experience is an individual one, and every map is subjective. If they were to be drawn again in one, or two, or five years from now, one could expect to observe changes in the experiences and places they described. If the mental maps were nothing but unique expressions of individual experience, however, they would have little to contribute to the exploration of larger questions about religious experience, but common ground exists between them. They all compress space, making long distances seem short and large, urban spaces more intimate. The conception of the eruv as a kind of communal Jewish home might lead us to anticipate this characterization. The maps emphasize the public, shared parts of the city (as opposed to private, enclosed, or domestic environments) within the eruv. This is more surprising, since the public street is an unusual (though by no means unprecedented) venue for encounters with the holy.[10] Finally, the maps stress social connection and the urban infrastructure that facilitates it. The Sabbath and the eruv underscore social interaction as a means of the creating of meaningful religious experiences. My intention with this project was not to be representative—for that, a much larger sample would be necessary—but to deepen my understanding of the quality, variety, and complexity of religious experiences generated in and through a dynamic urban environment. As a group the Sabbath maps attest to the ways in which Jews might encounter the city, each other, and God in the process of observing the Sabbath in a twenty-first-century neighborhood.

The Purpose of an Eruv

In order to understand the ways in which eruvim altered the experience of the Sabbath and of urban space in London, it is important to understand the function of an eruv. On the Sabbath all productive work is forbidden to Jews, but several other categories of activity are also suspended, including carrying objects from one type of "domain" (as defined by Jewish law) to another, or within a public "domain."[11] The prohibition on carrying applies not only to objects but also to people, and not only to carrying per se but also to pushing and throwing. Thus parents may not carry their infants or push them in a stroller. The elderly may not walk with the assistance of canes, and wheelchair-bound people may not be pushed in their chairs nor may they propel them by themselves. An eruv creates an enlarged symbolic private domain within a continuous perimeter, thereby making it possible to undertake such acts as carrying on the Sabbath within the parameters of Jewish law. The first eruv to be implemented in London was activated after fifteen years of planning. By virtue of the presence of the North West London Eruv, the fabric of the city could be regarded in Jewish law as a private domain (the technical term is *reshut hayachid*) for the purposes of the Sabbath.[12] A first and somewhat technical answer to the question of why one might build an eruv might be to permit carrying and related activities on the Sabbath in order to make the day a pleasurable experience within the confines of Jewish law. The remainder of this chapter shows that the eruv was not only a means to fulfill a religious obligation but also a catalyst for the enhancement of Jewish spirituality and community.

When the eruv was first declared to be "up," what was meant was that the eruv boundary (the technical term is *mechitzah*, or partition), which encompassed a large section of North West London, was intact and therefore functional for the purposes of Sabbath observance. As a consequence, Jews were free to carry outside their homes on the Sabbath. By constructing the eruv perimeter, Jews had asserted in material terms that religion in general, and their religion in particular, had legitimate claims to make on urban public space. News coverage of the reaction in Britain to the construction of the North West London Eruv, as well as to other expressions of public religion, has shown that the idea of religion having a place in British public life cannot be taken for granted.[13] Open hostility to the visible practice of religion, regardless of the sectarian identity of practitioners, was part of the context into which the eruv was built.[14] The construction of the physical boundary of the eruv, however, was only part of the life of the eruv. Every Sabbath–that is, between Friday at sundown and nightfall on Saturday–the eruv would be invoked and affirmed through the actions of the Jews who used it. What might it mean for Jews to experience the holiest day of the week by means of and within the spatially fixed reality of the eruv?

Ordinary Acts as Sabbath Ritual

First, Jews experienced the holiness of the Sabbath through a series of ordinary acts and gestures performed in public space. These acts were rendered part of the Sabbath by being performed in accordance with Jewish law. While the freedom to circulate across a significantly expanded network of newly domesticated streets and neighborhoods was a much-acclaimed benefit of the eruv in London, the foremost mundane acts that it enabled were carrying or pushing. All the mental maps drawn by participants in my research outline places to which they would typically carry on the Sabbath. A seemingly straightforward act, something one does almost without thinking unless the burden is great, carrying is symbolically freighted in the context of the Sabbath.[15] For Jews in London, certainly during the early days of the eruv, carrying in public was not undertaken without serious consideration of how such an act might affect the sanctity of the day. Some worried that after years of not carrying in public on the Sabbath and carrying only during the working week, the act would feel profane by association and thus lower their perceptions of the sanctity of the Sabbath. Indeed, a number of Jews refrained from carrying on the Sabbath for that very reason. But many Jews felt that the holiness of the Sabbath lay not in refraining from such ordinary acts, but in elevating them by performing them outside their homes yet within the eruv, which sanctioned them. These Jews proceeded to carry, despite any initial misgivings about the novelty of the act for them. Even after only a few months of eruv use, the act had already been refined according to neighborhood, necessity, custom, social group, ritual inclination, family priorities, and personal preference. Undoubtedly, between 2003, when the research for this chapter was conducted, and the present, the practice of the eruv has changed to reflect shifts in the needs and ritual priorities of London's Jews.

If transferring, or carrying, became a part of the ritual vocabulary of the Sabbath, we must ask what was carried and how. Jewish law constructs a typology of objects that can be transferred on the Sabbath, limiting it to those things that can be defined as necessary for the enjoyment of the Sabbath. While in theory the range of objects that can be carried would seem to be limited by concept of necessity, in practice many types of things (including people) can be transferred. For those Jews for whom the presence of an eruv made a significant difference in the experience of the holiness of the day, the permission to carry or push their young children was critical. Carrying children, or pushing them in a stroller, was "necessary" in order for the area's Jewish women to fully enjoy the Sabbath. Women who could not leave the house without a stroller were effectively housebound and barred from participation in Sabbath prayer, study rituals, and community celebrations. The same can be said for the use of wheelchairs by their users. Mrs. Channi Nussbaum, an elderly Jewish Londoner, had been wheelchair-bound with multiple sclerosis for many years as well as housebound on the Sabbath because of the lack of an eruv. The head of the North West London Eruv Committee, David Schreiber, told the following story of the first Sabbath on which the eruv was functional:

> Once it was decided that we would go live that *shabbat* [Sabbath], I placed a call to Channi Nussbaum to make a date to take her to *shul* [synagogue] and frankly I sat in my room and cried. Channi is the lady who suffers from MS, to whom I made a promise fifteen years before to push her to shul on the first shabbat with an eruv. I remember making the promise to her, really to commit myself and give myself a target and the truth is that it helped me through some very bleak periods in the intervening years. The anticipation of pushing Channi to shul undoubtedly gave me strength and purpose. [When they came to take her], Channi was beaming! Nero Yisrael [synagogue] had reserved a spot for her wheelchair and we were able to wheel her in with no fuss.[16]

While these words express Schreiber's elation at the changes in ritual practice engendered by the eruv, one can only imagine how Mrs. Nussbaum herself might have felt moving through the city and participating in public prayer on the Sabbath, possibly for the first time in her life.[17]

In addition to the strictly necessary, such as a wheelchair, other objects entered the category of material culture of the Sabbath with the implementation of the North West London Eruv, including keys, baby gear, canes, ritual items (such as prayer books), food and drink to be consumed on the Sabbath, clothing, and medication (among others). All of these objects were interpreted as enhancing the experience of the Sabbath by virtue of the physical comfort or psychological security with which they provide eruv users. One woman related how her experience of the Sabbath had been enhanced by the ability to carry objects of personal comfort, such as "wet weather clothes":

> If you're not sure it's going to rain, you can take something and you don't have to worry about wearing it all the way there and all the way back. So we do take wet weather things and the odd extra cardigan when the weather is iffy and up and down, and small things that are there to increase your comfort level.[18]

Another act that characterized the use of the London eruv was walking or, for those who used wheelchairs, walkers, or canes, assisted mobility in various forms. It was among mothers with young children, like Anushka Levey, as well as people who were not independently mobile, that the profound spatial consequences of the expansion of domestic space by means of the eruv were felt most keenly. The outline of Levey's house can be taken as representative of her pre-eruv Sabbath spatial experience, where she spent much of the day in her home at 5A Sinclair Grove in the neighborhood of Golders Green (figure 5.1). The full map, which shows three friends' homes, three synagogues, two nearby neighborhoods, a park, and the major streets of the area, implies a much more spatially varied Sabbath experience. All the maps produced by my informants echo this perception of significantly expanded Sabbath space once the eruv was in active use. Before the eruv, unless they had taken the trouble to arrange for child care in advance of the Sabbath, many women spent the Sabbath in their homes or, if they were lucky, their yards and gardens. In London these tend to be fully enclosed by fences or landscape elements such as tall hedges, creating a kind of small-scale eruv. Once the eruv was implemented, women could much more easily navigate their neighborhoods, along with their families, and they gained

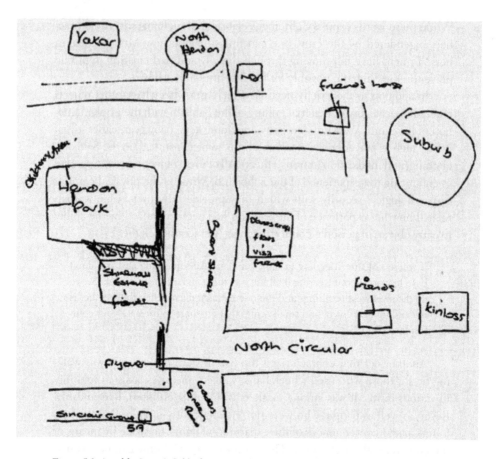

Figure 5.1. Anushka Levey's Sabbath map, produced June 2003.

access to a variety of urban spaces that had previously been closed to them on the Sabbath. Anushka Levey described her pre-eruv Sabbath spatial experience as one of physical confinement: "Shabbat is a wonderful time that is meant to be shared with family and friends. But if I have a newborn baby who obviously can't walk and I can't push a pram, it means that for twenty-five hours–between sundown and sundown–I'm stuck at home. [The eruv] will mean that we are no longer prisoners in our own home."[19] The ordinary acts of walking and carrying, which the eruv facilitated for this woman and many others like her, became part of a new ritual vocabulary of the Sabbath. Though ordinary, these acts enabled a broad spectrum of people to participate in the communal celebration of the Sabbath. The ability of people like Anushka to enjoy the Sabbath outside the family home, however, came at a price.

The Eruv as a Theater

Acts of transfer on the Sabbath are significant only when they occur publicly–that is, outside private space. The eruv boundary theoretically privatizes such acts by bringing them into a symbolic Jewish household. From a visual perspective, however, transfer on the Sabbath became part of the public "scene." Though the so-called walls of the eruv household may have been invisible to those who were not aware of their precise locations, their presence was invoked through every visible act of transfer that occurred among Sabbath-observant Jews. The streets and alleys of Golders Green and Hendon became ritual theaters in which the practice of or protest against the eruv was the main production. The mental maps convey the public and visible nature of transfer on the Sabbath (figures 5.1–5.3). They construct a typology of urban environments where Jews might circulate on the Sabbath and to which they might carry. Most of them are public — streets, sidewalks, alleys, parks, synagogues, and other households (which, though privately owned, become shared spaces on the Sabbath and in that sense have a public dimension). What the maps do not reveal is the level of discomfort that some Jews felt at having their behavior exposed and potentially judged by other people within and without their communities.

Sometime during the first few weeks after the eruv had been completed, a remarkable image was circulated by e-mail among eruv-supporting members of the community.[20] The image can be interpreted as conveying a strong message about the nature and consequence of public religious observance. It depicts two men dressed in black hats, black suits, and white shirts, with long beards. Their overall appearance suggests that they are strictly Orthodox Jews. They are seated in a ski lift that hangs high above a snow-covered landscape. The caption reads "Checking the North West London Eruv over the North Circular." This image may have been intended as a humorous comment on the self-consciousness that the presence of the eruv seemed to foster among Jews in the area. The two men, the image implied, were not just checking the eruv boundary, something that happens on a weekly basis, usually on foot or motor vehicle. They were dressed less like the Modern Orthodox Jews who used the eruv than like other Orthodox Jews who opposed and did not use it. They could therefore be understood as watching and judging eruv users, as God might, from on high. The image could also express the feeling of some eruv users that their ritual practices were being observed by co-religionists whose leadership looked with disfavor on the eruv. The image might also suggest that women's Sabbath behavior, in particular, was subject to the control of male authorities in Jewish law and that their bodies were being closely watched as they emerged into urban public space on the Sabbath. One woman described the experience of observing others within the eruv, noting where they were located, what they wore, and what or whether they carried or pushed. On the basis of a few Sabbaths worth of observing, she had formed a general impression of what type of Sabbath behavior was practiced in what place and has also speculated on the ritual choices of people she had seen carrying or not carrying:

> I definitely noticed some people who weren't carrying. It's hard to tell, you know, if they're not carrying because they're *not carrying*, or if they're not carrying because they don't happen to feel the need to carry at the moment. I did see some wheelchairs up there [in Golders Green]. Not vastly *be-sheitled* [wig-wearing] people. The impression from one or two journeys is that there are more wheelchairs in Hendon than in Golders Green.[21]

This type of judgmental people-watching was common, especially in the early months after the eruv was constructed. It is not surprising, then, that eruv users developed a number of different carrying strategies to help them manage their feelings of vulnerability and to mitigate the social consequences of public carrying in a community where not all Sabbath-observant Jews agreed that the North West London Eruv was completely "kosher," or acceptable. Some Jews carried objects in a hidden way, such as inside pockets, while others chose to carry objects in certain streets and neighborhoods but not in others. A coat might be worn in a neighborhood populated by objectors to the eruv and then taken off and carried when the wearer passed into a neighborhood that was more receptive to the eruv.

The intense scrutiny of Sabbath activity arising out of the implementation of the North West London Eruv drew attention to the beliefs underlying people's actions. The decision of a certain segment of the Jewish population to make use of the eruv was, in many cases, a decision to make their religious commitments public. When women began to push strollers about North West London on the Sabbath, in the words of one of my participants, they were "nailing their sails to the mast."[22] After all, children, however small, can hardly be concealed in a pocket. Every person who saw a woman pushing a stroller or carrying her small children on the Sabbath, acts that on any other day would have gone unnoticed, could reasonably assume that the woman believed that an urban-scale Jewish home had been created within the boundary of the eruv.[23] Unlike the decision to keep kosher or to pray, religious obligations that may be carried out privately, using the eruv was not something a Jew could do in her home. By carrying within the eruv, Jews were making the profound theological statement that they accepted the authority of the Torah as interpreted through the lens of the rabbinic tradition, which supported the use of the eruv. Jews who chose to carry on the Sabbath also made clear their allegiance to certain local rabbinic authorities rather than others who objected to the eruv. More than that, the range, variety, and distribution of urban spaces depicted in the Sabbath maps suggest that by using the eruv, some women were asserting a symbolic spiritual ownership of the city. This was not an exclusive type of ownership, but one in which women were participating alongside all citizens as free users of urban space. Jewish law, as expressed through the construction of the eruv, supported their claims to greater spatial freedoms, and to the fuller enjoyment of the Sabbath that came with it. When my informants were asked to depict their typical Sabbath spaces and trajectories, none hesitated to make claims of use over both the private and public spaces they inhabited on the holiest day of their week, as is reflected in their Sabbath maps.

The Eruv Community

An important dimension of the sanctity of the Sabbath for London Jews was its construction through social relations in the context of one or several Jewish communities. The rabbinic tradition in general discourages isolation from one's community, and the Sabbath maps that document eruv experiences constitute a visual rejection of the possibility that the Sabbath could be fully enjoyed alone. People's Sabbath places consistently included friends' houses, synagogues (in several cases eruv users frequented more than one), local parks, and the arteries that provided physical connection between the family home and other homes or communal spaces. Second only to the family home itself, the traditional sites for Sabbath spiritual observance and social life are synagogues, and their more humble cousins, shtiblach—ordinary houses converted into places for prayer. Until the eruv was constructed, synagogues in London were, by and large, male spaces. This is not to say that women did not attend services; they did, but women who had young children attended only with great effort and infrequently. Synagogues like Ner Yisrael (where an eruv committee was first convened) embraced the eruv and welcomed new attendees. Both rabbis and congregants at the synagogue noted a positive change in the general atmosphere, which they described as celebratory.[24] They also commented on the increased noise level brought about by the presence of small children. Women who began to come to synagogues made clear that they did not always come to pray; their young children were simply too young to follow the long Sabbath services. They came to engage with other Jews who had set aside the twenty-five hours of the Sabbath for rest and thus shared their values and practices. Many were close friends and extended family members who might not see each other during the busy work week. For London Jews, to be among one's fellows was, on some level, to encounter God. Almost three months after the eruv was completed, one woman described her altered experience of Sabbath space in terms of increased involvement with other Sabbath-observant Jews:

> From my point of view, Shabbat is supposed to be a family and community day. In order for it to be a proper break from everything that you do in the week, you want to share it with your family and your community. And up until now it's been quite isolating for either women with children, or people in wheelchairs or who needed crutches. What has been wonderful is that now we can do things together as a family. It's not just my husband going off to shul. It's all of us. We can go on family trips on Shabbat to the park, and, importantly, we can share it with our friends and with older members of the family who previously would have had to have been in their own home. I can be part of the community again, rather than having to wait until our kids are old enough to walk.[25]

At the time I interviewed the women, their Sabbath experiences had come to include communal-institutional as well as domestic buildings, a much enlarged streetscape, an expanded social network, and a new set of leisure spaces. Their maps speak to a sense of enlarged social life: they document purposeful, sanctified movement across an urban environment that had been reshaped and dedicated to support social connection and the active creation of community. The communities constructed in the maps cover several square miles in area and contain over a dozen synagogues and thousands of Jews. By these measures alone, women's experience of space on the Sabbath had been radically altered by the implementation of an eruv. When I interviewed them in June 2003, the urban environment had become embedded in a variety of ways in the religious practices of people who previously existed apart from it. Follow-up research has affirmed the positive impact the eruv continues to have on the women who use it in North West London, and the appearance of several other eruvim in London and throughout England suggests that they have become desirable as a means of enhancing the ritual and social lives of British Jews.[26]

While the eruv contributed to the increased movement of Jewish bodies through urban space, it also played a role in the perception of the urban environment by its inhabitants, especially in relation to the Sabbath. The eruv prompted reimaginings of the city around new eruv-related practices. Both women and men whom I interviewed discussed the emergence of what one man called "no-carry zones."[27] A no-carry zone is an area inhabited by or perceived to be the territory of a rabbi or a congregation that objected to the eruv and its use. Some Jews, feeling watched or judged by the fact that they carried, chose to avoid "no-carry zones" altogether when they were pushing strollers or carrying objects. For some people, the urban space inside the eruv thus became fragmented. While on the one hand it fostered some types of communities, on the other it revealed preexisting fissures in ritual practice among London Jews.

The experience of one mother of two small children attests to the acute sensitivity of Jews to their heterogeneous social environment. Sara Morris (pseudonym) and her husband belonged to a synagogue in Golders Green, where the rabbi was known not to condone the use of the eruv, although he did not publicly declare himself against it. In general, this couple reported, the rabbi's congregants respected his position and thus did not push strollers to the synagogue or carry items in a visible manner. Sara took even greater measures in an attempt to navigate the conflicting values of those who used or did not use the eruv. She lived in a small house on a quiet street in the Hampstead Garden Suburb (figure 5.2). A note on her Sabbath map, under the word "shul," which marked the location of her synagogue, states "don't use the eruv to shul." Not only did she not take her children to her synagogue, but when she did take them out in their stroller, she avoided the street on which the synagogue stood. On her map she marked the direct route from her home to the synagogue, which was the route her husband usually walked. She also marked the alternative route by which, one Sabbath, she circumvented the synagogue on her way to a lunch engagement at the home of one of the synagogue's members. For her, not only was the synagogue itself a kind of prohibited area, but the street on which it stood was also one long "no-carry zone." Describing the emotional experience of using the eruv, and expressing her perception that she was being observed by her neighbors, she said, "I don't want to offend anybody by using it [the eruv], especially my husband. You know, I think, I'm not breaking Shabbos [the Sabbath], yet I feel a kind of embarrassment, almost. I'm using it and having to walk in the other direction which just seems crazy. I don't understand why I'm doing it, but I wouldn't have felt comfortable walking near the shul."[28]

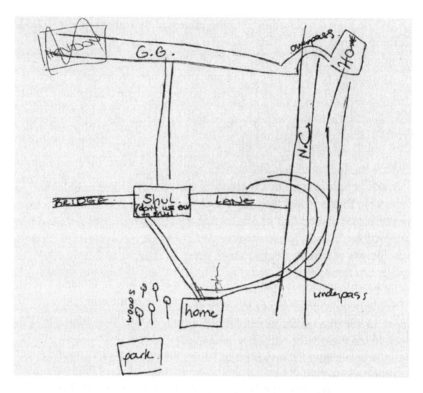

Figure 5.2. Sara Morris's Sabbath map, produced June 2003.

In addition to revealing that she felt watched and judged on the street when she was seen using the eruv by people who did not, the statement also reveals a somewhat common split in ritual practice between husbands and wives. Since some husbands had not felt restricted by the lack of an eruv before it was built, they did not feel the need to rely on it once it was. Their wives, both literally and metaphorically, carried the entire burden when they went out together on the Sabbath. Couples agreed to be inconsistent with each other in practice because of their deeply felt and mutually exclusive needs–one to escape the house and the other to express his piety by applying Jewish law more strictly. The woman's use of the eruv to carry in public and the husband's election not to, though introducing a minor rupture into their home and marriage, opened up new social connections for the woman. She reported feeling a bond with other people she saw in the neighborhood who were either carrying objects or pushing strollers, even when she didn't know who they were.

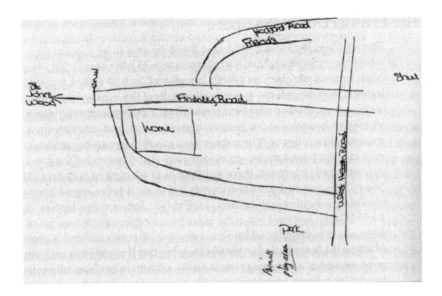

Figure 5.3. Rachel Cohen's Sabbath map, produced June 2003.

Having considered the actions, perceptions, and beliefs of eruv-using Jews, I would be remiss if I did not address the emotional dimension of the Sabbath with an eruv. What, if any, contribution did the eruv make to the inner life of Sabbath-observant Jews? This is not an easy question for many reasons, not least of which is that Jewish law tends to focus on creating correct outward ritual forms as a means of developing a proper inner spirituality. Further, the emotional dimension of religious experience is intensely personal. This kind of evidence is more difficult to access than information about seemingly more neutral activities like walking and carrying. Nonetheless, my informants suggested that their inner lives were indeed profoundly affected by the implementation of an eruv in their city. They repeatedly returned to expressions of joy, autonomy, and connectedness. Rachel Cohen, a mother of four young children, and an apartment dweller (figure 5.3), described the emotional and physical intensity of her pre-eruv Sabbath experience: "I was going crazy in this apartment. I just couldn't get out at all. It was horrible. And the kids were sitting at home climbing the walls. [Before the children] I always went to synagogue. I wasn't used to staying home. Here I was on Shabbos morning sitting here waiting, waiting, waiting. My husband would come home, I'd go out."[29]

For Rachel, the spatial autonomy offered by the eruv was essential to an emotional and spiritual reengagement with the Sabbath day. She also spoke of the community feeling that was created when people she knew stopped and shared the fact that they, too, were carrying. Anushka Levey's description of her experience of the synagogue underlined the spiritual quality of the place, but qualified it by saying that its spirituality lay as much in the ways it allowed for enjoyable meetings of community members with each other as in facilitating encounters between individuals and their God through communal prayer. This picture emerged consistently among Jewish women with small children, who might not be able to engage in formal prayer but could always talk, laugh, and eat with the people in their community.

A final example offered by Rabbi Alan Kimche, the rabbi of Ner Yisrael synagogue and the person responsible for initiating the eruv project in the late 1980s, captures the sense of spiritual elevation and pure joy the eruv could foster. On the first Sabbath the eruv was activated, Kimche had invited Dayan Hanoch Ehrentreu, the distinguished head of the London rabbinical court, to join him in his synagogue to celebrate the first Sabbath with an eruv. Ehrentreu was not only a much loved and respected figure in the community, but he had also contributed enormously to the implementation of the eruv. When he arrived, Kimche said:

> The shul was packed with people. Women were there with babies whom I'd never seen before. Some of them, I didn't even know them. I'd speak to them on the phone a few times, but they could never come on Shabbos. They don't come to shul during the week so I'd never actually met them. Must have had about four or five hundred people there. We laid on a big celebration, and we were drinking toasts, and it was a very nice atmosphere in the shul. And at a certain point, Dayan Ehrentreu arrived to toast with us. And it was very interesting. We hadn't planned anything at all, but there was a spontaneous dance. People started dancing like at a wedding. Yes. And it was quite spontaneous. The men got hold of Dayan Ehrentreu's hand and they started dancing, singing, and the little kids started. And for about a quarter of an hour, it was quite moving, because everybody clearly felt that something had changed.[30]

Something, or rather, a number of things, had changed. The extension of a Jewish home through the mechanism of the eruv to the scale of entire neighborhoods had an immediate, profound, and mostly positive effect on the neighborhoods' Jewish inhabitants. Women who had felt socially and spiritually isolated for years as a result of their religious choices emerged from their homes and created new kinds of communities—of friends, neighbors, and extended families. The construction of the eruv, at least temporarily, created a consciousness about newly public acts that were incorporated into an expanded set of Sabbath rituals. The eruv prompted new perceptions of neighborhood space that, once unified by the lack of an eruv, would henceforth highlight differences in ritual priorities. It also fostered the deep sense of joy that can result from making the celebration of the Sabbath a common cause rather than an individual one.

While covering the visit of Pope Benedict XVI to England in 2010, Canadian priest and journalist Raymond de Souza noted "the almost complete marginalization of religious voices in shaping public arguments in Britain, including the leadership of the Church of England."[31] The North West London Eruv represents an important exception in this vacuum. During the fifteen years of its construction, religious Jews found themselves very much at the center of public debates over what and whose values should prevail in the public domain. At that time, however, when there was a real chance that the eruv might not get approval from the municipality, eruv advocates downplayed the idea that sanctity might in any way be associated with the eruv. They described the eruv boundary in mundane terms as a series of poles and wires, without reference to the shift it would engender in the spiritual lives of Jews.[32] What eruv proponents could not state in a context that was hostile to public religion was that religion can and does frequently permeate even the most mundane aspects of everyday life. In his study of Anglican material culture in North Carolina, Louis Nelson argued convincingly that "the distinction between sacred and profane is a theological construct that has limited impact on practiced religion."[33] The Jews of London did not have to separate themselves from their day-to-day urban environment in order to experience the Sabbath to the fullest. Rather, the more they were a part of their neighborhoods and the communities that they inhabited, the more celebratory—and holy—the Sabbath became for them. The practice of the eruv demonstrates that everyday actions and neighborhood places are not peripheral to meaningful religious experience, but can be at its very core.

This study of the relationship between space and religious experience, though rooted in the particular experiences of Jews, has significance beyond the study of Judaism. The work of theologian Belden Lane, deeply influenced by cultural geography, asks how people "experience the holy within the context of a spatially fixed reality." His work directed what was initially a study of urban spatial politics toward questions about the intersection of human experience, space, and theology.[34] Lane sees religious experience as "placed experience." For him, place is not just a stage on which religious experiences might unfold, but is actually an integral part of the experience itself. Lane's work on what David Hall and others call "lived religion" offered a point of departure for exploring the ways users of space confront the holy, and the ways in which the built environment is implicated in that confrontation.[35] Following these scholars, this chapter offers a phenomenology-based approach to answering questions about religious experience.[36] Recent work in phenomenological studies stresses that space does not contain bodily experience, but is a component it. As such, space must be understood as dynamic and constantly in flux; how much more so when the space under consideration is not a discrete building but an entire neighborhood, or a number of them? My work on the experience of the eruv bears out the idea that space is not a container for human activity, but represents a field for both physical and conceptual relationships—relationships between family and community members, between Jews and non-Jews, between women and men, parents and children, and inhabitants of neighborhoods and cities. Indeed, since it was established, the eruv has added to the holiness of the Sabbath by expanding the possibilities for human interaction.

NOTES

1. This is a fictional scenario based on a series of oral histories gathered by the author in May and June 2003. Parts of this chapter were adapted from Jennifer Cousineau, "The Domestication of Urban Jewish Space and the North West London Eruv," in *Jews at Home: The Domestication of Identity*, ed. Simon Bronner (Oxford: Littman Library of Jewish Civilization, 2010), 43–74.

2. Although it is important for users to know where the boundary is in order to remain within the eruv, it is not essential that they be able to see the boundary.

3. Davina Cooper, "Talmudic Territory? Space, Law, and Modernist Discourse," *Journal of Law and Society* 23 (1996): 529–48; Jennifer Cousineau, "Rabbinic Urbanism in London: Rituals and the Material Culture of the Sabbath," *Jewish Social Studies* 11, no. 3 (2005): 36–57; Manuel Herz and Eyal Weizman, "Between City and Desert: Constructing the North London Eruv," *AA Files* 34 (1997): 68–76; Miriam Levy, "Encounter with the Eruv: A Project toward the City of Open Enclosures," master's thesis, Massachusetts Institute of Technology, 2000; Adam Mintz, "The History of City Eruvin, 1894–1962," PhD dissertation, New York University, 2011; Calvin Trillin, "Drawing the Line," *New Yorker*, December 12, 1994, 50–63; Oliver Valins, "Stubborn Identities and the Construction of Socio-Spatial Boundaries: Ultra-Orthodox Jews Living in Contemporary Britain," *Transactions of the Institute of British Geographers* 28, no. 2 (2003): 158–75; Sophie Watson, "Symbolic Spaces

of Difference: Contesting the Eruv in Barnet, London, and Tenafly, New Jersey," *Environment and Planning D. Society and Space* 23 (2005): 597–613.

4. David Chidester and Edward T. Linenthal, eds., *American Sacred Space* (Bloomington: Indiana University Press, 1995).

5. Robert Orsi, *Gods of the City: Religion and the American Urban Landscape* (Bloomington: Indiana University Press, 1999), 45.

6. The bibliography on women and Jewish law or tradition is too extensive to cite in detail here. The following list represents some of the most important scholarly and popular work of the past two decades, as well as the work that has had the greatest influence on my thinking about Jewish women and space in the context of Jewish law and tradition: Rachel Biale, *Women and Jewish Law: An Exploration of Women's Issues in Halakhic Sources* (New York: Schocken Books, 1984); Daniel Boyarin, *Carnal Israel: Reading Sex in Talmudic Culture* (Berkeley: University of California Press, 1993); Charlotte Elisheva Fonrobert, *Menstrual Purity: Rabbinic and Christian Reconstructions of Biblical Gender* (Stanford, Calif.: Stanford University Press, 2000); Blu Greenberg, *On Women and Judaism: A View from the Tradition* (Philadelphia: Jewish Publication Society, 1981); Susannah Heschel, ed., *On Being a Jewish Feminist: A Reader* (New York: Schocken Books, 1983); Miriam B. Peskowitz, *Spinning Fantasies: Rabbis, Gender, and History* (Berkeley: University of California Press, 1997); Judith Plaskow, *Standing again at Sinai: Judaism from a Feminist Perspective* (San Francisco: Harper, 1991); Tamar Ross, *Expanding the Palace of Torah: Orthodoxy and Feminism* (Waltham, Mass.: Brandeis University Press, 2004); Elizabeth Shanks Alexander, *Gender and Timebound Commandments in Judaism* (Cambridge: Cambridge University Press, 2013).

7. Abraham Joshua Heschel, *The Sabbath: Its Meaning for Modern Man* (New York: Farrar, Strauss, and Giroux, 1951), 21.

8. Peter Gould and Rodney White, *Mental Maps* (London: Penguin, 1974); A. R. Kearney and S. Kaplan, "Toward a Methodology for the Measurement of Knowledge Structures of Ordinary People: The Conceptual Content Cognitive Map," *Environment and Behavior* 29, no. 5 (1997): 579–617; R. W. Kulhavy and W. A. Stock, "How Cognitive Maps Are Learned and Remembered," *Annals of the Association of American Geographers* 86, no. 1 (1996): 123–45; Greg Hise, *Magnetic Los Angeles: Planning the Twentieth-Century Metropolis* (Baltimore: Johns Hopkins University Press, 1997).

9. Tim Ingold, *The Perception of the Environment: Essays in Livelihood, Perception, and Skill* (London: Routledge, 2000), 223–25.

10. See introduction to Orsi, *Gods of the City*. David Morgan and Sally Promey also discuss the visible, public dimension of religion in America, in many cases within an urban context. See David Morgan and Sally M. Promey, *The Visual Culture of American Religions* (Berkeley: University of California Press, 2001).

11. The rabbinic authorities who set the parameters for Jewish law during the first three centuries of the Common Era considered all Jews to be bound by Jewish law. Not all Jews today, however, consider themselves bound by Jewish law, although very few reject it altogether.

12. In Jewish law the word "eruv" refers to the process of merging the disparate spaces within the boundary, but in contemporary colloquial usage it generally refers to the physical boundary itself.

13. Herz and Weitzman, "Between City and Desert."

14. During the late 1980s and 1990s, and certainly after the bombing of the World Trade Center in 2001, there was a heightened sensitivity to the public and visible practice of non-Christian religious traditions. Muslims drew criticism over what sociologist John Eade has called the "Islamization" of space, which included the design of mosques and Muslims projecting the daily calls to prayer too loudly in their neighborhoods. See Talal Asad, "Multiculturalism and British Identity in the Wake of the Rushdie Affair," in *Genealogies of Religion: Discipline and Reasons of Power in Christianity and Islam*, ed. Talal Asad (Baltimore: Johns Hopkins University Press, 1993), 239–69; John Eade, "Nationalism, Community, and the Islamization of Space in London," in *Making Muslim Space in North America and Europe*, ed. Barbara Daly Metcalfe (Berkeley: University of California Press, 1996), 217–33. In a series of newspaper articles during the time of Pope Benedict XVI's visit to England, however, Raymond de Souza characterized Britain as a "post-Christian" society and called attention to the intense hostility there toward public expressions of Christianity. See Raymond de Souza, "Above All Holiness," *National Post*, September 23, 2010; and "Britain Makes Room for Benedict," *National Post*, September 20, 2010.

15. This has been the case from a very early period in Jewish history. The prohibition on which the rabbinic authors of the Mishnah and the Talmud focused was not carrying per se, but the transfer of objects from one domain to another or within a public domain. As a result of the close practical and conceptual associations of the transfer of objects with commerce and the construction of the Tabernacle, transfer itself became one of the thirty-nine categories of forbidden Sabbath labor. From the second century on, acts of transfer between different domains were subject to elaborate exegesis in the Jewish legal texts and meticulous circumscription in practice. See Charlotte Fonrobert, "From Separatism to Urbanism: The Dead Sea Scrolls and the Origins of the Tannaitic Eruv," *Dead Sea Discoveries* 2 (2004): 43–71.

16. Interview with David Schreiber, June 2003.

17. It should be stated that many of the Sabbath-observant Jews I interviewed had experienced eruvs in other places, primarily North America or Israel, and were conscious of the enhanced Sabbath experience they offered. Although I interviewed Channi Nussbaum about her experience of the Sabbath before the eruv was built, she died before I was able to speak to her after the eruv was completed. It struck me as remarkable that although she made clear that her Sabbath experience had long been compromised by the lack of an eruv, her faith in and practice of halakhic Judaism remained strong and consistent throughout her life.

18. Interview with Leya Todd, June 2003.

19. "Work Begins on UK's First Jewish Boundary," BBC News, World Edition, August 20, 2002, http://news.bbc.co.uk/2/hi/uk_news/england/2205486.stm.

20. This unpublished image was provided to the author by the office of Dayan (Judge) Hanoch Ehrentreu, the Rosh Beit Din, or head of the London Rabbinical Court in June 2003. Dayan Ehrentreu's approval of the North West London Eruv guaranteed its "kosher" status according to Jewish law, and his office is responsible for ensuring the integrity of the eruv boundary from week to week.

21. Interview with Leya Todd, June 2003.

22. Interview with A. P., May 2003.

23. "Every person" here includes non-Jews. By the time the eruv was finally implemented, it had received so much publicity in local, national, and even international news sources that it was a widely recognized phenomenon in England.

24. Interview with Rabbi Alan Kimche, R. C., L. T., and J. G., June 2003.

25. Interview with Anushka Levey, May 2003.

26. A second London eruv was created in Edgeware in 2006, a third in Borhamwood in 2007, and a fourth in Stanmore in 2011. Jewish communities in St. John's Wood and Maida Vale, and Camden, all in London, as well as in the Greater Manchester area are all in the process of creating eruvim.

27. Interview with A. P., May 2003.

28. Interview with Sara Morris, June 2003.

29. Interview with Rachel Cohen, June 2003.

30. Interview with Rabbi Alan Kimche, June 2003.

31. Raymond de Souza, "Pope Benedict Fighting Extreme Secularism in Visit to Britain," National Post, September 15, 2010, http://life.nationalpost.com/2010/09/15/pope-benedict-fighting-extreme-secularism-in-visit-to-britain.

32. Interviews with Edward Black and Alan Perrin, November/December 2000, and May/June, 2003.

33. Louis P. Nelson, *The Beauty of Holiness: Anglicanism and Architecture in Colonial South Carolina* (Chapel Hill: University of North Carolina Press, 2008), 367.

34. Belden C. Lane, *Landscapes of the Sacred: Geography and Narrative in American Spirituality* (1988; New York: Paulist Press, 2002), 6.

35. David D. Hall, ed., *Lived Religion in America: A Theory of Practice* (Princeton, N.J.: Princeton University Press, 1997).

36. Maurice Merleau-Ponty, *The Phenomenology of Perception* (1945; London: Routledge, 2002); Tim Ingold, *The Perception of the Environment: Essays on Livelihood, Dwelling, and Skill* (London: Routledge, 2000); Lindsay Jones, *The Hermeneutics of Sacred Architecture: Experience, Interpretation, Comparison* (Cambridge, Mass.: Harvard University Press, 2000).

6.

"Art, Memory, and the City" in Bogotá: Mapa Teatro's Artistic Encounters with Inhabited Places

KAREN E. TILL

Project Prometeo: Acts I & II, Downtown Bogotá, December 2002 and 2003

A young woman wearing a pink formal gown walks through a recreated bedroom. Candles and spotlights illuminate her figure as she steps atop a bed and begins jumping on a mattress. Rather than speak lines, her performance—part of a collective interpretation of Heinrich Müller's *Prometheus* titled *Project Prometeo: Acts I & II*—is an embodied one.[1] Her body is framed by her live-time performance as projected upon one of two very large screens (more than three-stories high); on the other screen we see historical and contemporary images and listen to sound recordings of the neighborhood that once existed upon the empty fields where she performs (figure 6.1). She continues climbing up and down off of the bed as other performers begin or continue to enact their own interpretations of the myth. We see a married couple sitting at a dining room table playing cards, a clown performing in a playroom, a man sitting at an imagined doorway lighting matches.

As the audience watches, they learn more about how the performers— as well as thousands of other former residents not on stage—were displaced from their homes when the performers' neighborhood, El Cartucho, was slated for urban renewal and razed in its entirety during 2000–2003. Within less than a year after the second performance of *Project Prometeo*, a new city park was unveiled. Sitting in what was once El Cartucho and would soon become an urban park, audience members of *Project Prometeo: Acts I & II* became witnesses to the stories of former inhabitants. Displaced residents

Figure 6.1. *Project Prometeo: Act II*. Former residents of El Cartucho perform in downtown Bogotá, December 2003. Photo by Fernando Cruz. © Mapa Teatro.

performed legends and truths about a place, their home, through their personal interpretations of the Prometheus myth. At the end of their performance, audience members were invited to become performers by joining the former residents "on stage," dancing to bolero music and sharing their own stories.

This artistic encounter with a once inhabited place encouraged residents and guests to attend to the unfolding and open-ended pathways of memory and belonging.[2] Former inhabitants remembered, visited, and attended to the place that was their home; they shared their stories about El Cartucho with each other and with citizens of the wider city. Through *Project Prometeo* former residents, in collaboration with the artistic collaborative Mapa Teatro (who curated and produced this project), created a temporary community that conveyed their embodied knowledges about place to each other and to guests attending the performance.

I understand the artistic process that led to this performance and other related creative projects as embedded and embodied alternative mappings of the city. These artistic mappings, unlike Cartesian two-dimensional maps, make visible the contours of particular histories, social networks, myths about place, inhabitants' stories, and "mazeways" of individual lives. Not only did inhabitants' quotidian routines become visible through this artistic performance, but also audiences became witnesses through these mappings. According to Diana Taylor, "*to witness*, a transitive verb, defines both the act and the person carrying it out . . . We are both the subject and product of our acts."[3] Those who were displaced and those who witnessed these stories were also encouraged to become caregivers to each other, to a particular place, and to the city. By creating a temporary community through the performance, residents and guests returned to a place where people experienced loss; performers and audiences were invited to engage in memory-work and what I call a place-based ethics of care.[4]

In contrast the city planners and government authorities who privileged so-called green agendas that legitimated the razing of El Cartucho did not try to listen to or learn from inhabitants' experiences, memories, and embodied knowledges. Instead, the area and residents were seen as undesirable. El Cartucho was not "seen" as a place; rather, it was objectified on a planners' map as a site of development potential. When places are understood as sites of development, the relational and complex qualities of already-lived-in places are not respected. The richness, messiness, and unpredictability of the places of everyday dwelling are contained and systematically destroyed in the name of "progress." Place is rendered a location in abstract, absolute space that can be emptied out (of its residents, stories, natures, networks, buildings, infrastructures) and filled in with "better" buildings, activities, things (and peoples). Thus to map places as mere locations is to assert authority over space; design and planning professionals map the present and design the future. In short, this attitude toward designing a "healthy" new park disrespected local inhabitants' routines through, meanings of, and rights to the city. It is far from clear, almost ten years later, if the new "Park of the Third Millennium" will succeed even by its own stated goals.[5]

What would happen if planners and urban designers set their priorities based upon what they learned from inhabitants and places? First, they would have to learn how to listen to inhabitants and attend to places. One way to do so is to learn from and with artists who work in an embedded way with places and inhabitants. This would mean that planners and urban professionals would need to respect artistic practice as a process that might enable a range of what planners call "stakeholders" to learn about and from place rather than treat art as objects (public space ornamentation) or outcomes that attract revenues (creative capital potentials). Artistic practice may also offer ways to rethink the failures of the public consultation practice in planning. Rather than come up with a design and see how residents respond, planners might be a bit more humble and recognize that the people inhabiting places are the experts. Inhabitant-experts acquire and communicate knowledge about both the possibilities and problems of their social ecosystems through their daily routines. At the same time, embedded artistic encounters with existing and once inhabited places may encourage residents and guests to become responsible for each other and for places in ways that result in longer-standing socially sustainable processes. If creative projects enable inhabitants to become caretakers of places (where they live, work, and play) and other inhabitants, their quality of life would be enhanced locally as well as across a number of urban environments, and over a longer period of time.

To make these arguments, I explore the artistic practices and methodologies of the artistic collaborative Mapa Teatro Laboratory of Artists, who curated a series of place-based projects with inhabitants of El Cartucho and other citizens of Bogotá that ran from 2001 to 2005.[6] I begin by providing an overview of the context within which this artistic collaborative worked together with residents—namely, the razing of a densely settled historic area.

Stories of Displacement: Santa Inés, Bogotá

In Bogotá the historic Santa Inés neighborhood was known locally as El Cartucho (after the name of one of the streets in the neighborhood). Located near the government district downtown, by the end of the nineteenth century it was home to many elegant colonial buildings and elite families. Following the interrelated processes of urbanization and suburbanization, economic restructuring, and migration that accelerated from the 1960s, populations and activities moved to different parts of the city, thereby affecting the neighborhoods they had left behind. After elite residents moved away from downtown, the central bus depot was located near Santa Inés. The neighborhood soon became the first stopping place for the many families and individuals who left the poverty and violence in the countryside seeking better opportunities for their children in the city. Growing rates of homelessness and unemployment contributed to the rise of so-called informal economies. Thousands of people survived for decades in El Cartucho working in the neighborhood's warehouses, bottle and paper recycling works, streets and alleyways, stalls, variety stores, little hotels, and pawnshops. Gangs, drugs, guns, and sex work also interpellated the lives of many of the residents living here. With the entry of the drug cartels and strongmen to Santa Inés, the neighborhood soon had one of the highest rates of homicide and insecurity in the city (and hence the nation). The historic fabric of the area deteriorated as state funds were used for projects elsewhere.[7]

Although El Cartucho became the target of urban renewal policies beginning in the 1990s, it was under the Liberal Party's Enrique Peñalosa Londoño that the neighborhood was demolished to make way for the "Public Park of the Third Millennium" (Parque Tercer Milenio), unveiled in March 2005. In office from 1998 to 2001, Peñalosa called the neighborhood "a symbol of chaos and of government impotence"; part of his mayoral campaign included the promise to "reclaim El Cartucho for the public."[8] Replacing a "symbol of chaos" with the promise of a clean public park was tied to Peñalosa's larger 1997 election campaign under the banner of the "green" and "sustainable" cities movement.[9] While Peñalosa accomplished much in his short term, including establishing the Transmilenio mass transit system (which meant breaking the mafia's hold on the bus system), many of his other projects resulted in the displacement of the city's poor and unwanted from downtown areas.

Renewal in Santa Inés meant the razing of twenty hectares (200,000 square meters); by 2003 families and individuals were displaced, largely without compensation. Some were housed temporarily in the nearby slaughterhouse because of the public fear of encountering those who once lived in El Cartucho. And yet the Third Millennium Park is a rather sterile space today and is still considered unsafe. As Rolf Abderhalden Cortés of Mapa Teatro described, "In 2006, the Parque Tercer Milenio was awarded the prize for the best public works project at the Bienale de Arquitectura in Colombia. It was a prize awarded, in truth, to a cemetery."[10]

Many planners consider the sustainable and liveable cities movement to be progressive. But when planning practice ignores residents' values and uses "expert" knowledge to view and "know" a place, then sustainability may ignore the very social-spatial relations needed to assure healthy environments over a longer period of time. Planners have traditionally classified densely settled, historic neighborhoods that have not received public or other investment funds according to the pejorative land use category "blighted." This development category, however, overlooks inhabitants' use values and contributions of social capital. Moreover, when "best practice" planning approaches and designs are imported from other cities without consideration of these local resources and ideas to supposedly "fix" or "clean up" a "blighted" area, the richness and potentialities of inhabited places are at best considered temporal aberrances on planning and development maps. Urban renewal of this sort means that the task of city officials and planners is to replace "bad" landscapes—and the things and people associated with them—with "good" urban design. (Indeed, the people who lived in El Cartucho were often referred to as "disposables."[11]) Land use and zoning maps that represent places as blighted sites assume that space is a container. Moreover, the temporal is separated out from the spatial. Urban renewal assumes sequential re-occupancy—whereby one set of (undesirable) users and uses occupying a parcel of space is replaced by a better set of users/uses—defined by a moralized temporality; in other words, a negative present will be replaced by a new, desired future. An area is thus classified as blighted, reappropriated under eminent domain, and razed; it is filled in and re-aestheticized; and it is re-presented as good for the body politic.

The mapping of places as sites on land use and zoning maps thus shifts the understandings of place as a lived and rich center of meaning, memory, and experience and as created by and enabling complex networks and mazeways that lead through and connect peoples and places over time to an atemporal, spatially bounded location. When place is understood according to this abstract conception of space, the complex social relations, memories, and affective and environmental networks that define and create places and peoples are not plotted; they are not valued on maps that define ground according to land use and development or property value.[12]

Once the extent of Peñalosa's plans for the removal of most of Santa Inés became public, there was an intense political backlash. In 2000 Antanas Mockus Šivickas of the Green Party (and affiliated with the Indigenous Social Alliance Movement and Yes Colombia parties) successfully ran for office and inherited the park project in 2001.[13] The Mockus administration argued that the plans and contracts were already too well advanced to prevent the project from proceeding legally; the razing of Santa Inés continued through to 2003. Drawing upon his previous work encouraging civic responsibility through creative and artistic happenings in public space (known as Cultura Ciudadana [Citizen Culture] programs), Mockus nonetheless organized an urban community development and public art working group that would work with the neighborhoods affected. The Mockus administration invited Alicia Eugenia Silva at Colombia National University to create a team of historians, anthropologists, social workers, students, and artists, which included Mapa Teatro, to develop projects in collaboration with local residents. The City of Bogotá Mayor's Office and the United Nations Development Program (UNDP) sponsored these projects. While this may be considered a liberal approach to recognize past wrongs—it did not resolve larger social and structural inequities in the city, it did not bring economic assistance to those displaced through jobs or housing, and it conceived of community development and artistic processes in managerial terms as outcomes—some of the projects resulted in unexpected, and for some citizens life-changing, collaborations and outcomes.

City authorities initially suggested creating some sort of tangible marker in the landscape in Santa Inés, a permanent memorial that would function as a testimony to the life experiences of those who once inhabited this part of the city. But the working group rejected that idea. Daniel Vargas, the executive director of the group, argued that the city's initial idea of building a memorial depicted "a population [as] without a memory, without any intention to remember, [and asked them] to assimilate," and expected outsiders "to leave a testimony and pay homage to its most painful and happiest life experiences." Such a gesture, he argued, is indicative "of a society that has problems *recognizing itself*."[14] As Vargas's comments indicate, although the working group was funded by the mayor's office of development, they did their best to maintain a critical distance from local administrative authorities. They rejected the proposal to create a memorial and developed instead *Project C'úndua: A Pact for Life*, three transdisciplinary, multimedia projects that ran at multiple locales throughout the city during 2001–2003, managed or curated by directors of different working groups.[15]

Mapa Teatro (or Mapa) was designated the artistic director of one of these projects. Their members initially worked with residents in two communities in 2001–2002: informal neighborhoods in Usaquén, on the outskirts of the city, and Santa Inés/El Cartucho in central Bogotá. For *Project C'úndua*, they curated and collaborated with residents on intergenerational memory-books, "the house in the street" installations along the historical route Avenida Jimenez, site-specific performances, and live-time video installations, simultaneously broadcast in both locations. Building upon this experience, they continued working with El Cartucho residents on their second project, *Project Prometeo: Acts I & II* (2002–2003). Although work funded by the city ran only from 2001 to 2003, Mapa continued their collaborations with residents using their own funding sources.

Mapa Teatro identifies their artistic work with former El Cartucho residents under the title *Arte, Memoria, y Cuidad* (Art, Memory, and the City) on their website.[16] In addition to *Project C'úndua* and *Project Prometeo*, they continued to work with El Cartucho residents on at least three other projects, including *Re-Corridos* (Run-Throughs), interactive "video-sonic install-actions" that included theater, performance art, installation art, and activism to reflect upon their work together. *Re-Corridos* was held in an old, deteriorating building in downtown Bogotá in 2003, which Mapa began using (and later purchased) to host workshops with residents. Another project,

La Limpieza de los Establos de Augías (The Cleaning of the Augean Stables), made visible the "clean-up" of El Cartucho and building of the park taking place behind fences, and projecting images of comfortable museum visitors watching the videos to the construction site, through simultaneous live video installations (venues: El Cartucho, Santa Inés, and the Museum of Modern Art, downtown Bogotá, 2004). Third, *Testigo de las Ruinas* (Testimony to the Ruins) included live performances, moving-screen video installations, with spoken narratives and recorded sounds by Mapa Teatro and El Cartucho performers (venue: downtown Bogotá, 2005, following the opening of the Parque Tercer Mileneo, and ongoing at various international theater venues). A final project, *Cartografía Movedizas* (Cartographic Quicksand), which was more a response to Mapa's reflections on their work with El Cartucho residents, was a series of live and performed walks throughout the city inspired by daily journeys of those who cannot afford public transportation (venue: from the outskirts of the city to the center and back again, Bogotá 2010). In the following section I briefly introduce Mapa's embedded methodologies through a discussion of *Project Prometeo* and *Re-Corridos*. In the concluding section I reflect on lessons that city planning, urban design, and landscape professionals might learn from artistic practice more generally.

"Art, Memory, and the City"

Colombian artists (and siblings) Heidi, Elizabeth, and Rolf Abderhalden founded the Mapa Teatro Laboratory of Artists in 1984 and have since become well known in the Latin American art world and internationally for their innovative productions in theater, radio, and multimedia installations.[17] After they agreed to participate in the city project, Mapa Teatro members did not want predetermined outcomes to set the parameters for their creative work, which resulted in some differences in how they and the social scientists in the *Project C'úndua* team did their research and designed their methodologies. Mapa Teatro's artists understand creative practice as open-ended, not designed according to predetermined outcomes and objects. Through their previous experiences working with marginalized residents on creative projects, moreover, they also understand their creative practice as a means to develop safe and open environments wherein experimental communities can be formed from strangers. These communities can then work together — try out new things, take risks, share stories, be co-present — and learn to trust each other when conceptualizing and implementing "social laboratories of the imagination." Consequently, their first step as nonresidents of

El Cartucho was to confront their own understandings of the place and explore the landscape in transition. They also began to do some research about the history of the area. Next, members of Mapa began to listen to residents' stories. After building relations of trust, they collaborated with former residents on projects that ran beyond the original larger working group and secured a run-down colonial building to meet in downtown to do so.

Before working with residents the Mapa artists knew they first had to face their own biases, fears, and fantasies associated with the "legendary" El Cartucho. Most, if not all, of the Mapa Teatro team had never set foot inside this neighborhood. As Abderhalden Cortés explained:

> The Santa Inés barrio, commonly known as *El Cartucho*, was a stigmatized area burdened not only by its own long, rich urban history, but also by a plethora of mythologies that all of us in the city carry around with us: some more than others, perhaps, depending on our proximity to or distance from that physical and symbolic location. For me, as a child growing up in a distant neighborhood in the north where I had little contact with it, the Santa Inés barrio was the object of fears and fantasies. It was a specific site of fear — the city's *center of fear*.[18]

After acknowledging their own stories about this place, in 2001 the Mapa team went to Santa Inés for the first time. There they encountered a rapidly changing landscape. To ensure that the Parque Tercer Milenio would be built (and perhaps due to growing public indignation at the scale of the overall project), city authorities had quickly decided to turn one smaller part of Santa Inés, about 15 percent of the larger area, into a green space, which members of Mapa interpreted as a political, symbolic, and economic promise that the larger park would be built.[19] Thus, already by 2001 many phases of "renewal" were occurring simultaneously and in close proximity: ongoing negotiations with property owners over the purchase of existing buildings; evictions of existing families; the razing of buildings and structures; the removal and clearance of debris; and the creation and installation of the park. Mapa artists recall being disoriented by the experience of witnessing demolition when people were still living in the area, moving through El Cartucho according to now disrupted day-to-day routines. Confronting this juxtaposition of a "partially devastated urban landscape" with everyday life was "terrifying" and "devastating" for the Mapa team. Abderhalden Cortés recalled that the image of "the demolition of vacated houses immediately made us want to stop time, to keep the tangible traces of history from being erased. The city's architectural patrimony was collapsing before our eyes and before the eyes of its inhabitants."[20] He noted that they were witnessing the loss both of a foundational memory and an "intangible patrimony" of the city.

After filming and making sound recordings of this landscape, they began researching archival documents about the history of Santa Inés and making preliminary contact with the former residents of El Cartucho. They first approached the public workers who were "processing" displaced residents. Many people evicted from the neighborhood didn't have state documentation, which may explain the derogatory label "disposables" that was sometimes used to refer to El Cartucho residents. For this first phase of demolition only, as part of a social inclusion and integration program, former residents could obtain identity cards, health exams, vaccinations, and possibly replacement housing. According to Abderhalden Cortés, although people could live without government documentation in El Cartucho because of the informal economy, that would not be the case when they were relocated to other parts of the city.[21]

With government identification some individuals and families were able to get a single room in a temporary housing shelter for a limited period of time. While the social workers processing former residents may have been well intentioned, Mapa members noted that some authorities were demeaning in their attitudes toward the individuals they "processed." For example, when Mapa asked about possible interview and working partners for their projects, authorities at the temporary shelters mentioned they should avoid particular individuals, including a younger person who was described as "mentally retarded" and unable to speak. (This person later became an important performer/collaborator of the Mapa–El Cartucho resident artistic team.)

Working initially with former residents, but later also with those individuals still living in the neighborhood, Mapa members began to listen closely to the stories, needs, and wishes of El Cartucho residents. They also visited the temporary housing shelters daily. Of course, Mapa artists received a range of responses from the residents. Many did not want to participate in the project; some asked for money, clothing, food, or housing, assuming the artists belonged to the government's relocation team; some individuals ignored their presence; still others were hostile. But they began to build relations of trust with a small group of individuals. Abderhalden Cortés noted the sense of urgency that framed their relationships with residents. The temporal was intensified: lives were being lived and re-lived in a very short period of time. According to Abderhalden Cortés, "Time was concentrated; from day to day, people lost their homes, lost contact with friends and family, needed help. . . . There was a sense of closeness because of this extreme situation. Within this temporal context of urgency and extreme change, moreover, the intensity of our interactions—one to two years of interacting with people—seemed like a much longer period of time."[22]

As Mapa artists gained trust with some residents, they began to record, follow, and move with residents as a way of learning and receiving knowledge about the important places, mazeways, and life stories of El Cartucho residents. Some individuals gave Mapa artists permission to videotape their belongings and personal stories at their temporary room or (later) still-standing homes. The collaborative also convinced authorities of the need for individuals to leave the temporary housing units for their artistic project (they were not given permission to leave these premises). Individuals thus were able to return to their former homes, their favorite hanging-out places, or to other special places and to witness what was happening to their worlds without having to explain themselves. Walking through the former neighborhood with residents, the artists paid attention to how former residents moved, where they pointed out where things used to be, how they recalled events, and the ways they reflected on their situation; when appropriate, the Mapa team video- and audio-recorded these memory walks. They also used archival materials to ask for reflections or created sketch maps as part of their place-based interactions with residents (either at the temporary housing units or in El Cartucho). Through these place-based methodologies, former residents introduced the Mapa team to people they knew who were still living and working in El Cartucho, some of whom later participated in the collaborative projects.

Some residents also began to work offsite with members of Mapa at the old colonial building. The collaborative provided a safe, supportive, and comfortable environment for individuals to visit regularly. In an old building near downtown that may have reminded residents of some of the older buildings in El Cartucho, residents visited the artists and each other, had teas and meals, and participated in workshops and projects that would move beyond the telling of personal stories. They were encouraged to work with, perform, and think through their memories, experiences, dreams, fears, and personal fictions of El Cartucho and the city. Some former residents stayed or worked there for different lengths of time. With what became *Project Prometeo* and *Re-Corridos*, the Mapa collaborative co-curated their work exclusively with these individuals.

Mapa's members understood that leaving El Cartucho meant many things, including abandonment and exile, as well as liberation and new possibilities. Because Mapa artists often work between documentary- and dream-like aesthetic and narrative forms in their art, they intuitively allow embodied storytelling and remembering to create the spaces of possibility for their art forms. They recognized that residents' contradictory experiences might be touched up obliquely, even worked through unconsciously, through myth-making and embodied movements rather than through linear narratives. As Abderhalden Cortés explained: "Myth is the consummate *story*. Its generative nature makes it a catalyst for stories; they repeat themselves like dreams, continually forming and deforming in a mobile structure that always reanimates itself. The community's stories were a substantive part of the architecture of the neighborhood's memory. A form of resistance in the face of oblivion, a potential footprint among the ruins."[23]

Mapa's previous work with prison inmates on various projects taught them that when working with individuals who have experienced violence and loss, words and narrative could close down memory and creativity. They developed theater and movement techniques for preliminary workshops. Heidi Abderhalden developed these bodywork workshops based upon her training in the "functional integration" approaches of the Feldenkrais method, approaches that encourage individuals to explore their well-being and self-awareness through different movement repertoires.[24] Preliminary workshops included bodywork and communal meals rather than face-to-face dialogue. Only in later workshops did they introduce texts.

The Mapa team also introduced former residents to Heinrich Müller's interpretation of the Prometheus myth because of its unexpected ending; it could work as a kind of "found object" taken out of context that residents could interpret and resignify through their own stories, "readings, gazes and gestures."[25] Recall that Prometheus steals fire from the gods and gives it to humans. When the gods discover that he broke his pact with them, he is condemned to exile in the Caucasus, chained to a rock where an eagle feeds on his liver. To survive, Prometheus feeds on the eagle's excrement. Three thousand years later the gods decide to free Prometheus and send Heracles to scale the wall of filth created over thousands of years and tell the good news of his liberation to Prometheus. But once he hears the news, Prometheus becomes afraid. Heracles can't understand his response, but Prometheus explains that he has grown accustomed to the eagle and is unsure he can live without it.

In the workshop discussions about the myth, Mapa artists had no idea of what to expect, because they were following the "footsteps" of residents through their terrains of memory as outsiders. The contradictory ending allowed for multiple possible interpretations; the myth resonated in quite distinctive ways for individual residents. "As the text was being read, each person reinvented his or her own story, updating the original text and re-writing his or her own myth."[26] Encouraged by residents' responses, the artists asked each person to take just one part of the myth that they most identified with and consider a way to interpret and perform it for the group. Some people knew right away what part they wanted to interpret. A man who had one leg said he wanted the last section, when Prometheus said he was more afraid of freedom than the eagle pecking at his liver. Other residents were more reserved, but once each person had a part of the story, they came up with many possibilities through another series of workshops, one for each of twelve parts of the myth that residents selected. Through this creative process, residents together or alone developed images and self-narratives of their barrio, drawing inspiration from the sites and struggles of their own myths, legends, and stories. The final outcome of these workshops resulted in the creation of a flexible script. According to Mapa's members, the collective script and performance of *Project Prometeo* became yet another "paper record of the disappearance of a neighborhood."[27]

By December 2002 fifteen residents from El Cartucho performed an evening rendition of *Project Prometeo: Act I* in a half-razed, half-standing neighborhood. All residents of the city, including Mayor Mockus, were invited, and many people living in the neighborhood and from other parts of the city attended. "We staged the stories and the visual, aural and gestural narratives born from the experience of the laboratory."[28] Two large video screens (one about three stories high and a second about five stories) were erected, and upon them were projected the residents' "archive," previously recorded and then edited by the artistic collaborative, as inspired by their conversations, the workshops, and residents' feedback (figure 6.1). Voices of interviewed residents and the work the collective had done became the video soundtrack for the performance. One year later, in the same place and again in December, the city center and the razed lots of the entire "old" Santa Inés neighborhood functioned as a backdrop and stage for *Project Prometeo: Act II*. The performance offered a new record of the lives of the people involved in the previous year's performances in the last moments of the neighborhood's demolition. As was the case in the first performance, thousands of candles were used to mark former streets and buildings of the neighborhood, and two screens framed the actors' stories. With no material trace left standing of buildings or other physical structures, for this second performance Mapa artists suggested that each participant choose the "most meaningful place in the house." Residents then either brought their furniture and belongings, or the artists helped them furnish a room, creating a kitchen, living room, bedroom, or bathroom as a stage upon the stage of the razed fields.[29]

As residents performed their interpretation of Prometheus in formal attire, they did not speak, but enacted their version of myth, their story, such as by sequentially lighting matches while sitting atop of chairs, eating fire, playing cards at a dining room table, and releasing doves from a magic box. Throughout their performances, projected images and soundtracks that the artists created from the range of engagements they had with residents and the neighborhood framed the embodied enactments of residents atop of their former homes. At times the "performers" mimicked the recorded images of themselves being projected on the large screens, which also allowed audiences to recognize the residents and actors in their multiple roles. In this way audiences became witnesses to the spectacle of themselves witnessing stories of loss.[30] What places and stories were "real" and what were imagined in this performance? What fantasies and memories did the actors and audiences bring to these city spaces in transition? What did the actors, as residents performing in their reconstructed homes and former locations of their old neighborhood, remember as their story unfolded behind, in front of, and around them? To integrate the audience physically into the performance, *Project Prometeo: Act II* concluded with a grand ball, which became a celebration of this place and an invitation to reflect upon how this place had been perceived. The audience was invited to come to the stage; about a hundred people joined the performers to dance to the music of a bolero tune on the ruins of their home. In this way the many spaces and stages were blurred, between the performer and audience, between recorded images and lived experiences, between memory and imagination. The dance also allowed for these witnesses and caregivers to tell new stories, create new imaginaries, and possibly even forge alternative futures. For Diana Taylor, because witnessing involves responsibility as well as the "heavy weight of sorrow," it "might help broaden the scope of the possible . . . and allow for a wider range of responses."[31]

Re-Corridos was another project curated and created by Mapa Teatro with former El Cartucho residents. Using the stories, recollections, found objects, fieldwork, memory walks, and sound and audiovisual records of their work, they made a series of interactive video-sonic installations in the old colonial building they used for their workshops. More than six thousand

Figure 6.2. *Re-Corridos* exterior installation: "The Witness." Downtown Bogotá, 2003. Photo by Mauricio Esguerra.© Mapa Teatro.

visitors came in just over two weeks in December 2003 to witness, experience, and interact with the living memory of El Cartucho during its final phases of the demolition. Twelve physical spaces, starting with "The Witness" recreated aspects of the neighborhood's "niche" memories (figure 6.2).

An important part of *Re-Corridos* was the spatially concentrated "sonic portals," installations in different areas of the building that brought the routine sounds and sound testimonies of Santa Inés into the interior spaces of the house. Near the entrance, the visitor would ring a bell and experience the sound installation "The Bellringer," a sonic threshold of voices—of vendors calling out from avenues, alleyways, and carts of the (now razed) neighborhood—through which the visitor would walk. These voices may have recalled (or not) the visitor's memories of particular places or experiences

Figure 6.3. *Re-Corridos*: "The Rubble," video-sonic installation of the demolition of El Cartucho, using various materials and projections. Interior courtyard of colonial building in downtown Bogotá, 2003. Photo by Mauricio Esguerra. © Mapa Teatro.

in the city, memories that the visitor might bring into the other memory "niche" installations throughout the house. A video-sonic installation called "The Rubble" transformed a larger interior room/courtyard into a place of devastation through sonic, visual, and material "testimonies" of the destruction of the built environment of El Cartucho; some buildings were similar to the spaces in which the visitor stood (figure 6.3). As the colonial building itself was in partial decay, the visitor could see up into the other floor and ceiling; at some angles the building appeared fragile, about ready to collapse in the ruins below.

At the top of the stairs, the visitor encountered a resident-performer who sat at a small desk in front of a wall of projected images of the interior spaces

Figure 6.4. *Re-Corridos*: "The Car" (*La bascule*), video installation with recycled televisions and recycling cart. Upstairs room of colonial building, downtown Bogotá, December 2003. Photo by Mauricio Esguerra.© Mapa Teatro.

of a destroyed home. Depending upon how the visitor entered the space, the performer would ask a question, ask for documents, tell a story, sing a song, or ignore the visitor. The adjacent installation, "The Car" (*El Carro/La báscule*), was a darkened room with eight or so recycling carts, each filled with eight to ten old televisions (figure 6.4). Paying tribute to one of the most important economies of the neighborhood, in each cart televisions played videos of inhabitants recalling or engaged in their trade, which created a sonic cacophony and arresting visual montage of talking heads and moving bodies. While one could gain a sense of the diversity of the recyclers, at some moments common visual or aural commonalities emerged, such as the songs of the recycler, the materials found or needed to engage in their work, or stories about discovery and destruction. A tactile ceiling of inverted bottles, "The Bottle," encouraged visitors to walk under and reach up to the glass and in the process create music and multicolored shifting light through the thousands of bottles. The final memory niches, "The Rest" and "The Voice," also included recycled materials to tell stories of life in El Cartucho, such as the "collection of old radio carcasses" that were installed to create a "forest of radios" in which the visitor would have to walk up to a radio, "tune in," and get in close to listen to a recorded story.

Tucked away somewhat in the back, after "The House" and "The Room," was "The Skin." Listening to personal stories through backlit deliberate cracks in a false wall, visitors learned about the stories behind an individual's scars; in a different false wall the visitor could look through to see images of wounds and scars. "The Skin" thus was a metaphor and metonym for the wounded body of the city. Many of these wounds were received in the process of negotiating life in El Cartucho. This installation resonated with what I have found in my ethnographic work in other wounded cities, including Berlin, Cape Town, and Roanoke.[32] For Mindy Fullilove, places are an important part of individual emotional and social ecologies; our everyday routines and interactions with places help create mazeways, an external system of protection that allows individuals to maintain the external balance between themselves and the larger world.[33] When a person's mazeway is damaged, such as when individuals are forced to leave their neighborhoods, or familiar places are destroyed, Fullilove argues, a person will go into "root shock"; the emotional and physical damage resulting from root shock may stay with a person for a lifetime. Because the physical fabric of the neighborhood one grows up in also provides individuals with the cues and opportunities for the intergenerational transmission of knowledges and stories, root shock may affect multiple generations. Thus root shock can be inherited through social, bodily, and place memory.

During a period of urban transition, the Mapa Teatro collaborative understood their artistic work with residents as engaging El Cartucho as a place not so much in terms of loss, but as a living eyewitness to the process of urban change. During the five years of the "Art, Memory, and the City" collaborations, residents worked with each other and the (changing) psychic and material qualities of place to access voices, inheritances, and resources that might provide them with a language of belonging. Residents were asked to understand and care for the places they once inhabited as a process of taking care of themselves; their embodied placemakings would remain with them as they faced unknown futures and searched for new homes and ways of life. Mapa Teatro members noted that their work with the residents of Santa Inés changed how they worked, and they believe it also affected many individuals with whom they collaborated, some with whom they still work. For Rolf Abderhalden Cortés, "its unique resonance was due to its particular qualities and implications, which were not only aesthetic but ethnographic, anthropological, sociological and above all human and *relational.*"[34]

Concluding Lessons

The gaps created in the wake of political, social, and spatial displacements, such as the case of El Cartucho, as well as the ways that such traumas are witnessed, remembered, forgotten, and inherited by different groups of residents raise ethical questions about the politics of urban renewal.[35] I have suggested that arrogant planning solutions to "problems" identified by politicians and city authorities delineate places as blank spatial palettes for urban design rather than as unfolding, resulting from multiple networks, temporalities, and pathways, and, consequently, as historically, symbolically, and spatially dense. If we, as citizens, understand that our duties include a responsibility to each other and to the rights of all citizens to inhabit the city, those who have the authority to plan for and build our cities should become especially aware of what inhabitants value about particular places. In other words, a place-based ethical responsibility tied to a sense of active democratic citizenship calls for a different approach to planning, policy, and development agendas than currently exists.[36]

The distinctive creative and embedded practices of the Mapa Teatro collaborative remind us that places are lived and relational, not locations of property and land use. As Rolf Abderhalden Cortés later reflected about their work with El Cartucho residents, the creative processes resulted in an "intimate relationship" with places and peoples, as shaped through art and the city.[37] Working with residents, Mapa artists made visible the quotidian textures of place. They created, with residents, alternative city mappings and walks; domestic installations; video projections on exterior walls of buildings and in public squares; street, body, and landscape ethnographies; and post-demolition archaeologies and installations. Their artistic practices meant that residents told stories about place (and were listened to), they returned again and again to a place as it dramatically changed, and they communicated embodied knowledges about place during a time of rapid transition and personal loss. Even as residents were unfairly and structurally excluded from accessing the central spaces and resources of the city as a result of urban renewal, the artists created a safe setting for displaced individuals to return. As they worked in teams of different capacities in unanticipated ways, residents could share their fears and memories with others; they could feel unsettled about their loss and unwanted transition as they explored their attachments to a place that would always be with them.

Although it is unclear how the displaced residents of El Cartucho were affected by these interactions and collaborations, I would argue that the memory-work of the Mapa collaborative and the residents resulted in positive personal changes, however small. Moreover, their artistic collaborations reflect what I call a place-based ethics of care. According to Joan Tronto, care is a type of engagement, a rational practice.[38] It is an "activity that includes everything that we do to maintain, continue, and repair our 'world' so that we can live in it as well as possible." Tronto identifies four types of care that result in ethical qualities: (1) "caring about" someone or something (and I would add particular places) results in attentiveness; (2) "taking care of" someone, some place, or something produces responsibility; (3) "giving care" produces competence in caring work; and (4) "receiving care" produces responsiveness. Mapa Teatro members and El Cartucho residents asked other residents, politicians, urban professionals, and audiences to "care about" the stories and lives of Santa Inés through projects such as *Project Prometeo* and *Re-Corridos*. They did so by "taking care of" the neighborhood when it was being materially destroyed: they documented stories, helped each other through the transition, went on memory walks together, talked and listened to each other, trusted Mapa artists and each other in their workshops, and tried to imagine a way to share that memory-work with others. The realization that the city's patrimony was to be materially lost initiated a creative, ethnographic, and relational artistic process that resulted in the giving and receiving of care. Through the teas, meals, bodywork, and workshops, the artists initially "gave care" to the residents in multiple ways, continuing to honor their stories and rights to the city; but they also encouraged residents to take care of themselves. In later workshops, as residents gained confidence in their interpretations and collaborations, they gave each other care and offered performances and installations for others in the city to experience and partake in. Thus, both artists and residents "received care" in unexpected ways, changing how they worked and interacted with others and the city. Some of those relationships continued beyond the life of these projects. Ethically, citizens became responsible for each other and for particular places.

This is a critical lesson for planners and urban designers who are interested in socially sustainable cities. Urban professionals should learn to listen to inhabitants' place-based knowledges and create the possibilities of place-based forms of stewardship by working with residents and artists *before* they begin conceptualizing, designing, and implementing planning and development projects. Some cities in Germany and cities in the United States, such as Minneapolis, already do so.[39] Why? Residents know the ways that places are made, the mazeways that sustain them, and the ways places and peoples are connected through various networks. They know where and how cultural, sacred, historical, and social places are made and used in different neighborhoods and parts of the city. They know which pathways are fluid and which ones are dead ends. They are aware of the economic and social resources, as well as the needs, of an area. Artists, using embedded and creative practices, can help residents and nonresident experts learn to listen, see, experience, and think about places and lives differently, such as through collaborative research, exploratory workshops, experiments, and other creative projects. Working with artists and residents, landscape architects and planners might consider developing site-specific walk-throughs (from documenting historical traces to thinking about water drainage), and learn to run community-based design charrettes, intense workshops devoted to design and planning activity with a range of urban experts, based upon inhabitants' needs and perspectives. (Planning and design students should be required to work on at least one community-based and embedded artistic project as part of their professional licensing.) If a project appears to be imposed by a government authority, planners should not only offer expert understandings of socio-demographic and environmental data, legal and zoning requirements, and a list of important "stakeholders," but they also should understand and be able to explain inhabitants' needs, as well as the reasons why places are valued, to city officials.

In addition to learning to respect place and inhabitants' understandings of place, Mapa Teatro's methodology of working with and respecting residents, rather than focusing on final products, is also instructive. Mapa artists' insistence on pursuing their own goals and artistic practice independently of the larger *Project C'úndua* group and mayor's office meant that they worked on open-ended projects with no stated clear "outcomes" in advance, despite the threat of having their funding cut. Inhabitants' stories, memories, and experiences, as well as the artists' responses to El Cartucho and to residents, were the "raw data" needed to generate creative responses and to nourish the imagination. Rather than create projects that were limited by demands by developers to guarantee profit margins or by government authorities to provide outcomes-based criteria for their reelection campaigns, Mapa's members chose to explore new possibilities with residents.

The demolition of El Cartucho exceeded contemporary narratives of urbanization and public memory. El Cartucho, both a mythic and lived central place of Bogotá, was always more than a mere location for former residents and city dwellers. Mapa's artistic practice invited residents, citizens, and guests to reflect critically on their lives, their attachments to particular places, and larger urban processes. Because they followed the residents' mazeways and circulations of daily life that extended from and through bodies and places throughout the city, Mapa artists encouraged former residents and audiences to engage in alternative mappings by following the contours of previously unknown, but now known, embodied memories of place. Through the co-construction of experimental communities, evicted residents were also offered the possibility of caregiving and receiving care. The collaborative performances and installations thus had the potential to transform memories of violence into shared stories of relevance through collective witnessing rather than spectatorship. "Art, Memory, and the City" enabled at least some residents to claim their "right to the city," including the right to represent, narrate, remember, perform, and care for El Cartucho.[40]

NOTES

This chapter was supported in part by the Netherlands Institute for Advanced Study in the Humanities and Social Sciences (NIAS). I am especially grateful for the generosity of Mapa Teatro and the numerous insightful conversations over the years with Rolf, Heidi, and Ximenia. Thanks also to Arijit Sen, Lisa Silverman, and John Blum for their helpful suggestions and encouragement.

1. For a more detailed discussion of *Project Prometeo*, see Karen E. Till, "A Footstep amidst the Ruins," in *Urban Constellations*, ed. Matthew Gandy (Berlin: Jovis Verlag, 2011), 167–71; and Karen E. Till, "Wounded Cities: Memory-Work and a Place-Based Ethics of Care," *Political Geography* 31, no. 1 (2012): 3–14.

2. For a discussion about place, memory, and art, see Karen E. Till, "Artistic and Activist Memory-Work: Approaching Place-Based Practice," *Memory Studies* 1, no. 1 (2008): 95–109; Karen E. Till, "Urban Remnants: Place, Memory, and Artistic Practice in Berlin and Bogotá," *ENCOUNTERS* 1, no. 1 (2010): 75–88, 101–103, available online at http://www2.dokkyo.ac.jp/~doky0016/encounters/09/Contents .htm; and Karen E. Till, "Interim Use at a Former Death Strip? Art, Politics, and Urbanism at Skulpturenpark Berlin Zentrum," in *The German Wall: Fallout in Europe*, ed. Marc Silberman (Basingstoke: Palgrave Macmillan, 2011), 99–122.

3. Diana Taylor, "Trauma as Durational Performance: A Return to Dark Sites," in *Rites of Return: Diaspora Poetics and the Politics of Memory*, ed. Marianne Hirsch and Nancy Miller (New York: Columbia University Press, 2011), 276; emphasis in original.

4. I introduce the concept of a "place-based ethics of care" as tied to memory-work in Karen E. Till, "Resilient Politics and Memory-Work in Wounded Cities:

Rethinking the City through the District Six in Cape Town, South Africa," in *Collaborative Resilience: Moving from Crisis to Opportunity*, ed. Bruce E. Goldstein (Cambridge: MIT Press, 2011), 283–307; and Till, "Wounded Cities."

5. For a further discussion of the park project, see Karen E. Till, "'Greening' the City? Artistic Re-Visions of Sustainability in Bogotá," *e-misferica* 7, no. 1 (2010), available at http://hemisphericinstitute.org/hemi/en/e-misferica-71/till.

6. Mapa Teatro Laboratorio des Artes website, "Arte, memoria y ciudad," http://www.mapateatro.org.

7. As far as I know, no systematic history has been done of the community, but see Rolf Abderhalden and Juanita Cristina Aristizábal, eds., *Catalogue and Multi-Media: Project C'úndua, Years 2001–2003*, trans. Curtis Glick and Tony Hastings (Bogotá: La Silueta ediciones Ltd., multimedia: CD SYSTEMS, n.d.); Henry Mance, "Colombia's Most Legendary Slum," *The Big Issue in the North: UK*, October 9, 2007, http://www.streetnewsservice.org/index.php?page=archive_detail&articleID=1673.

8. Mance, "Columbia's Most Legendary Slum."

9. As I describe elsewhere, Peñalosa initiated five mega-projects during his three years in office (1998–2001): the bank of lands; a parks system, including a bike paths network; a system of libraries; the Transmilenio mass transit system; and road construction, maintenance, and renovation. Not all were completed, but he was able to push through such ambitious initiatives, in part, because he received a city in good fiscal condition after Mayor Jaime Castro's financial reforms and a relatively independent city council. Peñalosa also built upon existing traditions to encourage a sense of safety in public spaces, in particular *Domingo Ciclovia* (Cycling Sunday), launched by Augusto Ramirez in 1982, which closed the city's main arteries to vehicular traffic and encouraged bicycle use. Peñalosa challenged the city's reliance on Japanese transportation companies that rejected public transport options. See Till, "'Greening' the City?"

10. Rolf Abderhalden Cortés, "The Artist as Witness: An Artist's Testimony," part of a talk given in December 2006 at the *Academia Superior de Artes de Bogotá*, available at http://www.hemisphericinstitute.org/journal/4.2/eng/artist_presentation/mapateatro/mapa_artist.html.

11. Rolf Abderhalden Cortés, personal interview with the author, Berlin, 2008.

12. On the mapping of places as sites on land use and zoning maps, see Yi-Fu Tuan, *Space and Place: The Perspective of Experience* (Minneapolis: University of Minnesota Press, 1977). On relational understandings of place, see Tim Ingold, "Part V: A Storied World," in *Being Alive: Essays on Movement, Knowledge, and Description* (New York: Routledge, 2011), 141–76; Doreen Massey, *Space, Place, and Gender* (Minneapolis: University of Minnesota Press, 1994); and Till, "Artistic and Activist Memory-Work." On definitions of place and discussions about absolute, relational, and lived spaces, see David Harvey, "Space as a Keyword," in *David Harvey: A Critical Reader*, ed. Noel Castree and Derek Gregory (Oxford: Blackwell, 2006), 209–93; Dolores Hayden, *The Power of Place: Urban Landscapes as Public History* (Cambridge: MIT Press, 1995); Henri Lefebvre, *The Production of Space*, trans. D. Nicholson-Smith (1974; Oxford: Blackwell, 1991); Karen E. Till, *The New Berlin: Memory, Politics, Place* (Minneapolis: University of Minnesota Press, 2005); and Tuan, *Space and Place*.

13. Mockus had been mayor before Peñalosa but stepped down to run for national office unsuccessfully. Under his leadership, water usage dropped by 40 percent, the homicide rate fell 70 percent, and traffic fatalities dropped over 50 percent. Seven thousand community security groups were formed; drinking water and sewerage were provided to all homes. See María Cristina Caballero, "Academic Turns City into a Social Experiment," *Harvard University Gazette*, March 11, 2004, http://www .news.Harvard.edu/gazette/2004/03.11/01-mockus.html.

14. Daniel Vargas, *"C'úndua 2001–2003: A Pact for Life,"* in Abderhalden and Aristizábal, *Catalogue and Multi-Media*; emphasis in original.

15. *C'úndua* is the Arhuaca (Columbian indigenous) word for the mythological place we go to after death.

16. Mapa Teatro, "Arte, memoria y ciudad."

17. Unless otherwise cited, the information for this section is taken from Abderhalden Cortés, "The Artist as Witness"; Cortés, personal interviews with author 2008 (Berlin), 2009 (Bogotá); Rolf Abderhalden and Heidi Abderhalden, "'Y saldrás de ti hacia nuevos y vastos territorios donde la palabra y el gesto no caerán en el olvido,' Proyecto Prometeo. Colectivo Mapa Teatro- Proyecto Cúndua, dirigido por Rolf y Heidi Abderhalden," in *Ciudad-espejo*, ed. Natalia Gutiérrez (Bogotá: Universidad Nacional de Colombia, Facultad de Artes, 2009); Abderhalden and Aristizábal, *Catalogue and Multi-Media*; David Gutiérrez Castañeda, "*C'úndua*: Pact for Life: Prospects for the Social Imaginary of Mapa Teatro, Interview with Rolf Abderhalden," LatinArt.com: An Online Journal of Art and Culture, issue on "Art and Social Space," November 1, 2008, http://www.latinart.com/aiview .cfm?start=1&id=398; Mapa Teatro, "Arte, memoria y ciudad"; and email correspondence between Rolf Abderhalden Cortés and Heidi Abderhalden with the author (2008–2011). For more information about Mapa Teatro's history and range of artistic projects, see Mapa Teatro's website at http://www.mapateatro.org.

18. Abderhalden Cortés, "Artist as Witness"; emphasis in original.

19. Abderhalden Cortés, interview with author (2009).

20. Abderhalden Cortés, "Artist as Witness."

21. Abderhalden Cortés, interview with author (2008).

22. Ibid.

23. Abderhalden Cortés, "Artist as Witness"; emphasis in original.

24. On the Feldenkrais method, see Elizabeth Beringer, ed., *Embodied Wisdom: The Collected Papers of Moshe Feldenkrais* (Berkeley, Calif.: North Atlantic Books, 2010).

25. Abderhalden Cortés, "Artist as Witness."

26. Ibid.

27. "Proyecto Prometeo," on the Mapa Teatro website, http://www.mapateatro .org/prometeo.html; translation mine.

28. Abderhalden Cortés, "Artist as Witness."

29. "Proyecto Prometeo," on the Mapa Teatro website. For a short YouTube clip, see "Prometeo," with scenes of Mapa Teatro setting up the "stage" and of the 2004 performance at http://www.youtube.com/watch?v=VQcCRaJC9ug, uploaded by Sebastian Gutierrez, March 5 2007.

30. For a range of perspectives on witnessing, see Jane Blocker, "A Cemetery of Images: Meditations on the Burial of Photographs," *Visual Resources* 21, no. 2 (2005): 181–91; Jacques Ranciére, *The Emancipated Spectator* (New York: Verso, 2009); Diana Taylor, *Disappearing Acts: Spectacles of Gender and Nationalism in Argentina's "Dirty War"* (Durham, N.C.: Duke University Press, 1997).

31. Taylor, *Disappearing Acts*, 265.

32. Till, *New Berlin*; Till, "Artistic and Activist Memory-Work"; Julian Jonker and Karen E. Till, "Mapping and Excavating Spectral Traces in Post-Apartheid Cape Town," *Memory Studies* 2, no. 3 (2009): 1–31; Karen E. Till, "Heritage Landscapes: Making Community Stories Visible in Hurt Park, Roanoke," conference paper delivered at the Virginia American Planning Association (APA) annual conference, Norfolk, Va., May 2010; and Till, "Wounded Cities."

33. Mindy Thompson Fullilove, *Root Shock: How Tearing up City Neighborhoods Hurts America, and What We Can Do about It* (New York: One World/Ballantine Books, 2005). Tim Ingold, *Being Alive*, also discusses mazeways and way-findings as the primary form of knowledge transmission.

34. Abderhalden Cortés, "Artist as Witness"; emphasis in original.

35. Leonie Sandercock, *Cosmopolis II: Mongrel Cities of the 21st Century* (New York: Routledge, 2003).

36. On active citizenship, see Engin Isin, *Being Political: Genealogies of Citizenship* (Minneapolis: University of Minnesota Press, 2002).

37. Abderhalden Cortés, "Artist as Witness."

38. Joan C. Tronto, *Moral Boundaries: A Political Argument for an Ethic of Care* (1993; New York: Routledge, 1999).

39. See Grant Kester, *Conversation Pieces: Community and Conversation in Public Art* (Berkeley: University of California Press, 2004).

40. See Henri Lefebvre, "The Right to the City," in *Writings on Cities*, trans. Eleonore Kofman and Elizabeth Lebas (Oxford: Blackwell, 1996), first published in French as a separate book, *Le droit à la ville* (Paris: Anthropos, 1968), 147–59.

7.

Jewish Memory, Jewish Geography:
Vienna before 1938

LISA SILVERMAN

Alles aus Liebe (All for Love), one of the most successful cabarets in 1927 Vienna, was, according to a critic for the *Neue Freie Presse*, a show intended mainly "for the eyes."[1] Like the other cabarets that year, it featured an entertaining musical score and plenty of talented comedians, including the well-known Karl Farkas, who also wrote its more than fifty lighthearted sketches. Like much lowbrow entertainment, it poked fun at its audience by humorously reversing traditional gender roles and mocking class distinctions. But this revue also featured something different: a dazzling array of women in extravagant costumes that evoked all things Austrian and Viennese—from culinary favorites like Wiener schnitzel and *Sachertorte* (chocolate cake), to the castles and gently rolling green hills of the country's beloved provinces. Appearing toward the end of the first half of the show, this visual display culminated in a set of striking tableaux of women costumed as Vienna's iconic buildings: the Stephansdom (St. Stephen's Cathedral), Karlskirche (St. Charles's Church), Rathaus (city hall), parliament, Schönbrunn (the emperor's summer palace), and even the city's Prater district and its famous Ferris wheel. This panoply was not, however, simply a diverting spectacle; like the rest of the show in which it appeared, it too challenged Viennese assumptions about the seemingly self-evident, stable order of things.

Though the critic appreciated the eye-catching, humorous costumes, he dismissed them as little more than simple patriotic symbols like one might find in a tourist brochure or children's book (figure 7.1). But as photographs show, the revue's unique "Disneyfication" of the city did more than just boil Vienna down to the sum of its best-known parts and present them in an

Figure 7.1. Scene from *Alles aus Liebe* (1927), depicting Schönbrunn Palace, St. Stephen's Cathedral, and Parliament. D'Ora-Benda Atelier. Österreichische Nationalbibliothek 204941-D.

unexpected way. By unhinging Vienna's iconic features from their context in the cityscape, and by having actresses perform them, rather than merely showing their images, the sketch disrupted the supposed boundaries that separate people from the places they inhabit. With the kind of irreverent humor characteristic of a cabaret performance, the revue took its audience members on a visual adventure that both celebrated and poked fun at their identification with Vienna. In doing so, it also exposed the question that underlies the mutually constitutive relationship between people and place: do people make place, or does place make people?[2]

This cabaret sketch provides a perfect entry point to a discussion of how placemaking in Vienna can illuminate the relationship between Jews and the cities in which they lived before World War II.[3] That Jews have maintained a special relationship to cities, particularly starting in the nineteenth century, is a scholarly given, as is the especially strong identification of Viennese Jews with their city's culture. To be sure, a deep attachment to the city one calls home is a universal emotion.[4] Nevertheless, the particular circumstances of Vienna's Jews can illuminate the complexities of social identifications and their relationship to embodied placemaking in urban spaces.

Figure 7.2. The First Republic of Austria. Map by Emily Verch.

From the fin de siècle on, Jews played an important role in Vienna's cultural achievements; identifying with culture, so the story goes, was a crucial part of their assimilation process. Jews could easily reconcile an embrace of the educated German *Kulturnation*, a patriotic love for the Austrian emperor, and, if they chose, religious Judaism. But the collapse of Austria-Hungary after the end of World War I radically destabilized the lives of all its residents, who found their economic ties severed, their political power greatly reduced, and the terms of their self-definitions as Austrians in turmoil. The relatively stable self-understandings of Austrian Jews as one minority among many in the vast territory of Austria-Hungary was thrown into disarray by a war that left them residents of a state comprised of a residual territory and a reluctant population (figure 7.2). After 1918 Vienna's once-celebrated status as the cosmopolitan, cultural center of a vast monarchy was reduced to that of an overblown *Wasserkopf* (hydrocephalic), soon to be overtaken by Berlin as central Europe's international vanguard. Jews responded to the state of affairs in the reconfigured boundaries of the new Austrian Republic by strengthening their allegiance to Vienna via its cultural heritage; as one scholar noted, they considered themselves politically Austrian, ethnically Jewish, and, more than ever, culturally Viennese.[5]

Discussions of the oft-cited special relationship of Jews to Vienna between the fin de siècle and 1938 typically highlight Vienna's high culture (music, art, architecture).[6] But as *Alles aus Liebe* suggests, an attachment to the city's physical attributes was a key part of how Jews connected to

Vienna, and that attachment engendered a different kind of security than an association with abstract ideals of culture. In this essay I use interwar Vienna as a case study for arguing that the tools of spatial ethnography enable us to consider urban place not as an objective fixed set of coordinates, but as a bounded space that exists only in relation to those who create it. This theoretical framework allows us to see how the self-identification of Vienna's Jews—like so many other urban Jews in pre–World War II Europe—was grounded not only in their city's culture but also in its geography, which was itself produced and reproduced in their everyday actions and movements through the city. The written memoirs and oral testimonies of these Jews suggest that their successful navigation of the city required an intimate, if implicit, knowledge of how its social codes traversed its physical layout.[7] As Jews daily engaged these coded spaces, they constantly formed and re-formed their Viennese self-identifications. In other words, Vienna was not just an idea for interwar Jews; it was a powerful physical reality.

We see this reality in the way Helen Blank (née Bilber), who was born in Vienna in 1917 and forced to leave in 1939, explicitly articulates how her ability to easily navigate Vienna's streets and other public spaces had everything to do with the shape of the city. Blank begins a lecture at the New School in 1990 by drawing a map of the city for her audience, explaining the relationship of the Danube Canal to the Ringstrasse, and how "From the Ringstrasse radiate outer districts again in a semi-circle, which are surrounded by the Gürtel (the belt)." As the first few minutes of her lecture make clear, she believes her audience will not understand her experiences in Vienna unless they understand something of the city's geography: "It is a metropolis, yet small enough to get to know it intimately. Especially, because of its star-like formation, the center of the city is within easy reach. Perhaps that is why we felt at home in the entire city. That is, in the streets, in the many public parks, museums, and other places open to the public. Private life was a different matter."[8] Half a century after the city itself, in a sense, rejected her, the shape and spaces of public Vienna still resonate deeply.

The testimony of Lore Waller, who was born in Vienna in 1918 and fled to England in 1939, similarly illuminates the importance of physical legibility to her identification with the city. Not the shape of Vienna but the recognition of its iconic buildings triggers Waller's affectionate feelings. She says: "It's a lovely city. I grew up in the city. I recently thought: I'd love to be in Vienna again and to see Vienna. And I turned on the TV—I love to listen to music—there is a music station at night and there was Vienna! They showed Vienna, the beautiful opera and the castle in Schönbrunn, the Ringstrasse and I was really excited. Vienna was exciting."[9] Waller's words evoke the power of the city's cultural riches, which were indeed important to Vienna's Jews, but the city's built environment is the ultimate focus of her excitement.

The physical landscape of Vienna had long been important not just to Viennese Jews like Blank and Waller, but to Jews from all over Austria-Hungary. According to Marianne Hirsch and Leo Spitzer, Jews in Czernowitz helped fund urban construction and beautification projects designed to mimic the buildings and layout of Vienna that helped transform the city "from a provincial backwater into an attractive Viennese-inspired magnet for visitors and new permanent settlers."[10] Urban theorist Kevin Lynch refers to the "legibility" of a cityscape: the visual measure of the ease with which a city's residents and visitors can recognize its parts and organize them into a coherent pattern. A legible city, Lynch proposes, offers security and both deepens and intensifies human experience.[11] As the case of Czernowitz suggests, using clearly articulated and familiar tropes eases the process of visually identifying a city and, in turn, can make it easier to identify with a city. For the Jews of Austria-Hungary, like those from Czernowitz, it was not only Vienna's cultural legacy but also its high degree of geographic legibility that made the city itself such a source of security, order, and self-identification.

And yet the importance of Vienna's legibility to Jews was not simply physical, as reflected in the disappointment many expressed about their "downgraded" city after the end of World War I.[12] Joseph Wechsberg, who was born in 1907 in Moravia, specifically remembers his mother's postwar shift in attitude as incomprehensible to him as a child: "After 1918 my mother would often say that Vienna was 'finished.' I didn't understand. The big city was still there, wasn't it, the baroque palaces, the churches, the Burgtheater, the great streets? My mother shook her head. . . . Vienna was only a big city then, no longer a world apart that my mother had found there. Once people had made a pilgrimage to Vienna to see the magic of the Kaiserstadt, the Imperial City. Now the magic was gone, the Kaiser was gone."[13] It was thus not only the buildings, but what they stood for that made Vienna meaningful for Wechsberg's mother—and so many others. Indeed, during the first two decades of the interwar period, many Austrians longed nostalgically for "*Alt-Wien*" (old Vienna), a metropolis of untainted rural villages that they only imagined existed before the expansion and urbanization of the *fin de siècle*. For a number of Vienna's Jews, however, that imagined past had less appeal as it appeared more exclusive.[14] Still, both responses show us how a city whose geography remained physically intact could shift so substantially in its meaning after the end of World War I. Kevin Lynch defines public images as "common mental pictures" possessed by significant numbers of a city's inhabitants; he describes them as "areas of agreement which might be expected to appear in the interaction of a single physical reality, a common culture, and a basic physiological nature."[15] In that light, the common longing—and admiration—of Jews for Vienna as represented through its iconic urban images makes sense, as does their collective disappointment in the city's loss of after the war.

It is clear, then, that the iconic cityscape was, for Vienna's Jews, neither static nor merely physical. According to Michel de Certeau, mundane experiences like walking in a city illuminate a "cultural logic" of space that is not otherwise perceptible.[16] The challenge for historians is that the hidden ways Jewish difference affected daily life and space in Vienna and other cities are not necessarily visible in photographs or even explicitly referenced in oral and written testimonies. Luckily, the tools of spatial ethnography can help us dig below surfaces to uncover these cultural codings and how they affected the lives of Jews in cities. Spatial ethnography is an interpretive method that combines analysis of artifacts (buildings, streets, furniture, and other forms of material culture) with ethnographic and observational accounts of how people use and give meaning to these artifacts. Spatial ethnography allows us to explore aspects of human culture that may not be available through traditional readings of written texts, material culture, or oral evidence. It focuses on corporeal and embodied experiences and affective responses to the physical environment, opening up a world of meanings and symbols—that is, a cultural logic—that may not be immediately visible. If we specifically examine how Vienna's Jews lived "spatially"—foregrounding, for instance, how they described the particular places they lived "close to, nearby, remote from, and detached from," and exploring how they made sense of those spatial coordinates as they moved through the city in their daily lives—we can begin to see both the cultural codings of space in Vienna and how the terms of Jewish difference were reproduced through the movements of Jews about the city.[17]

Social Codes and Vienna's Circles of Class

As seminal thinkers like Henri Lefebvre and Georg Simmel remind us, constructed social orders play a crucial role in how we experience the physical environment.[18] The material world acquires meaning through individual and collective actions and interactions; that is, through the engagements of people with the constructed social orders that shape a space. In other words, far from being a neutral backdrop to human action, "every landscape is a particular cognitive or symbolic ordering of space."[19] The basis of place lies at the intersection of the material, political, and ideological conditions according to which individuals construct streets, buildings, and parks, and the imaginative projections of those who physically inhabit those environments. Like other social codes, the codes of place are real but remain just below the threshold of articulation and are thus not easily discerned, measured, and evaluated. Class, ethnicity, and other social criteria play an active role in shaping the ways people experience urban spaces, and in particular whether they feel excluded from or included in those spaces. In Vienna the fact that Jews were part of a minority population that for centuries had faced restrictions about where they were allowed to reside, as well as exposure to persecution and expulsion, shaped the way parts of the city came to be coded as "Jewish." This, in turn, affected Jews' daily lives, regardless of whether they actually lived in identifiably "Jewish spaces." Meanwhile, the coding of Vienna as a Jewish space within Austria, and the Leopoldstadt district as a Jewish space within Vienna, was an important representational strategy used by many Austrians to articulate both national and urban power struggles along the lines of Jewish difference.[20]

For Dell Upton it is the disjunction between the visible physical order and implicit social space—the "scene" and the unseen—that shapes the meanings of the spaces people inhabit.[21] While the visible order of a city may suggest one possible community, the spatial order often indicates another. Interpreting the meaning of a space thus requires finding some sort of equilibrium between the two. By the nineteenth century Vienna was already spatially coded according to a relatively strict class system: the inner core and the Ringstrasse (known as the Ring) were the seat of the emperor and the space of the wealthy and cultured; most of the districts immediately surrounding the Ring were up-and-coming or bourgeois; and working-class districts were located outside the Gürtel (to be sure, simple class codings did not strictly conform to physical reality; members of the working class lived inside the Gürtel, impoverished Viennese lived in the city center, and the well-to-do often owned villas in the upper districts).[22] In his celebrated cultural history of the city, Carl Schorske recounts how the reconstruction of the Ringstrasse at the end of the nineteenth century created a circular flow that cut off the inner city from the rest of the city. Instead of linking the outlying districts—and their lower-class residents—to the vibrant heart of the metropolis, he argues, the Ring formed a "sociological isolation belt" that kept undesirable members of the population from penetrating the center.[23]

In Vienna, then, even more than in other European cities, physical and symbolic district boundaries provided an imagined line of defense that protected the elite, wealthy residents at the city center from the supposedly dangerous working-class districts at the outskirts. The powerful implications of these physical and imagined district configurations inevitably affected how Jews decided where to live in the city, as well as the nature and degree of their identifications with the city and its districts.

For Helen Blank, who grew up in a district with few Jews, these class divisions played an important role in her self-identification. In her lecture she describes the social delineations of Vienna's layout like the historians above, but then she immediately moves on to the specifics of her own sense of location, class, and self:

> In the Inner City, and the neighborhoods immediately surrounding it lived the wealthier people. But as you got further away from the center, the neighborhoods became poorer (except for the villas further out) and you reached solid working class districts. In the area between the Danube and Danube Canal you would find mostly Jewish people. But here too, the wealthier ones lived in the more opulent areas . . . Although not from a working class background, as long as I can remember, I identified with the working people of Vienna. This working class neighborhood became my turf. Here people lived in two-room walk-up apartments, a dark kitchen and one other room which served as a living room, water, as well as the toilet, were outside in the hallway, shared by several neighbors on the floor. We, on the other side of the street, also had no bathroom. But the sink with running cold water and the toilet were inside the apartment. To take a bath or shower you went to a public bathhouse and for a minimal fee you took your shower.[24]

The coding of the neighboring streets as proletarian (that is, non-Jewish) enabled her to identify not only with the people who lived there but also with the place where they lived. The neighborhood, as she notes, was "her turf."

The Leopoldstadt and the (Self-)Construction of Jewish Space(s)

In 1850 there were relatively few Jews in Vienna, but in 1910 they made up 8.6 percent of the city's population, and by World War I their numbers had grown to almost two hundred thousand.[25] Although their numerical growth paralleled an increase in the general population, Jews nevertheless remained a distinct group in Vienna, their presence engendering significant geographic and cultural ramifications for all the city's residents. Marsha L. Rozenblit points out that the Jewish population grew rapidly after 1850 when the government lifted residence restrictions. Jews came from different areas of Austria-Hungary, generally moved as families, and were not unfamiliar with city life. When they came to the city, they tended to reside near other Jews, regardless of class—a trait that set them apart from the non-Jewish Viennese.[26] The Leopoldstadt, which had first functioned as the city's quasi-ghetto in the seventeenth century (until the Jews were expelled in 1670), again became Vienna's quintessentially Jewish space in both population—30 percent of its residents were Jews, making it the most densely Jewish district in the city—and the public imagination; it remained home to most of the city's observant Eastern Jews, as well as Yiddish theater and culture.

Yet if the Leopoldstadt retained its image as a sort of homeland, evoking *shtetl* (the Yiddish term for small town) life and in effect turning the rest of the city into a microcosm of the diaspora, other spaces in Vienna could be described as contested sites of Jewish difference, even if their boundaries were not as visibly rendered.[27] It is important to note that codings of Jewish and non-Jewish spaces in Vienna become apparent both in the words and deeds of antisemites and the spatial and cultural depictions of Austrian Jews. In fact, for many Jews who chose to live outside its bounds, maintaining the Leopoldstadt's status as a "Jewish district" was an important way to disassociate themselves from negative Jewish stereotypes, as the district's status as "Jewish space" became directly proportional to the imagined "non-Jewishness" of the rest of the city. Ironically, this distinction resonated most powerfully not for ardent antisemites (who considered Jews ubiquitous), but for Vienna's Jews themselves as they negotiated their place in the city and their own self-identifications as Jews.[28] Yet even as "Jewish space," the Leopoldstadt resisted unitary interpretation.

Actor Leon Askin, who grew up in interwar Vienna, dismissed any illusion of the Leopoldstadt as a unified whole. "When you talk about the Leopoldstadt," he said, "you have to talk about six Leopoldstadts." He divided the district into separate residential and garden quarters, as well as the Prater, the city's renowned amusement park.[29] Most visible manifestations of Jewish life centered on the Taborstrasse, the main street in the section of the district where Jews had lived the longest. During the nineteenth and early twentieth centuries, thousands of mostly impoverished Jewish emigrants and refugees from the east arrived in the Leopoldstadt via the Nordbahnhof, the city's northern rail station, and typically remained there, contributing to a thriving culture of Yiddish and other Jewish newspapers, theaters, cafés, and synagogues. For Eva Brueck, who grew up outside the district, it was a center of religious practice, international languages, and visually compelling Eastern Jews:

> I remember that area, mainly populated by Jews, as a place with coffee-houses, theaters, cinemas, with people speaking Yiddish, Polish, Russian, Roumanian, German with a foreign accent, Jews whose outer appearance characterized them as Rabbis, with their black hats, their beards, young boys with side-locks. . . . Many of my class-mates at school had lived in this area, where I had often been invited for a "Seder" or Khanukka celebration. It was an area full of vitality, with a varied cultural life enriched by the influence of the traditions of many countries.[30]

Ernst Epler, however, pointed out that Orthodox Jews tried to stay separate from the rest of the district's population, in effect producing a ghetto with "invisible walls."[31] This move is a clear example of what Michel de Certeau terms "tactics": everyday forms of engagement through which individuals resist, counter, circumvent, and transform the world around them when they do not have the power to transform their environment on a larger scale.[32] As scholars have pointed out, in order to understand the relationships of power and role of space in social relations and individual self-understandings, we must acknowledge the fact that, even in the most controlled environments—prisons being the most extreme—the relatively powerless still have the power to "carve out spaces of control" when it comes to living their everyday lives.[33] Thus, in the ghetto, as it were, those whom we might consider most ghettoized empowered themselves with their own self-restriction.

Yet the areas of the Leopoldstadt without religious overtones, like the nearby Praterstrasse and the Prater itself, were also coded as Jewish spaces, albeit multivalent Jewish spaces. There, other "tactics" were in play. Librettist Peter Herz describes the Praterstrasse as a microcosm of Jewish acculturation. Historically, non-Jewish Austrian aristocrats had built palaces adjacent to the park. Prosperous Jews followed, building their own beautiful residences. But eventually the street came to be seen as "too bourgeois," and the wealthy moved on, at which point Jewish musicians, artists, scholars, and doctors moved in and cemented the vibrant theater and café scene.[34] Lotte Hümbelin alludes to other "unseen" class-related "tactics." She claims that working-class Jews were separated from the "real" (that is, non-Jewish) working class by both their Jewishness and geography, since the working-class districts were located elsewhere in the city.[35] But she also suggests that other Jews in the district maintained social boundaries between themselves and working-class Jews, even when geography united them.

Negative or ambivalent descriptions of the Leopoldstadt suggest that its depiction as a world apart from the rest of Vienna was integral to how Jews engaged with it. Stella Klein-Löw devotes an entire chapter of her memoir to the district, not because it was where she was most comfortable, but because, as an acculturated, middle-class Jew who lived elsewhere, she felt least at home in what she termed the *Judenbezirk* (Jews' district): "There I didn't like it, the Leopoldstadt. It smelled bad, the streets were dirty, the people strange."[36] Even Benno Weiser Varon, who defended his original home district in his memoirs as the one space in Vienna where a Jew could feel that Christians were in the minority (and thus experience less antisemitism), followed the path of many other upwardly mobile Jews by moving away as soon as he could.[37] By linking residence with acculturation, we see how the Jewishness of the entire Leopoldstadt continued to be upheld in the minds of those who moved beyond its borders.

Leaving Leopoldstadt: Jews in Non-Jewish Spaces

Typically, we think of Jewish spaces in terms of ghettos *eruvim*, (bounded zones that make public areas private for religious practice), or specific buildings like homes, synagogues, or yeshivas. But examining how Jews lived spatially in the modern era requires us to broaden our definitions. Even such explicitly Jewish areas generate important symbolic meanings that extend far beyond their physical boundaries, while many spaces with little visible or quantifiable evidence of Jewishness—even some spaces coded as decidedly "non-Jewish"—can generate significant, albeit often implicit, associations with Jewish difference. One useful way to negotiate these complexities is to think of spaces not simply as "Jewish" or "not Jewish," but rather in terms of affective responses of inclusion or exclusion. As David Sibley notes, the term "geographies of exclusion" refers to the fact that feelings about the other "and the ambivalent sensations of desire and disgust which energize interpersonal and social relations" also affect the way people interpret their environments: the "literal mappings of power relations and rejection are informed by the generalized other."[38]

Having long served as Vienna's quintessential Other and persecuted minority, Jews in the interwar period remained finely attuned to the implications of their historical exclusions and the ongoing precariousness of their existence in the city.[39] Yet Jews could feel excluded from "Jewish space" as much as from "non-Jewish" space; indeed, for some Jews, "non-Jewish" space was central to their sense of security and stability in the city. Jewish space could physically overlap with working-class or aristocratic space or be at odds with it; the real or imagined presence of Jews was often intertwined with spatial codings of class, ethnicity, and religion. But as interwar property registers, memoirs, and other sources make clear, although more than half of Vienna's Jews lived in only three districts, the others made their homes in virtually every other district of the city.[40]

Jews began living outside the Leopoldstadt long before World War I. However, according to Rozenblit, even as they moved away from the "Jewish" section of the city, "the Jews of Vienna chose housing mainly with their Jewishness in mind." Rozenblit's research reveals that, even as their newly acquired social and economic mobility enabled them to disperse across the city, Jews still tended to live largely among themselves, belong to Jewish organizations, and socialize with and marry other Jews. However, rather than living in certain areas for religious reasons, they "adjusted their choice of neighborhood to conform to their changing occupations and social status." Between 1870 and 1910, for instance, the proportion of Jews in the Alsergrund doubled from 10 to 20 percent; in Mariahilf and Neubau it tripled from 4 to 12 percent. These percentages continued to increase during the interwar period. But although many Jews had become less observant by this time, most retained some form of secular Jewish self-identification and sense of community even when they moved beyond the bounds of the Leopoldstadt.[41]

Jews who distanced themselves from the "Jewish" areas of the city thus ended up maintaining the boundary between the Jewish and the non-Jewish. Even the poorest Jews chose to live with middle-class Jews over non-Jews of their own class, rarely choosing, for example, to live in working-class districts like Ottakring and Hernals. Anxiety about antisemitism was likely one of the reasons for this choice. Mark Monies, who was born in Vienna in 1921, recalls being subjected to antisemitic taunts from students at his school in Ottakring, where few other Jews lived.[42] In the working-class district of Favoriten, where Jews comprised only 2.3 percent of the population in 1934, the Suschitzky brothers, owners of the district's first and only socialist bookstore, faced a constant stream of attacks from accusers who deployed common antisemitic tropes of Jews as dangerous deviants and purveyors of pornography. In a district coded as non-Jewish, these slurs were particularly powerful.[43]

Historians claim that the Alsergrund, located directly adjacent to the Leopoldstadt, attracted so many white-collar Jewish business employees and professionals that it eventually became "the proper address for a new breed of urban Jew" seeking cultural cachet.[44] The testimony of a number of Austrian Jews supports this assertion. Weiser Varon recalls that he and his brother Max moved out of the Leopoldstadt as soon as they made enough money, even though they were still in *Gymnasium* (high school). They lived in a furnished apartment with a bath in the "much more classy Ninth District [Alsergrund]," although they "never missed a meal" back at their parents' home in the Leopoldstadt.[45]

Though many Jews who moved to the Alsergrund clearly sought to leave the Jewish Leopoldstadt behind, the unintended result of their collective migration was the creation of another contested space. Wherever they moved in any significant numbers, it seems, Jews brought with them the association of "Jewish space." In 1898 Adam Müller-Guttenbrunn, a zealous German nationalist, theater critic, and writer, indicated his discontent with these population shifts when he led the call for the establishment of Vienna's *Kaiserjubiläums Stadtheater* (Emperor's Jubilee Theater) on the border between the Alsergrund and Währing, the adjacent eighteenth district. From the beginning, the new establishment was intended as—and, indeed, became—Vienna's first "Aryan" theater. Hence Müller-Guttenbrunn's determination to construct the theater in Währing, which was separated from the northern border of the Alsergrund by the Gürtel, reflects a cognitive boundary directly related to the perception of the Alsergrund as a "Jewish" space.[46] The locations and intended audiences of theaters had been a major issue in Vienna since the middle of the century, when the demolition of the old city walls first made possible the construction of new buildings on the Ring.[47] While the Ring's Burgtheater, constructed in 1870, was run by and served the city's aristocracy and wealthy bourgeoisie, theater and music were important elements of acculturation for Jews, many of whom were deeply involved in the cultural life on the Ring as producers, creators, and audiences.[48] Jews were also visible theatergoers in other districts, including, of course, the Leopoldstadt, which featured Jewish-themed and Yiddish-language dramas.

Müller-Guttenbrunn and the other founding members of the theater's board made it clear that, although the official purpose of its founding was to celebrate the emperor, the underlying goal was the exclusion of Jewish playwrights, actors, and audiences.[49] In addition to declaring that theaters should be free of characteristics like "showy boxes," typically ascribed to Jewish parvenus, Müller-Guttenbrunn argued passionately for the importance of locating the theater on the border between Währing and

Alsergrund. At the same time that his insistence underscores his implicit perception of Alsergrund as "Jewish" space, it indicates that the theater was to serve as a physical buttress against a growing Jewish population.[50] The link between the theater's underlying purpose and its location is supported by Müller-Guttenbrunn's reflections on his childhood apartment, which was located on the same street. In his memoirs he nostalgically recalls the *ländlichen* (rural) condition of the district before it transformed into a *städtlichen* (urban) area, a distinction that easily translates as a transformation from non-Jewish to Jewish. In its untainted state during his youth, he laments, the district was bucolic and innocent, replete with grazing sheep and children's playgrounds. Then, he sourly complains, an editor from the *Neue Freie Presse*, whom he refers to as a "real estate speculator" (a stereotypical Jewish occupation), bought the houses next to the children's playground and planned to build a theater there.[51] By expressing his desire for urban spaces imbued with the slow-paced, pure, innocent nature of the romanticized provinces, and by associating Jews with the destructive forces of modernity and culture, Müller-Guttenbrunn reveals the social boundaries of the emerging Jewish space in the Alsergrund that his theater seeks to thwart—or at least redress.

The Intricacies of Vienna

During the interwar period, everyone in Austria's provinces knew about "Red Vienna" and its dangerous Jews and socialists. This coding was based in part on fact: over 90 percent of Austria's Jews lived in Vienna and most of the city's Social Democrat leaders were Jews, creating a distinct contrast to the rest of the country, which was led by Christian Democrats.[52] But within the city it was hard to imagine Vienna as a whole as "Jewish space," not least because of the uneven distribution of its Jewish population. By 1934 Jews may have comprised one-third of the population of the Leopoldstadt, but they also made up 20 percent of the population of its neighboring inner city and Alsergrund districts (figure 7.3).[53] Although the entire Leopoldstadt district was far larger than its relatively small Jewish quarter, and its residents included more non-Jews than Jews, both its history and its concentration of Jewish life and culture assured its continued coding as Vienna's most "Jewish" district, even as Jews moved to other areas. If the coding of the Leopoldstadt as "Jewish space" made most sense from outside, so did the coding of the whole city as "Jewish."

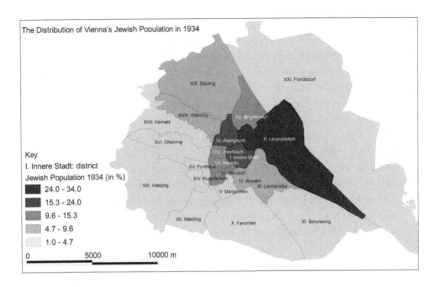

Figure 7.3. Jewish population of Vienna, by district. Map © Jobstmedia.

For Jews who lived in Vienna, the city's entire geography had meaning. While the importance of "Jewish space" depended on the person and the place, the experience of being "Jewish" in the city's space could never be fully escaped. In an interview, Ula Pommer, an Austrian émigré born in 1919, details not only where her family lived and worked but even the names of the streets that delineated the borders of her district:

> Interviewer: You wrote that your father owned a factory and where precisely?
> Pommer: Yes, in the third district [Bezirk] they made corks, fancy corks and bottle closings.
> Interviewer: And where was the third district [Bezirk]?
> Pommer: First in the Dietscheinergasse and then on the Landstrasse Hauptstrasse and then it went to the Erdberger Laende.[54]

The third district was home to relatively few Jews; in 1934 they made up only 9.1 percent of its population.[55] But when asked whether many Jews lived in the building where she grew up, Pommer replies that she had no idea. In response to questions about school, she good-naturedly complains that it is difficult (and unimportant) to her to remember exactly what years she was there, but she makes certain to emphasize the details she does remember: the names and locations of the schools she attended, as well as the discrimination she encountered as she attempted to begin a career in the textile industry:

Pommer: I went to the grammar school at Kollonitzplatz and then I went to the Gymnasium at the Kundmanngasse. Then I went to the Textile School and then in the Arts and Crafts School which was on the Ring whose name I have forgotten, between Café Prueckel and the Kai Stubenring.

Interviewer: That was the Arts and Crafts School.

Pommer: Before that I was in the Textile School on the Spenglergasse.

Interviewer: And how long in the Gymnasium?

Pommer: Up to the fourth and then in the Spenglergasse, another two years. Because I really wanted to get into the knit fashion. There it was two years and I learned the knit fashion. That meant drawing as well as a bit of tailoring. And then it turned out that as a Jew I had no chances to get a job anywhere. Because Palmers was friends with a friend of my parents, I went to him and he used to tell me: I am sorry I cannot hire you, because his Jewish quota is filled. If he had more, he would not be able to sell to Germany.[56]

The dynamic between Pommer's locational specificity and her testimony of professional exclusion suggests that she deploys her knowledge of the city's geography as an unconscious defensive strategy.

The testimonies of other Austrian Jews reveal a deep awareness of the city's strictly defined social boundaries. Gertrude Marmorek (née Neuron), who was born in Vienna in 1914, lived at Kandlgasse 23, in the seventh district (Neubau), before eventually emigrating to the United States. In 1934 the 5 percent of Vienna's Jews who lived in the district made up just 15 percent of its population. Neubau was thus far from a "Jewish space," a coding of which Marmorek was well aware: "It was a fairly poor neighborhood; . . . we went to temple in the sixth district, quite a walk, and I felt so bad. Vienna was very Catholic . . . and I felt so bad being dressed up to go to synagogue. I was afraid of being Jewish. There were very few Jews, more Catholics, not many Protestants, though I had a lot of Protestant friends."[57]

Others recall harassment at school, though this was a phenomenon more prevalent in Vienna's outer, less Jewish districts. There, being able to "pass" as non-Jewish was a distinct advantage, though it didn't necessarily mean one could hide one's Jewish background. Mark Monies describes his experiences living in the working-class sixteenth district: "I went to the *Volksschule* in Ottakring—they made fun of me because I was Jewish, already in the 1920s, in 1925 and 1926. There were very few Jews there. My friends were mostly Jews—Christians didn't want to make friends with me. My mother kept kosher. My father was a Jewish nationalist but not religious . . . I had red hair, I didn't look Jewish, I looked very Austrian."[58] Even within his own family and body, his Jewish identification was complex, but at school it was the fact of his being Jewish that mattered.

Charlotte R. Carter (née Wissboeck), who was born in Vienna to a Jewish mother and Catholic father, had no problems living in the tenth district (Favoriten), which had the city's largest overall population (over 157,000) but very few Jews (only 2.3 percent). It was a "a relatively poor Christian area of the city. It was not the Jewish area," according to Carter, and neither of her parents were observant. Her status as the child of a mixed marriage and her "non-Jewish" looks became problematic only when she and her mother were forced to move to the Leopoldstadt after the Nazi takeover of Vienna in 1938: "I was immediately called the *Shiksa* [Yiddish for non-Jewish woman, used mainly pejoratively], so I did not make friends in the neighborhood or among the people that I lived. I was humiliated by many people when I was made to turn on the lights on the holiday, and to go out of the ghetto to buy certain things for them, because I could pass."[59]

But even for assimilated Jews, living in a "non-Jewish" district could be a negative experience. Sonia Wachstein's parents built a house at the far west end of Vienna in Hütteldorf. The family's decision to live in a district with few Jews (only 4 percent of the population in 1934) deeply colored her childhood and underscored how different she felt from other Jewish families. The family clearly had a Jewish identity; although they rarely went to synagogue and didn't keep kosher, Wachstein's Galician-born father was the director of the Jewish community's library, lectured on Jewish philosopher Baruch Spinoza at the local B'nai B'rith lodge, and visited his favorite coffeehouse every Monday evening. Her father loved to hike in the Vienna woods where he went every week on his day off until his death in 1935. But the family paid a high price for such luxury: as the only Jewish child at her elementary school, Wachstein was often the target of antisemitic insults and attacks.[60] Employing a "tactic" for carving out a semblance of Jewish space, she describes how she dealt with threatening religious symbols: "A life size statue of Jesus, often prominent on a street corner, as there were many in Catholic Austria, was so frightening to me that every time I passed the spot by myself, I would cover my eyes and recite the 'Shemah.'"[61] On the other hand, she did not feel comfortable among her Jewish relatives in the Leopoldstadt, recalling that the close quarters and shabby surroundings made her feel like a "foreigner" who could not wait to return home to the "coolness of our house on the hill," "the spacious isolation of our rooms," and the "silent fragrant garden."[62]

Nazi Vienna and the Exclusion from Space

Nazi Germany's annexation of Austria in 1938 brought Vienna's ethnic and social coding into sharp relief as Jews faced more intense antisemitic
persecution on a tangible, geographic level. Lore Waller recalls the events
that took place in the heart of the "cultured" city and reveals much about the
newly destabilized terms of the city's legibility—and security—as well as the
altered tactics Jews used to navigate the city in the face of unexpected antisemitic incidents:

> On the day of the *Anschluß* I was in school, at the Institute. But I had a long
> way to go, because I lived in the 3rd district, in the Weihergasse, but the
> Graphic Institute was in the 8th or 9th district. It was a long journey with
> the tram. I was in the tram, there were many people and lots of talk. But
> I didn't know what they were talking about. Normally I would have gone
> home through the first district, but you couldn't because the Ringstrasse was
> blocked. You had to take a detour with the tram and with walking. It was
> hours before I got home. But I didn't know what was going on. Something
> was happening, but I didn't know what.[63]

That Waller remembers the first signs of her eventual exile from the city in
geographic terms—she was forced to veer from her normal route home—
indicates just how important the daily pattern of traversing the streets was
to her self-identification as Viennese. Forbidden to enter one of her regular areas of the city, she was forced to carve out a "negative space," spatially
performing the tightening noose of exclusion imposed by the Nazis upon
Vienna's Jews.[64] When Waller recounts one incident in particular, its location on the Wollzeile, one of central Vienna's main thoroughfares, becomes
more important to the story than the incident itself. These central streets
had been secure places for her, and her awareness of how the Nazis used
the terms of Jewish difference to exclude her registered in a sense of spatial exile.

As Paul Connerton notes, everyday forms of engagement with place can
be considered "products of habits and bodily practices that produce a combination of cognitive and habit-memory."[65] He points out that our repeated
and mundane place-based behavior tends to become so habitual and taken
for granted that its powerful influence is often not explicitly evident. With
that in mind, this incident also sheds light on the importance of geography
to Waller's self-identification as Viennese:

Yes, I guess I still was at the Graphic Institute because I was on my way home from school and—I believe it was on the Wollzeile—there was a group of Nazis. I wanted to get away from them and took a detour through the Baeckerstrasse and I had no makeup on, I was wearing simple clothes, and I just wanted to go home, my mother was waiting for me with lunch. On the other side, there was a boy in an SS uniform and another with an armband—not everyone had their uniforms then, it was a few days after the Nazis marched in. And he was only wearing an armband. The Baeckerstrasse is a narrow little street, they crossed the street and stopped me. They asked: are you Austrian? I said: yes. Are you a Jew? I said: yes. Come with us! I said, my mother is expecting me for lunch, can I call and tell her I'm not coming home? Yes! One went in front of me, the other behind me, and I acted as if nothing had happened. I had no idea where they were taking me and what would happen. Then we arrived at the Stephansplatz and there was a woman waiting for the bus, and they asked her the same questions. Whether she was Austrian, a Jew, and then they let me go. I have no idea why they took me, and no idea why they let me go.[66]

The fact that sixty years later Waller remembers the incident's precise location suggests that the incident was upsetting not only because of the threat of Nazi violence but also because it disrupted her ordering of the city's spaces, replicating the historical exclusion of Jews that was already written into the city's history. Despite their ever-present awareness of spatial codings, this generation of Austrian Jews had not encountered such challenges to status and self-identification so explicitly; it is no wonder, then, that asserting their familiarity and intimacy with the city through such descriptions is an important way to resist the terms of their expulsion from the community.

The spectacle of women as buildings in *Alles aus Liebe* was successful in part because it played to its audience's longing for an iconic cultural status that Vienna had once possessed and then seemingly lost. Knowing exactly where they stood was a crucial part of the interwar experience for the many Jews whose relatively stable self-understandings were thrown into disarray by the reshaping of Austria's borders after the end of the war. Just as a love for its language, food, music, and literature mark one's identification with a city, so does a deep familiarity with its geography and iconic buildings. In the Leopoldstadt or far afield, Vienna's Jews understood how codings of Jewish difference translated onto urban space—and how that space could have powerful political and social import.

NOTES

1. *Neue Freie Presse*, October 1, 1927, 15. See also Fred Heller, "Alles aus Liebe: Die neue Revue im Wiener Stadttheater," *Die Bühne* 152, October 6, 1927.

2. M. Christine Boyer, "The Great Frame-Up: Fantastic Appearances in Contemporary Spatial Politics," in *Spatial Practices: Critical Explorations in Social/Spatial Theory*, ed. Helen Liggett and David C. Perry (London: Sage, 1995), 81–109, esp. 97.

3. On Jews' extensive involvement in cabaret in interwar Vienna, see Christian Klösch, "'Wien das fidele Grab an der Donau.' Der Beitrag von Juden zu Kabarett und Kleinkunst im Wien in der Zwischenkrieszeit," in *Wien, Stadt der Juden: Die Welt der Tante Jolesch*, ed. Joachim Riedl (Vienna: Zsolnay, 2004), 198–208.

4. Louis Wirth, "Urbanism as a Way of Life," in *Classic Essays on the Culture of Cities*, ed. Richard Sennett (New York: Appleton-Century-Crofts, 1969), 143–64.

5. On the basis of research on autobiographies stemming from the first quarter of the twentieth century, Eleonore Lappin claims that many Jews reconfigured their self-identifications as politically Austrian, ethnically Jewish, and culturally Viennese. See "Jüdische Lebenserinnerungen. Rekonstruktionen von jüdischer Kindheit und Jugend im Wien der Zwischenkriegzeit," in *Wien und die jüdische Erfahrung, 1900–1938*, ed. Frank Stern and Barbara Eichinger, 17–38, esp. 25.

6. The literature on Jews' paradoxical place in fin de siècle Viennese culture is substantial. See Steven Beller, *Vienna and the Jews, 1867–1938: A Cultural History* (New York: Cambridge University Press, 1989) and *Was nicht im Baedeker steht: Juden und andere Österreicher im Wien der Zwischenkriegszeit* (Vienna: Picus, 2008); Gerhard Botz, Ivar Oxaal, and Michael Pollak, eds., *Eine Zerstörte Kultur: Jüdisches Leben und Antisemitismus in Wien seit dem 19. Jahrhundert*, 2nd ed. (Vienna: Czernin, 2002); Frank Stern and Barbara Eichinger, eds., *Wien und die jüdische Erfahrung; Akkulturation—Antisemitismus—Zionismus* (Vienna: Böhlau, 2009); Robert S. Wistrich, ed., *Austrians and Jews in the Twentieth Century: From Franz Joseph to Waldheim* (New York: St. Martin's, 1992).

7. Many of the testimonies quoted in this essay are part of the Austrian Heritage Collection, an oral history project available through the Leo Baeck Institute for the study of the history and culture of German-speaking Jewry in New York. The collection includes more than 350 written and oral testimonies of Austrians forced to emigrate after 1938.

8. Helen Blank, "Growing up in Vienna," AR 11286, Leo Baeck Institute (hereafter, LBI), Austrian Heritage Collection (hereafter, AHC), 3.

9. Interview with Lore Waller, LBI, AHC 64.

10. Marianne Hirsch and Leo Spitzer, *Ghosts of Home: The Afterlife of Czernowitz in Jewish Memory* (Berkeley: University of California Press, 2010), 32.

11. Kevin Lynch, *Image of the City* (Cambridge: MIT Press, 1960), 5. See also Boyer, "Great Frame-Up," 82.

12. Vienna and Lower Austria officially became separate states on December 29, 1921, though they already functioned separately in practice as early as December 1920. Post–World War I shifts in the physical boundaries of Austria and Vienna also changed how the Viennese perceived their city. On January 1, 1922, the city became an independent state (*Land*), which gave it more financial independence and autonomy but also isolated it even further from the rest of the country.

13. Joseph Wechsberg, *The Vienna I Knew: Memories of a European Childhood* (New York: Doubleday, 1979), 76.

14. For more on this phenomenon, see the exhibition catalog *Alt Wien. Die Stadt, die niemals war*, ed. Wolfgang Kos and Christian Rapp (Vienna: Czernin, 2004).

15. Lynch, *Image of the City*, 7.

16. Ian Buchanan, *Michel de Certeau: Cultural Theorist* (London: Sage, 2001), 81.

17. John Allen, "On Georg Simmel: Proximity, Distance, and Movement," in *Thinking Space*, ed. Mike Crang and Nigel Thrift (London: Routledge, 2000), 54–70, esp. 68.

18. Henri Lefebvre, *The Production of Space*, trans. Donald Nicholson-Smith (Malden, Mass.: Blackwell, 1984), 44–45. See also Georg Simmel, "Soziologie des Raumes," *Jahrbuch für Gesetzgebung, Verwaltung, und Volkswirtschaft des Deutschen Reiches* 27, no. 1 (1903): 27–71.

19. Tim Ingold, "The Temporality of the Landscape," in *World Archaeology* 25, no. 2 (1993): 152–74.

20. Ritchie Robertson notes that the contrast between city and country is a recurrent theme in Austrian literature between the wars. See "Austrian Prose Fiction, 1918–1945," in *A History of Austrian Literature*, ed. Katrin Kohl and Ritchie Robertson (Rochester, N.Y.: Camden House, 2006), 54. Ernst Bruckmüller maintains that Austrians first discovered the "value of natural beauty and cultural treasures" in a phase of serious self-doubt during the First Republic. See Ernst Bruckmüller, *The Austrian Nation: Cultural Consciousness and Socio-Political Processes* (Riverside, Calif.: Ariadne, 1996), 91.

21. Dell Upton, "Seen, Unseen, and Scene," in *Understanding Ordinary Landscapes*, ed. Paul Erling Groth and Todd W. Bressi (New Haven, Conn.: Yale University Press, 1997), 174–75.

22. Wolfgang Maderthaner and Lutz Musner argue that a solid ring of densely constructed working-class suburbs surrounds the districts within the Gürtel and the city center; those districts with villa estates alone were designed for upper- and upper-middle-class residents. See Wolfgang Maderthaner and Lutz Musner, *Unruly Masses: The Other Side of Fin-de-siècle Vienna* (New York: Berghahn, 2008), 34.

23. Carl E. Schorske, *Fin-de-siècle Vienna* (New York: Vintage, 1980), 32–33.

24. Blank, "Growing up in Vienna," 3.

25. Marsha L. Rozenblit, *The Jews of Vienna, 1867–1914: Assimilation and Identity* (Albany: SUNY Press, 1983), 17. In 1869, Jews represented 6.4 percent of the total population of Vienna. The percentage rose to 8.6 percent in 1910 and to 9.4 percent in 1934. However, between 1923 and 1934 the number of Jews in Vienna actually fell from 201,513 to 176,034. *Die Ergebnisse der österreichischen Volkszählung vom 22. März 1934*, Vol. 1, *Bundesstaat*, ed. Bundesamt für Statistik (Vienna: Druck und Verlag der österreichischen Staatsdruckerei, 1935), 50.

26. Rozenblit, *Assimilation and Identity*, 16–19. Nevertheless, other scholars point out that living apart from each other did not preclude their inevitable interaction, even in the Middle Ages. See Birgit Wiendl, "Jews and the City: Parameters of Jewish Life in Late Medieval Austria," in *Urban Space in the Middle Ages and the Early Modern Age*, ed. Albrecht Classen (Berlin: Walter de Gruyter, 2009), 273–308, esp. 283.

27. Rozenblit notes that registered members of the Jewish community tended to live on more major streets such as the Taborstrasse, Rembrandtstrasse, Untere Augartenstrasse, Stefaniestrasse, Praterstrasse, and obere Donaustrasse. The wealthier among them lived to the east of the Taborstrasse, while poorer Jews tended to live on side streets and in back alleys to its west. In 1910, Jews made up 33.9 percent of the total population of the Leopoldstadt. Rozenblit, *Assimilation and Identity*, 78, 84. In 1934, 50,922 of Vienna's 176,034 Jews (29 percent) lived there. *Die Ergebnisse der österreichischen Volkszählung vom 22. März 1934*, Vol. 3, *Wien*, ed. Bundesamt für Statistik (Vienna: Druck und Verlag der österreichischen Staatsdruckerei, 1935), 2–3. It retained its character as the "core Jewish district" despite the fact that Jews of all origins and social classes lived there; the highest concentration of Galician Jews remained in Brigittenau, which was part of the Leopoldstadt until 1900. Ivar Oxaal, "The Jews of Young Hitler's Vienna: Historical and Sociological Aspects," in *Jews, Antisemitism, and Culture in Vienna*, ed. Ivar Oxall, Michael Pollack, Gerhard Botz (London: Routledge, 1987), 29.

28. Daniel Vyleta points out that liberal publications were more likely to emphasize the Leopoldstadt as a site with a high crime rate than right-wing, antisemitic publications. See Daniel Vyleta, *Crime, Jews, and News: Vienna, 1895–1914* (New York: Berghahn, 2007), 161, 261.

29. Leon Askin, cited in *Wien II. Leopoldstadt. Die andere Heimatkunde*, ed. Werner Hanak and Mechtild Widrich (Vienna: Brandstätter, 1999), 9.

30. Eva Brueck, "Shadows of the Past: Childhood Years in Austria, 1933–1938," LBI ME 1121, 4–5.

31. Ernst Epler, cited in Ruth Beckermann, ed., *Die Mazzesinsel: Juden in der Wiener Leopoldstadt, 1918–1938*, (Vienna: Löcker, 1984), 75.

32. Michel de Certeau, *The Practice of Everyday Life*, trans. Steven Rendall (Berkeley: University of California Press, 1984).

33. David Sibley, *Geographies of Exclusion: Society and Difference in the West* (London: Routledge, 1995), 76. Here he quotes Eugene Rochberg-Halton, "Object Relations, Role Models, and the Cultivation of the Self," in *Environment and Behavior* 16, no. 3 (1984): 335–68.

34. Herz also names the smaller Roland-Bühne as a place of lively interest, especially the Budapester Orpheum in the Taborstrasse. Peter Herz, "Entzauberte Praterstraße," in *Die Mazzesinsel: Juden in der Wiener Leopoldstadt, 1918–1938*, ed. Ruth Beckermann (Vienna: Löcker, 1984), 82–83.

35. Lotte Hümbelin, *Mein Eigener Kopf: ein Frauenleben in Wien, Moskau, Prag, Paris und Zürich* (Zürich: Edition 8, 1999), 27, 46.

36. Stella Klein-Löw, *Erinnerungen* (Vienna: Jugend und Volk, 1980), 188–89.

37. As a refugee from Eastern Europe growing up in the Leopoldstadt, he said he felt he suffered less antisemitism than those Jews in other areas of the city. Benno Weiser Varon, *Professions of a Lucky Jew* (London: Cornwall, 1992), 21–22.

38. Sibley, *Geographies of Exclusion*, 11. For a development of object relations theory that incorporates the world as it is perceived, but mainly from a visual point of view, see Sander L. Gilman, *Difference and Pathology: Stereotypes of Sexuality, Race, and Madness* (Ithaca, N.Y.: Cornell University Press, 1985).

39. Wiendl, "Jews and the City," 299.

40. Recently, local histories have been written about Viennese Jews who lived in districts where few other Jews resided; all seek, to some extent, to "correct" the notion that Jews lived only in heavily Jewish-populated areas of the city. See *Das Dreieck meiner Kindheit: Eine jüdische Vorstadtgemeinde in Wien* (Vienna: Mandelbaum, 2008), about Jews in Rudolfsheim-Fünfhaus; and Herbert Exenberger, *Gleich dem kleinen Häuflein der Makkabäer. Die jüdische Gemeinde in Simmering, 1848–1945* (Vienna: Mandelbaum, 2009), about Jews in Simmering.

41. See Rozenblit, *Jews of Vienna*, 88–91. These trends continue through the 1930s, according to the Austrian census of 1934. See *Statistik des Bundesstaates Österreichs, Die Ergebnisse der österreichischen Volkszählung vom 22. März 1934*, Vol. 3, *Wien*, ed. Bundesamt für Statistik (Vienna: Druck und Verlag der österreichischen Staatsdruckerei, 1935), 2–3.

42. Mark Monies, LBI, AHC 2211.

43. Philipp and Wilhelm Suschitzky had difficulties obtaining permission to open a bookstore selling mainly socialist literature in the proletarian district of Favoriten, even though few Jews lived there. As Rozenblit notes, although Favoriten was a popular home for Viennese Czechs, few Czech Jews—or any Jews at all—chose to live in that district. Rozenblit, *Assimilation and Identity*, 96. Between 1920 and 1933, the Suschitzkys were obliged to appear in court at least seven times to respond to charges for supposed violations of the city's ordinance against selling pornography. They were found guilty only once, in 1933, for selling erotic literature. See Annette Lechner, *Die Wiener Verlagsbuchhandlung Anzengruber-Verlag, Brüder Suschitzky (1901–1938) im Spiegel der Zeit*, M.A. Diplomarbeit, University of Vienna, 1994, 147. According to Lechner's research, the Suschitzky brothers wanted to build their store on the Himbergerstrae between Keplerplatz and Landgutgasse, claiming in their application to the Ministry of the Interior that such a business was necessary in the district, since it had such a large population and numerous schools. (Vgl. Allgemeines Verwaltungsarchiv, Zl. 23.018 a.a.O., as cited in Lechner, *Die Wiener Verlagsbuchhandlung Anzengruber-Verlag*, 13.)

44. Rozenblit, *Assimilation and Identity*, 85.

45. Weiser Varon, *Professions of a Lucky Jew*, 21–22.

46. Lynch, *Image of the City*, 5.

47. The Burgtheater on the Ringstrasse was not finished until 1870, by which time new theaters had emerged focusing on operetta and targeting middle-class audiences who were moving to the districts surrounding the inner city. W. E. Yates, *Theatre in Vienna: A Critical History, 1776–1995* (Cambridge: Cambridge University Press, 1996), 159.

48. "The Viennese theater was, to a great extent, a Jewish affair. Though many actors were Gentiles, the stars and prominent playwrights and directors were predominantly Jews." Weiser Varon, *Professions of a Lucky Jew*, 29. For more on the preponderance of Jews in the audience of musical and theater performances in Vienna, see Leon Botstein, *Judentum und Modernität. Essays zur Rolle der Juden in der deutschen und österreichischen Kultur, 1848 bis 1938* (Vienna: Böhlau, 1991). See also the exhibition catalog *Quasi una fantasia: Juden und die Musikstadt Wien*, ed. Leon Botstein and Werner Hanak (Hofheim: Wolke Verlag, 2003).

49. Adam Müller-Guttenbrunn [Roderich Meinhart, pseud.], *Erinnerungen eines Theaterdirektors* (Leipzig: L. Staackmann Verlag, 1924), 15–16. The theater produced plays with antisemitic content and only occasionally broke the rule about not hiring Jewish actors or including Jewish playwrights on the program. The brief history of the original theater was filled with missteps, blunders, and financial mismanagement. See "Aryan Theater," in *A Historical Encyclopedia of Prejudice and Antisemitism*, vol. 1, ed. Richard S. Levy. Today the building houses Vienna's *Volksoper*. In its lobby are two large plaques honoring both Adam Müller-Guttenbrunn and Mayor Karl Lueger that make no mention of their original antisemitic intent.

50. Müller-Guttenbrunn, *Erinnerungen*, 10. In the decades before World War I, the districts of Währing and Döbling began to attract more Jews. See Rozenblit, *Assimilation and Identity*, 91.

51. The Jewish editor in question was Friedrich Schütz from the Viennese daily *Neue Freie Presse*.

52. Robert S. Wistrich notes that associating the "Red Fear" with the "Jewish Question" began as part of Mayor Karl Lueger's propaganda when he took office in 1897. See "Social Democracy, Antisemitism, and the Jews," in Oxaal, et al., *Jews, Antisemitism, and Culture in Vienna*, 111–20, esp. 116. According to Josef Hindels, both teachers and students, with few exceptions, expressed antisemitism by decrying "Red Vienna." "For them antisemitism was accepted, but they had only hate and scorn for the plans to build up Red Vienna. The students, with few exceptions, came from bourgeois homes, and were full of prejudices against 'the Reds' and 'the Jews.'" See his undated autobiography, 5, cited in Eleonore Lappin, "Jüdische Lebenserinnerungen. Rekonstruktionen von jüdischer Kindheit und Jugend im Wien der Zwischenkriegzeit," in *Wien und die jüdische Erfahrung, 1900–1938*, ed. Frank Stern and Barbara Eichinger (Vienna: Böhlau, 2009), 36. I argue that many Jews' association of the provinces/mountains as "non-Jewish" space is a tacit acknowledgment of the coding of Vienna as "Jewish." See, for example, *"Hast du meine Alpen gesehen?" Eine jüdische Beziehungsgeschichte*, Jüdisches Museum Hohenems and Jüdisches Museum Wien, 2009.

53. Rozenblit, *Assimilation and Identity*, 74–76.

54. Interview with Ula Pommer (LBI, AHC 61) (author's translation from German).

55. *Statistik des Bundesstaates Österreichs*, 2–3.

56. Pommer, LBI, AHC 61. Palmers Textil AG, a well-known textile company, was founded in 1914 in Innsbruck.

57. Interview with Gertrud Marmorek, LBI, AHC 760.

58. Interview with Mark Monies, LBI, AHC 2211.

59. Interview with Charlotte R. Carter, LBI, AHC 3298.

60. Sonia Wachstein, "Hagenberggasse 49: Memories of a Viennese Jewish Childhood," (unpublished manuscript, 1997), LBI, ME 1068, 9.

61. Ibid., 8–9.

62. Ibid., 16.

63. Interview with Lore Waller, LBI, AHC 64.

64. Here "negative space" recalls the work of Nancy Munn, as cited in Setha M. Low and Denise Lawrence-Zúñiga, *Anthropology of Space and Place: Locating Culture* (Malden, Mass.: Blackwell, 2003), 95.

65. Paul Connerton, "Bodily Practices," in *How Societies Remember* (New York: Cambridge University Press, 1989), 88.

66. Interview with Lore Waller, LBI, AHC 64.

CONTRIBUTORS

Swati Chattopadhyay is professor of history of art and architecture at the University of California, Santa Barbara. She is the author of *Unlearning the City: Infrastructure in a New Optical Field* and *Representing Calcutta: Modernity, Nationalism, and the Colonial Uncanny.*

Jennifer A. Cousineau is an architectural historian with the Heritage Conservation and Commemorations Directorate of Parks Canada.

Emanuela Guano is associate professor of anthropology at Georgia State University.

Setha Low is professor of environmental psychology, geography, anthropology, and women's studies, and director of the Public Space Research Group at the Graduate Center, City University of New York. Her books include *Politics of Public Space, Rethinking Urban Parks: Public Space and Cultural Diversity,* and*Behind the Gates: Life, Security, and the Pursuit of Happiness in Fortress America.*

Arijit Sen is associate professor of architecture at the University of Wisconsin–Milwaukee. He is co-editor (with Jennifer Johung) of *Landscapes of Mobility: Culture, Politics, and Placemaking.*

Lisa Silverman is associate professor of history and Jewish Studies at the University of Wisconsin–Milwaukee. She is author of *Becoming Austrians: Jews and Culture between the World Wars* and co-editor (with Deborah Holmes) of *Interwar Vienna: Culture between Tradition and Modernity.*

Karen E. Till is senior lecturer in geography at the National University of Ireland, Maynooth. She is the author of *The New Berlin: Memory, Politics, Place*; editor of *Mapping Spectral Traces*; and co-editor of *Walls, Borders, Boundaries: Spatial and Cultural Practices in Europe.*

INDEX

Italicized page references refer to figures.

CPSIA information can be obtained at www.ICGtesting.com
Printed in the USA
LVOW02s2349090614

389313LV00010BA/23/P